THE PAUPER'S COOKBOOK

THE PAUPER'S COOKBOOK

Jocasta Innes

FRANCES LINCOLN

Frances Lincoln Limited
4 Torriano Mews
Torriano Avenue
London NW5 2RZ
www.franceslincoln.com

THE PAUPER'S COOKBOOK

First Frances Lincoln edition 2003

First published 1971 by Penguin Books
Revised edition *The New Pauper's Cookbook*
published 1992 by Vermilion, an imprint of Ebury Press

A catalogue record for this book is available from
the British Library

ISBN 0 7112 2240 1

Designed by Anne Wilson
Printed in England

2 4 6 8 9 7 5 3 1

Contents

Introduction

The Pauper's Cookbook was my very first published book, appearing as a Penguin paperback original in 1971. Jill Norman, my brilliant editor, was dubious about my choice of title, unconvinced that potential readers would recognize or approve of its tongue-in-cheekiness. I argued that it was catchy, got the message across succinctly without the dismal connotations of words like 'budget', or 'economy'. Besides, I urged, pauperishness was not the shameful state it might once have been; sixties hippies had made poverty into something of a mantra, an anti-materialistic stance, sharing their macrobiotic messes as readily as they passed round their spliffs. A recent pauper myself, trawling through libraries and my friends' bookshelves for thrifty but attractive recipes for my family, I was confident that the people I was writing for – students, nurses, young marrieds, as well as hippies – would get the point and the joke. Jill allowed herself to be persuaded and my small paperback was launched: a rustic dish of 'pork and beans' on the cover, more than 120 'international, racially mixed and classless dishes promising good home cooking at Joe's Café prices', according to the blurb, all for a mere 60p. Three minutes airtime on the *World at One*, parrying some shrewd but not unkindly sallies from Bill Hardcastle – 'So tell me about these limpet stovies, Jocasta Innes, is this a regular pauper's dish?' – ensured a run on my book in the first few weeks, after which that precious aid word-of-mouth took over.

The Pauper's Cookbook was reprinted by Penguin almost every year for twelve years, twice in 1971 and 1976, and left a wake of friendly feeling no subsequent book of mine has matched. During this time I was warmly greeted by strangers assuring me *The Pauper's Cookbook* fed them through lean years scraping by on a student grant, and women confided, only half-joking, that it rescued their marriages in the early days before they learned how to cook. I had written the book from hands-on and hard-won experience, out of a genuine desire to pass on my discoveries and make them useful, so it was exhilarating to find that so many people agreed that it hit the spot and filled a need.

The high-rolling eighties supervened, the pauper tag felt a bit tacky to a generation revelling in conspicuous consumption, big cars, big hair, big shoulders, and extravagant restaurant meals. Sales of *The Pauper's Cookbook* petered out, Jill Norman was working for the European Commission and I had fallen into a whole new scene, as the 'paint guru' with the best-selling *Paint Magic*. But I still cooked daily, still preferred the traditional peasant dishes I wrote about in the seventies to the most exquisite *nouvelle cuisine* offerings dreamed up by fashionable chefs. In keeping with the mood of the times, we ate more pasta, more vegetable – if not vegetarian – dishes, more game than red meat, and, thanks to a box delivered weekly from a walled garden in Suffolk, we were discovering the palate-rousing delights of organic foodstuffs. My own two surviving copies of *The Pauper's Cookbook* were stained, sticky and falling to bits, but my affection for the book was undiminished; it wrapped up the enthusiasm and curiosity of a golden passage in my life, wading to rocks at low tide to scrape off mussels, humping a baby in a sling along Dorset cliffs in search of blewits or puffballs (fungi the locals found suspect), trying out eel, spider crabs, wild rabbit from a local poacher, the windfall of a line-caught baby bream, dizzyingly fresh, from a fisherman lurking round the Poole ferry.

I needed no persuasion to revive *The Pauper's Cookbook* concept, in the early nineties, when there was more than a whiff of recession in the air, retail sales drooping and the dread word 'repo' entering the language. My son's girlfriend, Kate, an inspired and inventive cook herself, helped bring my original recipes more into line with what the younger hard-up foodies ate and enjoyed. We had fun cutting, and tweaking, and the original 120 recipes grew to 250, despite axing entire sections ('Programmed Eating' now felt obsessive) and many of the original recipes on the grounds that they hadn't stood the test of time – too much hassle, too arbitrary, or – for a newly veggie readership – too offaly, too bloody. Pasta and Vegetarian recipes had new sections to themselves. My own cooking skills had developed considerably in twenty years, not just by cooking longer for more people, but from writing annual reviews for *The Sunday Times*, which delivered a yearly harvest of the latest glossy offerings by master chefs, TV chefs, and regional experts, all of whom expanded my culinary horizons once the frenzy of meeting a deadline had subsided and I could curl my mind around them, in bed.

The *New Pauper's Cookbook* – 'Over 250 delicious recipes for penniless cooks' – appeared under a different imprint in 1992. Another paperback, bigger and more stylishly presented, with a witty cartoon cover, it cost £8.99. Compared with the toppling piles of glossies overshadowing it in the bookstores, it was a snip. But though it made two editions, the *New Pauper's Cookbook* failed to catch on in the way its humble little predecessor had. Still basking in the afterglow of the eighties, I think people were unwilling to admit that they were experiencing more than a temporary downturn; to be hard-up, never mind a pauper, was not a larky challenge, it was flatly depressing. At any rate this is my take on the socio-economic reasons why this bigger, better version of my seventies cookbook ended up treading water instead of being carried along on the crest of a word-of-mouth wave.

But that was then. The early noughties already seem a long way off, and different, from the early nineties. National economies are straining, pensions being halved, corporations retrenching, workers being 'let go' in their thousands. A tightening of belts is audible. If media pundits have got it right a tough recession is just round the corner if not on our doorsteps. The concept I espoused with such enthusiasm thirty years ago – that frugal food can be good eating – seems newly valid and relevant. I am delighted that Frances Lincoln Limited (who published *Paint Magic*) agree with me that good ideas don't date or die. *The Pauper's Cookbook* (we are dropping the *New* tag), revised, updated and expanded, is once again available in a no-frills format, paperback, at the rock-bottom price of £7.99, less as you might observe than it cost the second time round. A book about eating cheaply should be easily affordable, if not by the student, by the parents thereof.

So what's new? Most of the advice I updated for my second version still makes sense, with a bit of tweaking. The surprise to me was how many of the Original Recipes (1970 ones), axed for various reasons, demand to be reinstated. There was a squeamishness about offal in the nineties but thanks to the bold enterprise of chefs like Fergus Henderson (he runs the trend-setting St John restaurant in Clerkenwell), dishes based on 'offal' – oxtail, brains, tripe – are not just acceptable but sought after. Hough, or brawn, made from a pig's head simmered with spices and seasonings, and yielding succulent nuggets of tender meat enclosed in a tasty jelly, is once again a gourmet treat, and a Pauper recipe. Ditto brain fritters, kidney dishes, oxtail soup and stew, many ways to make liver tasty and succulent. You won't find most of these in your supermarket meat section, but a good family butcher should oblige, aware of the competition. This is the man to sort you a hand of pork (brilliant recipe on page 246), caul fat, flead, or fill casings with your home-made sausage mixture.

Perhaps the most significant development, food-wise, over the past decade has been the surging popularity of organic foodstuffs, now worth over a billion pounds annually and still growing. Organic products cost more than their non-organic equivalents, it is true, but they taste like the real thing. Organic vegetables are so flavourful that meatless meals can be a treat, even for non-veggie households. With this in mind I have added more vegetable gratins, risottos, pasta dishes and salads to the veggie section, and elsewhere in the book. Savings here might go toward an organic chicken (incomparably richer in flavour) at the weekend, or dry-cured bacon or all-meat sausages. Organic dairy products are another taste revelation. Organic bread flour transforms a home-baked loaf. Organic products I pass on are rice, tea, coffee and tinned stuff where the benefits, taste- and health-wise seem negligible. Vegetarians should definitely go organic, in my view, and I think babies and toddlers should be fed organically wherever possible because the purity of their food is important to their long-term development. Home-made baby food not only costs considerably less than those nifty little commercially produced jars, but you have the comfort of knowing exactly what went into it.

If I have one serious concern about relaunching my book for a new generation it is this – do they really know how to cook? I doubt Delia Smith was off-the-wall when she started her last cookery series with a lengthy demonstration of how to boil an egg. And we oldies gaped incredulously as Jamie Oliver's final fifteen (weeded out from over six hundred applicants) coolly paraded incompetence and bad attitude over the months it took to train and cajole them – well, the ones who stayed the course – into becoming employable in Jamie's new restaurant. Anecdotal evidence, some gleaned in my own family situation, suggests that while many young adults today have a quite sophisticated appreciation of good food, thanks to the media, foreign travel, and parental indulgence, they are often surprisingly ignorant when it comes to feeding themselves on a daily basis. Most of them can do one signature dish – Sunday roast, with trimmings, a fry-up, Thai green curry – but what they don't know is how to shop and budget, how to deal with leftovers, what constitutes a healthy diet, how to make a béchamel sauce, stock, batter, shortcrust pastry, pizza dough or any of the other essential, thrifty ploys which have enabled people to stretch limited ingredients and come up with a reasonably varied diet over the centuries, across the world. The fast food, instant gratification, ethos is largely to blame of course; takeaways, microwave dishes, cook-in sauces, tinned soups, pizza bases, supermarket packs of vegetables, trimmed, washed and ready-to-go. Their parents, us, must take some of the responsibility too, I feel. Too busy bringing home the bread to teach them how to make it.

Necessity is a tough teacher. I was already a competent cook, but I learned a great deal more about cooking, planning, and shopping in my pauper days because I had to, to make ends meet; it was that simple. Pride came into it. I enjoyed the challenge of dishing up good food for our friends 'at Joe's Café prices'; this felt like a triumph, and I had fun doing it. But what really drove me on through the testing and tasting of hundreds of recipes was native greed, the most important item in any cook's equipment I tend to think. My definition of greedy – a person who prepares a treat for him or herself, when eating alone, rather than reaching for a tin of baked beans or boiling an egg. I am proud of having passed on the greedy gene to my children, all talented cooks and appreciative eaters. If my *Pauper's Cookbook* (maybe it should be titled *The Greedy Pauper's Cookbook?*) can kindle appetite in a new generation of readers, and point the way to satisfying it both thriftily and interestingly, I will be well pleased.

LEFTOVERS

Most of the recipes in *The Pauper's Cookbook* are straightforward and detailed enough to be achievable by beginner cooks, and cheap enough for the odd failure not to hurt too much. One addition I have made to the existing formula was a short section on leftovers. Whereas experienced cooks find cooking with leftovers stimulating, inspiring unexpected new combinations and surprise successes, I have a sneaky feeling that beginning pauper cooks might just dump them in the bin. Getting clever with leftovers is critical to stretching ingredients imaginatively, whether it's a bowl of cooked rice, a glut of milk cartons, a chicken carcass or the remains of a stew you have eaten hot two days running and wearied of. I hate waste, and I exert some ingenuity to use up and transform leftovers; cooking a couple of unused pints of milk into white sauce and freezing it, turning leftover rice into a salad or stuffing for a marrow or other vegetable container, hotting up the last of a stew with chillies, a splash of sherry vinegar, and cooking a few eggs in this decoction, in the oven, for a spin on Huevos a la Flamenca.

To a practised hand such moves are routine, though I am always on the lookout for new variations. But my guess is that to a new generation of aspiring cooks, weaning themselves off convenience foods, many of these tried and tested stratagems may be news, and welcome at that. For more leftover suggestions, and tips, see page 14.

Some leftovers just happen; others are planned for. Get into the habit of cooking up more than you are going to need of basic ingredients, or what I call 'padding' – rice, potatoes (mashed or boiled in their skins), lentils, dried beans and pulses, polenta, burghul, etc. Keep them in the fridge and plan to use them up in the next day or two for a second meal, not so much to save money (though it might cut fuel bills) as to save time, and mental fatigue.

RICE Mix with herbs, scraps of bacon, leftover mince or sausage, a spoonful of tomato sauce, and use to stuff vegetables in season – marrow, tomatoes, peppers, onions, aubergines – to be slowly baked under a lid or foil in the oven. Or combine with lentils, chopped spring onion and herbs for a salad doused with vinaigrette.

POTATOES Mashed potato can be combined with leftover cooked fish and chopped fresh herbs for fishcakes. For a quick snack reheat the mash, adding a little more milk, and make nests of this in ramekins, or a small shallow dish, and break an egg into the hollows. Dot with butter and bake in a medium oven till the whites are firm, about ten minutes. Cold boiled potatoes can be peeled, thickly sliced and fried in oil or goose fat with chopped onion and a sprinkle of rosemary.

LENTILS Add to soups, stuffing or salads. Or make the lentil and anchovy dish on page 104.

BEANS Cooked dried beans – haricots, black or red beans, etc. – can be added to soups, salads, or puréed with leftover gravy, or stock, for a side dish.

CHICKPEAS Mix with cooked pasta, small shapes like fusilli, not spaghetti, for a classic Italian salad, dressed with olive oil, lemon juice and chopped fresh herbs. Or use to make hummus, puréed with garlic, lemon juice, tahini and yoghurt.

WINE Use the remains after a dinner party to make a thick, deeply flavoured tomato sauce to store in the freezer. Tinned tomatoes or fresh ones, but reduce over low heat to thicken. Endlessly useful. Purists object to mixing reds and whites and different labels, but you can safely ignore them.

BONES/COOKING WATER Keep the water you used to cook a joint of gammon, and any bones, and make these the base of a minestrone or garbure soup. Check for saltiness - not a problem if the gammon was cooked as in the recipe on page 244.

COOKED MEAT Usually nicest eaten cold, neatly sliced, with baked potatoes and salad. Really small amounts can be diced, or shredded, and added to a potato salad, dressed with vinaigrette and/or mayonnaise, adding capers, chopped parsley, chives, tarragon as available. Larger amounts can be reheated *à la* Miroton, sliced and covered with a little stock or gravy and a spoonful of crème fraîche and Dijon mustard. The trick is to heat slowly in the oven, just to simmering point – reboiled meat tastes like cardboard.

FISH Cooked fish can give flavour and food value to a potato or rice salad. Use lemon juice to sharpen the vinaigrette or mayonnaise, and lots of fresh chopped herbs. Or combine with mashed potato for fishcakes. White fish, smoked fish, or salmon are all good here. Remove any skin and bones and flake. Scraps of smoked salmon in crème fraîche make a quick pasta sauce.

MILK A sudden glut can be made into a thick béchamel (white sauce) and frozen. Great for fish pie, or a vegetable gratin or onion-bacon-potato hotpot. A real time-saver.

CHEESE Hard, dry nuggets can obviously be grated for use in white-sauce-based dishes, or on toast for Welsh rarebit, adding mustard, a little stout or beer. Scraps of soft cheese can be processed for potted cheese flavoured with herbs, mustard, cayenne, using crème fraîche, yoghurt, even a splash of port or sherry to lubricate the mixture. Eat on toast or crackers.

VEGETABLES The easiest way to make cooked vegetables presentable is to purée them, and reheat with a little butter/cream/gravy or stock, seasoning well.

BREAD Day-old bread is needed for bread and butter pudding, summer pudding, French toast and stuffings. A stale country-style loaf can be sliced, rubbed with garlic and olive oil and baked till golden for crostini, or added to rustic soups and salads. Make offcuts into croûtons, or turn them into breadcrumbs.

TIPS

- To cut parsley fine, quickly, stuff into a mug and chop with kitchen scissors.
- To get the maximum pungency from spices, whether they are powdered or whole, heat them in a dry pan till you can smell them. Bash whole spices (e.g., coriander, cumin, allspice) in a mortar.
- For speed, trim French beans and mangetout in the supermarket plastic pack, pushing them down to one end, chopping across with a sharp knife. Repeat at the opposite end.
- Peeling onions goes faster and with fewer tears if you cut them across first – this gives you better purchase on the skin.
- A pinch of instant coffee counteracts the tinny sharpness of tinned tomatoes.
- Shallots baked in their skins add zip to fried or grilled chops, steak, fish and sausages.
- To make a fluid dressing for salads, add tepid water to homemade mayonnaise.
- For crisp, puffy fried onion rings shake them in a plastic bag with a little flour before frying.
- Animal fat (use tinned goose fat) makes the best chips because it heats to a higher temperature than oil without burning.
- Self-standing freezer bags with snap-shut closure are ideal for storing liquids (white sauce, tomato sauce, soups) in the freezer as they take up less room, and are reusable.
- Frozen broad beans, outer skins removed, have twice the class. A useful standby for starters and salads.
- Reducing garlic cloves to pulp goes faster and more tidily if you sprinkle peeled cloves with sea salt before chopping or smashing via pestle and mortar.
- Bacon rinds make appealing nibbles if you cook them on a flat dish in a low oven till brown and crisp.
- For neater poached eggs, break each egg into a saucer before sliding into bubbling water to which you have added a splash of vinegar.

- Browning bones before adding them to a stock or stew adds depth and richness of flavour.
- Enclosing a ham or large gammon joint in a huff paste (flour and water kneaded together to make a thick, elastic dough) before baking keeps flavour in and makes sure the meat stays tender and moist. Open it up, or remove, for a final glazing.
- Parsley looks cute in a jug of water, but keeps twice as long if you dip into cold water and store it wet, in a plastic bag in the fridge.
- Thyme, rosemary and sage dry successfully if you untie the bundles and leave them till brittle in a low oven, or on the back of an Aga. Crumble the leaves into airtight jars. I often dry strips of citrus peel – orange and tangerine are both good – in the same way, to brighten up casserole dishes.
- A pinch of bicarbonate of soda in the cooking water helps soften dried pulses and beans past their sell-by date. But don't add salt – it has the opposite effect.
- When draining pasta, keep a coffee cupful of the cooking water and add to the pasta before saucing – this helps stop it turning into a solid lump. Also have all serving dishes and plates really hot – cooling, congealing pasta is much less appetizing.
- Any joint of pork on the bone is improved in texture and flavour by dry-salting overnight or longer. Use cheap pouring salt, rub well in and leave in a cool place, or the fridge. Rinse off surplus salt thoroughly before cooking, and pat dry with kitchen paper. See recipe for hand of pork, page 246.
- Sausages (quality bangers, please) are useful for more than fry-ups these days. Use cooked leftover bangers or raw ones to stuff vegetables, poultry, cabbage leaves. In both cases extract meat from their casings before mixing with rice, herbs, whatever. A real time-saver.
- For an instant marinade for steaks, chops, etc., use a standard vinaigrette plus a sprinkling of thyme or *persillade* – a finely chopped mix of parsley and garlic.

For new readers here is a short breakdown of the sections:

STANDARDS Everyday dishes one does not tire of, on the substantial side, with an emphasis on one-pot meals, including recipes for everything from soups to puds.

PADDING Basic know-how and some recipes for stretching more expensive ingredients with cheap, useful staples – rice, batter, pulses, grains, etc.

FAST WORK The emphasis on speed, with some reliance on store-cupboard items and the freezer.

PASTA FASTER No spag bol (well, you know that one already) but some corkers: simple, sophisticated and sophisticatedly simple.

VEGGIES Non-meat and non-fish eaters (not vegans, however) should find this a mini-cookbook, going through from soups and salads to solid dishes and party food.

FANCY WORK Recipes for special occasions. They may cost a bit more, take a bit longer, or introduce exotica. Paupers, especially, need to splurge occasionally; these dishes let you splurge safely.

PRIVATE ENTERPRISE Extras like home-made preserves, bread and mayonnaise add a welcome dash of luxury to a scrimping budget. They may also be cheaper than the bought kind.

Where the Money Goes

Indisputably, it goes. But it is possible to control the outflow and see that you get value for your money. Sensible shopping, the domestic equivalent of a planned economy, does save actual money, largely by cutting down on wastage, and it should also ensure that you have good-quality materials to cook with.

Without going to the lengths of keeping itemized accounts of everything you spend, you will need to introduce a little system into your shopping, to avoid fetching up broke and hungry halfway through the week. The first thing is to decide how much you want, or can afford, to spend on food each week. Make a rough estimate of your weekly consumption of essentials like bread, butter, eggs, tea, milk, and what this costs. Subtract the figure from your weekly budget, divide the remainder by seven, and you are left with a pretty good idea of what your daily expenditure should be. If you keep well within this figure for half the week, you will have accumulated enough to buy something special for the weekend, or stock up on cans, extra herbs, sauces, etc.

A shopping list is the most effective curb on overstepping your daily food budget. Decide what you are going to eat, check the recipe against what you have already got, list what you need, and *stick* to the list. Elementary, I know, but for every steel-trap mind there must be ten impulse buyers bumbling round the shops, trusting to association of ideas to come up with the right answers. A fallible system at any time, and positively dangerous in supermarkets. On the other hand, don't become too inflexible – if a good buy crops up unexpectedly, cheap pheasant, say, or herrings, you should be able to revise your other purchases accordingly. A little homework with this cookbook ought to help there.

The foregoing three paragraphs, written thirty years ago, still seem to me sensible advice. I still shop around for shops, though like most busy people living in a big city I tend to do one massive weekly session at the nearest supermarket for boring basics. For the rest, I supplement these with sorties to specialist shops, markets, farm shops, foodie boutiques, church fêtes. There is a sameness about supermarket food: one can live with it, or off it, but sometimes paupers need a bit of the genuine article, the taste, the smell, even, of excellence. This means more to people hemmed in by cash restrictions than to fat cats. I journey to Islington for fresh fish. Meat I buy from a family butcher, who also sells game. The only meat products I buy in supermarkets are sausages, in all their variety but preferably organic, and joints of bacon, or gammon, smoked and unsmoked, which are invariably tasty, tender and versatile, cooked as on page 244.

Asian food stores catering to the restaurant trade are well worth investigating, not just for daals, spices and curry-making ingredients. Look for fresh spinach, mooli radishes, pumpkin sold by the slice, tinned coconut milk (far superior to milk made from desiccated coconut), burghul, couscous; all startlingly cheap by supermarket standards. I find their keema (minced lamb-going-on-mutton) beats all but the swankiest butcher's mince for freshness and flavour, at less than half the price of supermarket packs. I shop in farmers' markets as often as I can, looking for seasonal produce and regional or local specialities, organics where available. London's Borough Market has a sensational range of fresh vegetables, fruit, herbs (mostly French imports), while Spitalfields makes a point of organics.

I always end up lugging some food treasure back from trips abroad – olive oil, air-cured ham, salami, strings of garlic, Tunisian spices. Does this sound like a lot of trouble to go to? I enjoy the discoveries, which add a point to so many trips, here and abroad. Some of these things are luxuries, but there is a trade-off: the money I save not buying packaged sauces, frozen dinners, tubes of garlic purée, bottled mayonnaise and so on ad infinitum (convenience foods, in a word) seems prudently invested in such items as free-range eggs, fine tea and organic vegetables.

SHOPS

Before deciding which shops to patronize, compare prices and the range and quality of goods on display. The butcher for you is one who stocks a wide range of good-quality cheap cuts as well as offal, rabbit and pigeons. Your fishmonger should offer bargains like mussels, fresh herring and sprats in season. Your greengrocer ought to stock a selection of local produce (this applies less to large towns, of course) as well as imported stuff. Where two shops are much of a muchness, go for the one with the friendlier staff. Having made your choice, try and stick to it. Shopkeepers take more trouble over their regulars.

Paupers, my mother crisply observed, cannot afford to be squeamish, and she has a point. Don't be cowardly about trying something new, odd, or unprepossessing-looking. Most shoppers go for the obvious, safe and familiar, particularly in the meat line – chops and frying steak, according to my butcher – with the result that these get pricier while offbeat items are often absurdly cheap. The less snob cuts of meat like shin of beef, hand of pork, many varieties of game, and most of what goes under the unfortunate name of 'offal' – kidneys, liver, etc. – are all good buys and make good eating when properly cooked. In the fish line, try mussels, sprats, coley and bream as well as mackerel and herring. I often find humble vegetables like kale and spring greens more rewarding, carefully cooked, than expensive foreign imports.

PLANNING

My food planning for the week is definitely broad brush; I buy one good-sized chicken, a pound or so of smoked fish, and a ring of smoked sausage, regularly. These, plus any leftovers and by-products (chicken stock, haddock stock), and padded out with potatoes, grains, pulses or whatever, will see us through four or five meals. On Sundays we get large packs of fresh mussels (the new food of the poor, with frozen chicken livers) to eat first as soup, then with pasta. I usually have smoked salmon and bacon scraps in the fridge. Both are versatile, and a little goes a long way. I am lucky in having a box of organic vegetables delivered once a week, nine months of the year. These spoil fast so I have to rush into action; we have lots of cooked salads (beets, turnips, broad beans) as well as raw ones. I make gratins, ratatouille, purées to freeze for soups later, impromptu *salade niçoise* combinations to eat with hard-boiled eggs, canned tuna and aïoli. We eat red meat less often than we used to, preferring game in season. If I buy pork I salt it overnight (just rub in salt well all over) to leach out some of that sinister moisture it seems to be pumped with; I find this, *pace* Jane Grigson, improves taste and texture. Every time I finish a book I promise myself to take up bread-making again, using Fleur's recipe (see page 275), because my family eat bread like it was just invented and home-made bread is such a luxury. Here is a list of thrifty buys, little altered since 1970.

OLIVE OIL Buy the largest size you can afford of the strongest tasting oil (usually green, from Cyprus, Greece or Spain). It is now accepted as healthier than butter or margarine for cooking, and it is nicer than the other vegetable oils. You can extend it with safflower or sunflower oil.

RICE Asian cash-and-carries sell whopping bags of patna or basmati rice, at a price that works out markedly cheaper. Rice keeps well, stored in a mouse-proof bin. Or you could go shares with friends. Uncle Ben's long-grain rice can replace Italian arborio for risotto. Brown rice is good for salads.

SPICES It's daft to buy all your spices in those titchy jars in supermarkets. Get black peppercorns, coriander seeds and cumin in 450 g (1 lb) packs from Asian supermarkets, likewise turmeric, ginger and garam masala. The best-value saffron is powdered, in sachets, from Italian and Spanish delis. Use fresh chillies sometimes instead of dried; they are high in Vitamin C, and smell ineffably fresh, like cucumber but more so.

SPECIALITY STORES Get your Chinese sauces, seasonings, wonton wrappers, etc., from a Chinese foodstore. Healthfood shops tend to be pricey, but may be the only source of unusual items like dried seaweed, laver bread, buckwheat, brown lentils, agar-agar and millet.

TEA Teabag tea tastes like dust to me. I buy packets of favourite oriental blends, like Lapsang, and mix them with cheaper but not rubbishy standard blends, for their fragrance.

BACON/GAMMON Supermarkets have taken to selling packs of off-cuts of bacon and gammon which one can do a lot with in a pauper kitchen. A bonus is, quite often, that the meat itself seems rather better quality, not so watery. Trim pieces into neat chunks or strips and cook as usual.

BITS AND BONES Get to know a family butcher, and a good fishmonger and charm them into giving you marrow bones, fresh suet, caul fat, pigs' trotters, odd white fish heads, bones and trimmings for stock.

PULSES, GRAINS, ETC. Best bought in moderate-size bags (1–2 kg/2¼–4½ lb) from wholefood or healthfood shops. These deteriorate more rapidly than rice, on the whole, so go for a store with a rapid turnover.

HERBS You can get seedlings everywhere nowadays, potted up. Basil, thyme, chives and parsley grow well for me in windowboxes or large tubs, in a sunny place. Dill grows like a weed in the ground, as does fennel.

CRÈME FRAÎCHE Mix yoghurt with fresh cream and leave overnight to develop that faint refreshing acidity characteristic of crème fraîche.

PASTA Forget the so-called 'fresh' pasta, unless from an Italian deli; it is floppy and tasteless. Get a good brand of dried durum wheat pasta, cheaper and nicer. And try making your own (see page 157).

STOCKING UP

The following is a list of useful things to have by you at all times and especially for the Fast Work recipes in this book. No need to rush out and buy them all at once; the most useful are in italics.

CANS Tuna, *anchovies,* corned beef, *peeled tomatoes, tomato purée.*

FROZEN FOODS *Peas, broad beans, sweetcorn, chicken livers.*

SAUCES/CONDIMENTS *Dry mustard, Dijon mustard, soy sauce* (Japanese brands are best), Worcestershire sauce, Tabasco, *white wine vinegar,* honey, molasses.

PULSES/GRAINS/CEREALS *Green and brown lentils, chickpeas,* flageolets, barley, buckwheat, burghul, couscous, channa daal, *polenta, strong white bread flour,* cornflour, easy-cook long-grain rice (or arborio), *brown rice.*

SPICES Buy in small quantities – *juniper berries,* allspice, cinnamon sticks, vanilla pods, *whole nutmegs,* coriander berries, cumin seeds, turmeric and cloves. Whole spices keep better than ground; heat in a dry pan for a minute or two, then crush with pestle and mortar.

DRIED FRUIT *Raisins, sultanas,* prunes, dates, apricots.

VANILLA SUGAR This improves most puddings, cakes and biscuits, used in place of ordinary granulated or caster sugar. You can make your own very easily by buying a few vanilla pods from a good grocer or delicatessen and storing them in a covered jar or tin of caster sugar. The vanilla pods can be used for flavouring milk puddings and custards, rinsed, dried and put back in the jar. They can be used three or four times.

OPTIONAL EXTRAS Capers, *olives*, dried tomatoes, oyster sauce, *black bean sauce, dried red chillies*, bitter chocolate, pine nuts.

You will also need a supply of *lemons* (a pauper's answer to wine marinades), peanut oil for deep-frying, *garlic, fresh ginger*, breadcrumbs (home-made from stale bread dried in the oven and pounded), fast-action yeast in packets. Use Parmesan or Pecorino where it matters, bought in a chunk and grated, although Cheddar or a sharper hard cheese can be substituted – Lancashire, Cheshire, mature Gouda, etc.

WHEREWITHAL

Improvisation is the keyword here. Paupers are often pushed for space as well as cash and the logical answer is to have a minimum of equipment, which can double up for different purposes.

STORAGE The simplest, cheapest and handiest way of keeping it out of the way when not in use is to borrow a practical French trick and hang as much as possible from hooks, or plain nails, in the walls.
  If you are short of working surfaces, and your kitchen space can accommodate another piece of furniture, look for a low cupboard (waist-height, or lower) in a junk shop. Cover it with formica, or a slab of marble off an old washstand – the latter makes the ideal pastry board. The cupboard will take casseroles, etc., and groceries. Fifties utility kitchen units are good for storage.

WHERE TO BUY Junk shops, charity shops and boot sales are fruitful locales for kitchen equipment. For once the consumer society works in your favour. Households which have gone mad for stainless steel or enamelled cast-iron often throw out a mass of serviceable pots, pans and utensils. Dingy to look at, perhaps, but often surprisingly good-quality. Weight is a reliable indication of quality – the heavier your saucepan or casserole, the better it holds and diffuses heat.

Look out for: aluminium pans and stoneware casseroles, the latter usually brown or green outside, cream within. They often arrive lidless, but inverted plates or foil will substitute in most cases. You can't have too many china mixing bowls – a 'slight fault' doesn't matter if you don't bash it too heartily. Glass storage jars (must have tops) and canisters are useful for storing perishable foods. Breadboards, rolling pins and carving knives are all worth looking out for. Asian food stores sell the best pestle and mortar sets, massively weighty to make short work of crushing spices, garlic, fresh or dried herbs; these stack to save space. Also small glass-topped metal containers for spices. Antiquated gadgets, if you can work out what they are *for*, are often good buys and usually work very efficiently with a little cleaning and oiling.

For anything else, try a good ironmonger's.

WHAT YOU WILL NEED

The following is a skeleton selection of equipment but it should prove adequate for the recipes in this book. Again, there is no need to buy all of it at once – keep adding to it as occasion arises and cash permits.

COOK'S KNIFE One thing you cannot do without. It should be medium-size, sharp as a razor, and good-quality. You need it for slicing and trimming meat, chopping vegetables and herbs, peeling potatoes, derinding bacon, and a host of other jobs. Quality pays off here. If you can't wangle one as a present, save up, and in the meantime hunt for an old carbon (non-stainless) steel knife at boot sales, brighten it with scouring powder rubbed on with a cork and sharpen on a carborundum 'stone'. Stainless steel serrated-edged knives are adequate for peeling and scraping vegetables.

SWIVEL-BLADED PEELER A tiny but invaluable gadget for paring carrots, etc., as well as for peeling spuds.

CHOPPING BOARD Essential. The back of a wooden breadboard will do. Scrub it often or garlic will permeate everything.

SAUCEPANS Two is the minimum. One medium-to-large, one a size or two smaller. The big one for soups, pasta, rice, which need a lot of liquid; the smaller one for vegetables, etc. You can improvise a double boiler by standing the smaller pan inside the larger one. A very small pan is best for boiling eggs or heating milk and sauces.

CASSEROLES Two again. Big one for stews, pot roasts and bulky dishes. Smaller for milk pudding, pâtés, soufflés, fish pie, etc. I find stoneware the most versatile material for the money.

SIEVE A fairly capacious one for sieving, or puréeing soup, sauces, stewed fruit, flour. Metal is strongest, good-quality plastic adequate, as long as you don't hold it over direct heat. You need a nylon sieve for sieving acidic fruit.

COLANDER People muddle along without, by juggling with saucepan lids or plates, but colanders save time and scalds and you can pick them up cheaply in junk shops – the metal ones are better than plastics, as they don't melt.

FRYING PAN One medium-sized one will cope with most frying jobs. It should be a heavyweight one, but the lighter kind is adequate if you use it with a heat-diffuser mat to prevent food sticking and burning. A non-stick one is brilliant for pancakes, frittata, tortilla.

ROASTING PAN The cheapest is all right. A medium-sized pan will take shepherd's pie and upside-down puddings, as well as roasts.

MIXING BOWLS One sturdy, large one for mixing batters, etc. A small one for beating up egg whites, mayonnaise. But you can always do with more, so keep your eyes open.

FLAN TIN One 20 or 23 cm (8 or 9 inch) tin is essential. Better still, two, so you can bake two pastry cases at once, freezing the extra one.

MEASURING JUG I have a large plastic beaker which cost a few pence. It gives ml/fluid oz, litre/pint, sugar and flour measurement tables separately, and I find it invaluable. Kitchen scales are not so vital because exact measurements are less important with bulky dishes, but for pastry and cake-making, where accuracy matters, the beaker is essential.

IMPLEMENTS You will need two or three wooden spoons, a metal spatula for lifting fried foods, an egg whisk, a coffee strainer and a grater. The last is essential for grating cheese, lemon rind, vegetables, and worth every penny it costs. Best are the four-sided plastic graters – stable and less painful on the knuckles.

When you can add to this basic selection, you should concentrate first on extra saucepans and casseroles. Other useful oddments are a loaf tin, good for baking meat loaf, caramel custards and cakes; a shallow ovenproof dish for baking fish and vegetables, or milk puddings; a garlic press (chefs swat the bulb with a heavy chopper but, in less skilful hands, the fragments tend to fly round the room). If you have an odd pound to spare any time, a mouli food mill is a gadget to invest in. Childishly simple to use, it takes the slog out of mushing soup, fruit and vegetables. But, of course, if you can persuade a parent or relative to pass on their superannuated food processor, you are laughing. These can be serviced and new blades obtained.

One last aid to cooking without tears. Free, too! When making mayonnaise, put the oil in a corked bottle with a deep notch cut in one side of the cork. This regulates the flow of oil, greatly simplifying the task of adding it drop by drop to the egg (see page 260).

Rules of Thumb

Not surprisingly, paupers' kitchens tend to be light on equipment. When money is tight, one spends it on food rather than kitchen scales, sets of mixing bowls or measuring spoons. Bearing this in mind, there are few recipes, if any, in this book where quantities or timing are critical. Relative proportions – rather than hairbreadth accuracy – are important in making a béchamel sauce, soufflés or cakes. Timing obviously counts when roasting meat or cooking soufflés and such items as pasta and rice. Largely, though, cooking successfully is a matter of common sense. If you are short of meat for a casserole, bung in more vegetables, slices of garlic sausage, pulses, barley, dumplings, etc., etc. If one ingredient in a list is missing, you can often do without, or substitute another, without wrecking the outcome. Again, use your loaf about this. Onion soup cannot be made without onions, or bread without flour (though this doesn't have to be wheat flour), but chicken recipes are also suitable for rabbit, and vice versa; swedes or parsnips can supply the sweetness of carrots in soups and stews; Worcestershire sauce can stand in, at a pinch, for soy sauce; nutmeg can be used instead of cinnamon or cloves; and many herbs are interchangeable. The dish will be different with different ingredients, but you might even prefer it that way, your way.

The following tips and suggestions are dedicated to making cooking feel relaxed, not frantic.

QUANTITIES

- 1 level teaspoon = 5 ml
- 1 level tablespoon = 15 ml

As a rough but useful guide, the following tablespoon quantities yield 25 g (1 oz):
Butter/margarine – 2 level tablespoons
Caster sugar – 2 level tablespoons
Uncooked rice – 2 level tablespoons
Unsifted flour – 3 level tablespoons
- 1 glass = approximately 175 ml (6 fl oz)
- 1 teacup = approximately 150 ml (¼ pint)

A plastic measuring jug or beaker, with quantities marked off on the sides, will see you through most recipes. Use it to weigh out sugar, flour and rice as well as liquids. Failing this, many foods you buy have their weight marked on them – a quarter of a standard butter pack weighs 50 g (2 oz), for example.

In estimating serving quantities, I work on the following per person (these are approximate and a little on the stingy side):
- For pasta and rice – 75–125 g (3–4 oz)
- Other pulses and grains – 75 g (3 oz)
- Meat and fish – 125 g (4 oz)

TIMING

MEAT AND POULTRY The basic rule for roasting meat and poultry is to give it 20 minutes per 450 g (1 lb) and a further 20 minutes 'for the pot'. Pork should be cooked for 30 minutes per 450 g (1 lb) plus 30 minutes. Braising and boiling times are the same. Remember to check the weight before you throw the wrapping away.

To check that poultry is cooked, insert a knife in the fleshy part where the leg joins the body – the juices should run clear.

FISH Fish is delicate stuff. If you are baking it in foil or in a dish, put it in the centre of a preheated oven at 180°C (350°F, gas mark 4), and allow 8 minutes per 450 g (1 lb) for a whole fish, plus 10 minutes, and 10–20 minutes in total for fillets and steaks.

To check that fish is cooked, insert a knife near the backbone – the flesh should be opaque and flaky.

Roast meat and birds should 'rest' in a warm spot for 10 minutes before serving, covered loosely with foil. This makes for juicy, tender eating. Fish dishes are best eaten straightaway as their delicate flesh continues cooking in its own heat.

RICE White, long-grain rice should be boiled fast in lots of salted water for 12 minutes, then rinsed and dried off in a low oven. Cooking times for brown rice vary – it usually takes upwards of 40 minutes.

PASTA With dried pasta, check the makers' instructions, but start testing it sooner rather than later. 'Fresh', especially home-made, pasta cooks in a much shorter time – test after 2 minutes.

Standards

All the recipes in this chapter come into a category unrecognized, so far as I know, by cooking literature, but familiar to every reasonably experienced cook, who usually makes his or her personal selection as time goes by. Quite simply, these are dishes which one can, and does, go back to, over and over again, with renewed pleasure and appetite. They extend over the whole field of eating – soups, salads, main dishes, puddings. They must taste good, certainly, in a homely rather than subtle fashion. They are often, though not always, easy to make successfully. Their components tend to be straightforward, and associative as well – pork and beans, frankfurters and red cabbage – which makes the shopping easier, especially from memory. They are, of course, thrifty, but without appearing stingy. Still, in the last resort, their appeal is elusive, and just why one should keep returning to these, after many promising alternatives have been discarded, is something of a mystery.

There is nothing mysterious, however, about my reason for choosing to start my book with a whole collection of cooking Standards. I am convinced, from analysing my own experience and the food offered up regularly by friends, family and acquaintances, that these are the most useful recipes for an inexperienced cook to start on, a good foundation on which to build a more elaborate repertoire as experience and confidence grow. Once you have mastered a selection of these recipes, you will be able to feed yourself and others cheaply, efficiently and well, and you will have picked up some useful knowledge along the way.

A few specific points:

SOUPS Ideal pauper's food – cheap, nourishing and good for you. If your experience is limited to canned or packet varieties, you have no idea how good soup can be. A solid minestrone, with grated cheese, or a French onion soup poured over slices of bread, is almost a meal in itself. Certainly a light lunch. A lighter vegetable soup is, say, half a meal, and should be rounded out with a light main dish – grilled fish, pâté and salad, or an omelette.

MAIN DISHES Most in this chapter are substantial and need no more than one vegetable dish or salad as accompaniment. Many have their own stodge built in. Leftovers can be warmed up – indeed many of these dishes improve with keeping, within reason.

PUDDINGS Fresh fruit addicts probably won't bother with these. All the same it is worth learning up a few because they are useful when you have a lot of people to feed. Children love them, and so, oddly enough, do most men. A simple sweet like bread and butter pudding rounds off a skimpy meal pleasantly.

A guiding rule is that a meal can either be built round one solid dish, needing very little with, before or after, or a succession of lightweight dishes. The first is less trouble, the second offers more variety and is a better summer formula when salads and fruit are cheap and plentiful.

Simple Stock

What might be called serious stock-making, involving long cooking of selected meats and bones, plus clarifying with egg white, belongs today to the world of professional cheffery. However, any domestic cooking, and pauper meals especially, benefit enormously from the enriching properties of an easily made bowl of simple stock that can be kept in the fridge for several days, and used as the basis of soups, sauces, casserole dishes and much else. I tend to cook chicken, or one of the game birds in season (pheasant is sometimes as cheap as chicken) once a week, knowing that it will provide not only two meals, at a pinch, but also a supply of fresh, versatile stock to build into the week's meals.

I apply the same method, if anything so rough and ready can be called a method, to the remains of whatever bird we have eaten. Collect up all the bones, plus the carcass, plus any jellied cooking juices or congealed gravy, then chop them all across with a cleaver (to release the bone marrow), and dump the lot in a casserole with cold water to cover. Cover and cook in the oven at 140°C (275°F, gas mark 1) for several hours to extract whatever flavour and richness remains. What starts off as an unappetizing-looking panful of skin, scraps and bones (I mention this because too often people chuck these useful remnants away simply because they look so grungy) gradually yields up a quantity of lightly coloured, potentially savoury, broth with manifold uses.

Strain off the debris, leave the stock to cool in a bowl, then you can store it in the fridge for a few days or for several months in the freezer. This stock, as it is, will enormously enhance soups, pasta sauces, etc., 'rounding out' their essential flavours. A good simple stock sets to a light jelly with a layer of fat on top which can be scraped off and used to fry potatoes or croûtons.

Two points should be noted about this simple stock: it should not be seasoned at this stage, because any salting and peppering will become exaggerated during further reducing, and if it contains any vegetable ingredients, such as onions, herbs, stuffing, etc., during the time it is in the fridge it will need boiling up for a few minutes every couple of days (religiously every 48 hours to be on the safe side) to prevent it souring and spoiling.

Simple Fish Stock

Most fish dishes are improved by the addition of fish stock, which intensifies the flavour markedly – whether you are making a fish soup or a prawn curry, baking whole fish, or looking for the makings of a simple sauce to accompany poached, grilled or baked fish. This need not be a performance. For instance, if you make a point of buying prawns in their shells, it is no great bother to cook up the shells with water to cover and maybe a few chopped spring onions, for 20–30 minutes. This is more trouble than reaching for a packet of frozen shelled prawns, I agree, but the pay-off in terms of taste is seriously interesting. Not everyone realizes how much fishy taste there is in prawn shells, not to mention in other fishy debris, such as bones, skin and fish heads. I doubt that many paupers are so organized they cook up a regular supply of fish stock, to freeze, just in case, but any time you are contemplating a big fish dish, for a party perhaps, it is common sense to grab whatever 'bits' are available (a wise fishmonger will always let you have odds and ends, for a pittance, that would otherwise be thrown away) and cook the lot up for stock. Fresh fish is exquisite food, worth taking a little or even a *lot* of trouble over.

The fish trimmings to use for stock are best taken from so-called white, that is non-oily, fish. Oily fish – mackerel, herring, fresh sardines – have too pronounced a flavour, which when reduced down overpowers everything else. In this sense, fish stock should be neutral, but *fishy*. The making is simplicity itself. Put all the 'bits', including any prawn shells if you have them, into a large pan, cover with cold water, and bring very slowly to the boil. Skim off any scum that rises, reduce the heat and simmer for about 30 minutes. Strain off the liquid. Reduce by further simmering, uncovered, for another 10–15 minutes or until the broth begins to waft a marine tang, and looks less watery and a little more coloured. This is now the ideal liquid to add to any of the above-mentioned dishes, either solo or sharpened with wine, cider, a drop of wine vinegar or lemon juice. Keep the initial stock as plain as possible if you plan to freeze it or keep it in the fridge. It is the vegetable or herb additions which turn stock sour faster. And skip the salt and pepper, too, because reduction strengthens these flavours undesirably.

NOTE: *If you really can't be fashed to make your own, look for commercially prepared fish stock in small cartons or jars, and keep in the freezer. A clear liquid, this adds helpful fishiness to a dish.*

Vegetable Stock

A vegetable stock is a must for vegetarians, but non-veggies may find it useful for vegetable soups. Cookery writer Frances Bissell points out that basing vegetable soups on chicken stock clouds the pure taste of the main vegetable ingredient. I have adapted her recipe slightly. Any surplus is best frozen, as vegetable stocks rapidly sour.

1 large onion
2 carrots
2 stalks celery
1 leek
1 tablespoon vegetable oil
a bunch of parsley stalks (more flavour than the leaves)
3 large ripe tomatoes or half a tin peeled tomatoes
1.5 litres (3 pints) water

Peel and chop the first four vegetables, and cook them in the oil in a non-stick pan, stirring often, till just softening. They should be lightly coloured, but not burnt. Add the parsley and tomatoes, pour over the water, bring to simmering point and cook gently for 2 hours, skimming as needed. Strain the liquid from the vegetable matter. Use immediately, keep in the fridge for up to three days, or freeze.

NOTE: *Cooking water from boiling or steaming asparagus, broccoli, leeks, celery provides an ad hoc vegetable stock, a useful addition to gravies and sauces, when braising a chicken, or added to a béchamel (white sauce) mixture for a vegetable gratin, replacing milk. The sauce will not be so white but will taste more intensely of the vegetable concerned.*

Artichoke Soup

This soup is made with Jerusalem artichokes, which look like small knobbly potatoes, not the leafy globe variety. Artichokes have a pronounced, though delicate, flavour, which makes for a very good soup.

4 SERVINGS

450 g (1 lb) Jerusalem artichokes
25 g (1 oz) butter
1 litre (2 pints) water and 1 stock cube,
or 1 litre (2 pints) Simple Stock (see page 31)
salt and pepper
freshly grated nutmeg
a little single cream

Peel and slice the artichokes, then heat them gently in the butter for a few minutes. Add the water and stock cube, or Simple Stock, making sure the artichokes are covered by about 2.5 cm (1 inch). Season with salt, pepper and nutmeg, bring to the boil, then reduce the heat and simmer gently for 45 minutes to 1 hour or until the artichokes are tender.

Press the soup through a sieve into a bowl, then return it to the pan and add a little cream. Heat through gently before serving.

If you have time, make some croûtons (see page 41) to eat with this. The small cubed sort are best, sprinkled over the soup.

French Onion Soup

4 SERVINGS

a knob of butter
4 large or 6 small onions, thickly sliced
1 litre (2 pints) Simple Stock (see page 31)
salt and pepper
4 thick slices of bread
125g (4 oz) Cheddar cheese, grated

Melt the butter in a heavy-based saucepan and fry the onions over a moderate heat until golden brown. Stir from time to time to prevent them sticking. Pour in the stock and bring to the boil, then reduce the heat, cover and simmer for 30–45 minutes. Taste and season.

Toast the slices of bread and remove the crusts if you are fussy. Serve the soup in individual bowls. Float a slice of toast on each serving and sprinkle generously with grated cheese.

Celery Soup

An excellent, easily made soup, which really tastes of the vegetable.

4–6 SERVINGS

a knob of butter
1 small head of celery, trimmed and roughly chopped
(leaves included)
1 large potato, peeled and chopped
1 litre (2 pints) stock, or 500 ml (1 pint) stock and
500 ml (1 pint) milk
salt and pepper
freshly grated nutmeg
a little butter, to serve (optional)

Melt the butter in a large saucepan and gently stew the vegetables in it until well coated. This preliminary stew-frying of the vegetables makes the soup richer and tastier. Add the stock, bring to the boil, cover the pan and cook steadily for 45 minutes, or until the celery is soft. (It needs to be soft because you have to press it through a sieve.)

After sieving, return the soup to the pan, add the milk now if you are using milk, stir well and heat through. Taste, and add salt and pepper and a little grated nutmeg. Just before serving, you can stir in a little butter. Croûtons (see page 41) go well with this.

Borscht

Borscht is to Russia what Scotch Broth is to Scotland. It is a cheering soup to look at, ruby red, and the beetroot and soured cream give it an interesting acidulated sweetness. If you have any pickled beetroot, 1 tablespoon of the juice can be added to the Borscht. The soup can be made equally successfully with vegetable stock.

4–6 SERVINGS

1 litre (2 pints) Simple Stock (see page 31)
450 g (1 lb) uncooked beetroot, peeled and diced
1 onion, roughly chopped
1 carrot, roughly chopped
salt and pepper
150 ml (¼ pint) soured cream

Put the stock in a large saucepan, add the vegetables and bring to the boil, then reduce the heat, cover and simmer for 1–2 hours or until the beetroot is very pale and the soup very red. Add salt and pepper.

The Russian way would be to strain off the vegetables, but if you prefer a thicker soup you could sieve them and return them to the pan. A spoonful of soured cream is added to each helping of soup.

Minestrone

More a meal than a soup, this is economical, because only the greediest people would demand more than an omelette to follow. You can play about with the ingredients according to what is at hand, adding odd scraps of boiled bacon, a bacon bone, and such vegetables as are cheap and in season, but keep to the rule of putting slow-cooking vegetables in ahead of the quicker cooking ones. Other vegetables which can go in include celery, beans, peas, a Jerusalem artichoke or two, even a few spring greens, well trimmed. Of course, using Simple Stock (see page 31) instead of water and stock cubes gives a much richer soup.

4–6 SERVINGS

1 tablespoon vegetable oil
125 g (4 oz) belly of pork or bacon rashers, de-rinded and chopped
3 onions, sliced
3 garlic cloves, sliced
1.5 litres (3 pints) hot stock
125 g (4 oz) dried haricot beans, soaked overnight and drained
1 bay leaf
a pinch of dried thyme
a pinch of dried marjoram
227 g (8 oz) can tomatoes, or 2 tablespoons tomato purée
3 carrots, sliced
1 turnip, sliced
2 or 3 potatoes, peeled and sliced
½ small cabbage, shredded
1 leek, sliced (optional)
a handful of small pasta shapes
salt and pepper
grated Parmesan or Pecorino cheese, to serve

Heat the oil in a large saucepan and gently fry the belly of pork or bacon, onions and garlic, stirring to make sure nothing burns. Add the hot stock, haricot beans, bay leaf, thyme and marjoram, and the tomatoes or tomato purée. Boil for 1½ –2 hours, or until tender.

Add the carrots, turnip and potatoes to the soup. Ten minutes later put in the cabbage, leek (if using) and the pasta. After a further 10 minutes, taste, and add salt and pepper as needed.

Serve this soup with a bowl of grated Parmesan cheese so everyone can help themselves, and large slices of bread and butter.

Smoked Haddock Chowder

The basis for this comforting and filling soup is the milk which has been used to cook just a small amount of smoked haddock. The milk leaches out a surprisingly strong, smoky taste, which you can reinforce with the reserved fish and a few mussels or prawns. But the basis remains the combination of flavoured milk, potatoes and onion.

4 SERVINGS

smoked haddock fillet
500 ml–1 litre (1–2 pints) milk
1 tablespoon vegetable oil
25 g (1 oz) butter
2–3 medium-sized onions, finely chopped
4 medium-sized potatoes, peeled and diced
salt and black pepper
freshly grated nutmeg
1–2 tablespoons cooked mussels (see opposite), shells removed,
or peeled prawns, or a mixture
1 tablespoon finely chopped fresh parsley

Put the haddock fillet in a shallow pan or flameproof baking dish, cover with milk, bring to a simmer and simmer gently for 15–20 minutes. Drain off the milk and reserve it. Flake the fish, removing any skin and bones.

Heat the oil and butter over a medium heat in a heavy-based saucepan, and, when hot, add the onions and potatoes. Give the pan a good shake to coat the contents in the buttery oil. Turn the heat down, cover the pan and leave to sweat over a low heat until the onion is transparent. Pour over the reserved milk, adding a little water to cover the ingredients, if necessary (this is a solid sort of soup). Re-cover the pan and cook gently for about 10 minutes or until the potato is tender. Season to taste with salt, pepper and nutmeg, add the fish and shellfish, and heat through over a low heat for a few minutes.

Ladle into shallow soup plates, sprinkle with parsley and serve.

Moules MacCormac

This excellent dish began life as moules marinières with knobs on, acquired an Asian fillip under the tutelage of cookery writer Daramjit Singh, plus modifications suggested by an exceptional mussel broth in Edinburgh, and was then surprised to find its twin in a medieval dish described in Dorothy Hartley's *Food in England*. Whatever its pedigree, it is always worth waiting for.

6–8 SERVINGS

1 kg (2 lb) fresh mussels
50 g (2 oz) butter
450 g (1 lb) onions, chopped
2 large leeks, chopped
2 garlic cloves, chopped
1 cm (½ inch) cube of fresh root ginger, peeled and chopped
125 ml (4 fl oz) water
1 teaspoon ground turmeric, or ½ teaspoon saffron threads
a pinch of cayenne pepper
salt and black pepper
300 ml (½ pint) dry white wine
200 ml (7 fl oz) cream (optional)
a small handful of fresh parsley or coriander, finely chopped

Clean mussels under a running tap, scraping off any barnacles and removing the beards with a sharp knife. Don't leave them in water – as many recipes suggest – because this encourages them to open, thus losing their briny juices. Mussels (or clams) which feel unusually heavy should be discarded (they may be full of mud), likewise mussels (or clams) which refuse to close after giving them a sharp tap.

Melt the butter in a large heavy-based saucepan with a lid and soften the onions and leeks over moderate heat, with the lid half on. Add the garlic and ginger and leave to simmer, without browning.

Drain the mussels and put them in a large pan with the water. Cook over a high heat and shake and turn them with a wooden spoon for 1–2 minutes or until they are all open. Remove immediately. (Discard any mussels that remain stubbornly closed.) The mussels should be just firm enough to remove from the shells. Using a slotted spoon, lift the mussels out on to a large dish and cool slightly.

Pour the mussel pan liquid through a fine sieve to remove any grit, directly into the vegetable pan. Add the turmeric or saffron, cayenne, salt and black pepper to taste. Simmer very gently, covered.

Remove the mussels from their shells (some people might prefer to leave them on the half shell). They should be added all at once, with the wine, to the oniony stock. Replace the lid and leave to simmer very gently for a further 3–5 minutes.

Add the cream (if using) and parsley, and serve in shallow soup plates with lots of hot bread.

Baked Eggs

My entire household has rediscovered baked eggs, with the result that the sink is now full of little ramekins instead of pans coated with burned scrambled egg. Baked eggs take longer to cook but taste subtly nicer, either quite plain, or fancied up with herbs, chopped mushroom, bacon, etc. The method may sound fussy for such a simple dish, but practice it until it becomes effortless because it makes for eggs which are sufficiently set to turn out, but still creamy and delicious.

1 SERVING

a scrap of butter and/or 1 teaspoon soured cream
salt and pepper
optional extras: ½ teaspoon chopped fresh herbs, or
1 teaspoon chopped mushroom or bacon
1–2 eggs

Put all the ingredients, except the egg, in a ramekin dish. Stand it in a shallow ovenproof dish with hot water in it to come about 1 cm (½ inch) up the sides. Pop this dish in the oven at 190°C (375°F, gas mark 5) for a few minutes or until the butter is hot and the mushroom, or whatever you are using, is starting to cook.

Wearing oven gloves, take the dish out and break the egg into the ramekin. Return to the oven with a lid or piece of foil on top. I find this speeds the cooking. Cook for 10–12 minutes or until the white is opaque and the yolk just setting.

Baked eggs can be eaten with teaspoons straight from the dish, or turned out on to plates to eat with fried bacon, or a salad, or buttered toast.

Spinach Salad with Frizzled Bacon and Croûtons

This is an update on the old rustic French salad of young dandelion leaves wilted in the fat rendered from diced bacon and served with a dash of vinegar.

If you can lay hands on some new dandelion leaves (the smaller inner ones), they add a certain *je ne sais quoi* to the spinach, which must be young, green and crisped in cold water beforehand.

4 SERVINGS

450 g (1 lb) spinach leaves
1 small slice of fatty gammon, cubed, or
4 rashers of streaky bacon, de-rinded and cut into strips
1–2 tablespoons white or red wine vinegar

FOR THE CROÛTONS
1 thick slice of day-old bread
1 garlic clove, halved
1 tablespoon olive oil
a knob of butter

Pick over the spinach, discarding any limp or yellowing leaves and pinching off coarse stalks. Leave in cold water for 1–2 hours to crisp.

To make the croûtons, cut the crusts off the bread and rub it with the garlic clove, then dice the bread into cubes. Heat the oil and butter in a frying pan and fry the bread cubes until golden. Remove from the pan and keep warm.

Put the gammon or bacon in the pan and heat gently until the fat runs and the meat is cooked.

Drain the spinach and dry it in a salad spinner or shake it in a clean towel, then put it in a bowl, and quickly add the gammon or bacon and the croûtons. Pour the vinegar into the pan, swirl round and pour over the spinach. Toss well and serve on cold plates.

Celery, Beetroot and Onion Salad

If you find beetroot cloying on its own, try this excellent winter salad, where the sweetness of the beet is offset by the crisp texture of celery and pungent taste of onion.

4 SERVINGS

**2 medium-sized cooked beetroots
4 celery stalks
1 mild onion
dressing**

Peel the beets and cut into dice. Scrub the celery well and cut crossways into thin strips. Slice the onion finely and separate the rings. Combine all the ingredients. Add dressing to taste and if possible leave for a few hours before eating.

An ordinary vinaigrette dressing is quite adequate for this but if you want to glorify the salad the following vinaigrette-plus will do the trick.

Mix together 1 tablespoon vinegar, 3 tablespoons oil, 1 teaspoon made English or French mustard, 1 teaspoon brown sugar, the sieved yolks of 2 hard-boiled eggs, a squeeze of lemon juice, salt, pepper. Beat this lot up together till it is a smooth emulsion and stir it into your salad – you may not need it all, so use your discretion. Just before serving stir in a couple of spoonfuls of cream.

Mashed Potato and Swede

It seems incredible that there was a time when I despised swedes, now a household favourite, especially cooked like this. I know the snobbery persists in France, however. I produced this dish for a Frenchman once; he pronounced it intriguing and good, and asked what went into it. On hearing it was swedes, he looked scandalized. But that is cattle food! Choose smallish swedes, which are likely to be younger, and tender once cooked. Every now and then one encounters a swede that retains a woody core even after the longest cooking; best chuck these, they have been around too long. A prime swede yields sweet, golden flesh of a delicious texture, less perfumed than parsnip, tastier than pumpkin. It can also be made into a flavoursome soup.

4 SERVINGS

1 swede, weighing about 450–700 g (1–1½ lb), scrubbed
700 g (1½ lb) 'floury' potatoes, such as King Edward
or Maris Piper, scrubbed
50 g (2 oz) butter
250 ml (9 fl oz) milk
salt and pepper
freshly grated nutmeg

Put the swede in a large saucepan, cover with cold water and bring slowly to the boil, then reduce the heat and simmer for 45 minutes to 1 hour or until tender.

Meanwhile, put the potatoes in another large saucepan and cover with cold water. Bring to the boil, then reduce the heat and simmer for 20–25 minutes or until tender. Drain the potatoes and peel them, wearing rubber gloves. Cut the potatoes roughly into chunks and put them in a heatproof bowl. Mash the potatoes with a potato masher until soft, then beat in the butter and milk to give a smooth, soft consistency. Cover and keep warm.

When the swede is tender enough to yield to a fork, drain, peel, cut into chunks and mash in the same way as the potato. Mix the swede with the mashed potato, beating with a fork to amalgamate thoroughly. Season well with salt, pepper and nutmeg, adding more butter and milk if the mixture seems too stiff. Serve hot.

NOTE: *Fashionable restaurants increasingly feature variations on mashed potatoes on their menus these days and some of their inventions are worth trying when you want a change from the basic mash of floury potatoes, cooked in their skins, peeled, and worked up with butter, milk and salt and pepper. Try adding a spoonful of Dijon mustard, a big spoonful of horseradish sauce, or a dollop of garlic purée (see page 266) at the seasoning stage, or include a bunch of chopped spring onions towards the end of their cooking time. Other root vegetables which can enliven a basic mash are celeriac, parsnip, carrots, cooked separately and puréed before mixing into the potato mash. Scraps of cheese (soft or hard, rind removed) add food value as well as flavour, as will the last scraping of cream, ricotta, cottage cheese. Chopped fresh herbs – chives, parsley, dill – also boost the flavour.*

Celeriac and Potato Mash

Celeriac, if you have not come across it before, is a large bulbous-looking root – it is, in fact, the root of the celery plant with a coarse brown skin. It has the flavour of celery, but is a more manageable vegetable for dishes like this one. It also makes an excellent salad, served raw with a mustardy dressing.

roughly equal weights of celeriac and potato

Scrub the celeriac, and cook, unpeeled, in water till it is quite tender. Wearing rubber gloves (the peel stains), peel and mash it, then put it through a sieve. Mix with boiled sieved potatoes. Return to the pan and beat in a good lump of butter and plenty of seasoning – salt, black pepper, a little nutmeg – over a low flame. If you have any cream stir that in too.

French Fried Onion Rings

There is a trick to making these crisp, puffy, golden fried onion rings, which is worth learning. Some people will eat almost anything provided you dish up a pile of these onions at the same time.

4 SERVINGS

4 onions, very thinly sliced into rings
salt
50 g (2 oz) plain flour
vegetable oil for deep-frying

Sprinkle the onions with salt and leave on a plate for 20 minutes or so, to sweat out their moisture.

Drain the onions, shake off excess salt and dredge with flour (the easiest way to do this is to put the flour in a paper bag and to shake the onions around inside it). Fry the onions in hot oil for 5 minutes.

Take the onions out of the pan with a perforated slice. Reheat the oil until it is good and hot, then return the onions to the pan and fry until as crisp and golden as you want them. Drain on kitchen paper.

NOTE: *This is also the French method of producing those delicious frites (chips) which taste so different from the sluggish white things most British chippies produce. The trick is to fry twice, with a pause between for the oil to reheat.*

Roast Onions

Not only are onions almost the cheapest vegetable, but if you believe time is money, this is a terrific recipe for paupers.

4 SERVINGS

4 even-sized onions

Stand the onions in an ovenproof dish and roast them in their skins in the oven at 180°C (350°F, gas mark 4) for about 1 hour. They give off a delicious smell of caramel.

Braised Cabbage with Apple

After washing the cabbage, don't be fussy about drying it; the water that adheres to the leaves will provide its cooking liquid.

6 SERVINGS

50 g (2 oz) butter
1 small onion, sliced
1 green or red cabbage, chopped
2 Cox's Orange Pippin, or other firm eating apples,
peeled, cored and sliced
2 teaspoons soft brown sugar
a pinch of salt

Melt the butter in a saucepan, add the onion, cover with a lid and cook over a very low heat, stirring occasionally, until the onion is soft but not brown. Add the cabbage, apple, sugar and salt. Stir, then replace the lid and cook over a very gentle heat for 20–30 minutes, stirring once or twice, until the cabbage is tender but still fresh-tasting.

NOTE: *If you want to make the cabbage more tart, add 1 tablespoon cider vinegar with the raw cabbage and other ingredients.*

Braised Celery

6–8 SERVINGS

4 heads of celery
450 ml (¾ pint) hot Vegetable Stock (see page 33)

Trim the celery heads, remove the tough outside stalks and scrape off any strings with a sharp knife. Cut each head in half lengthways.

Simmer the celery pieces in salted water for 10 minutes, then drain and put them in an earthenware or other gratin dish which is broad enough to hold them side by side. Cover with hot stock, cover and cook in the oven at 140°C (275°F, gas mark 1) for 1 hour or until the stock has reduced to a syrup.

'Hot' Cauliflower

4–6 SERVINGS

4 garlic cloves
3 anchovy fillets
cauliflower, broken into florets
2 tablespoons olive oil
25 g (1 oz) butter
4 tablespoons dried breadcrumbs
1 dried red chilli, finely chopped
2 tablespoons finely chopped fresh parsley

Crush the garlic in a pestle and mortar or in a strong bowl with the end of a rolling pin. Add the anchovy fillets and pound to a paste. Steam or briefly cook the cauliflower florets in boiling salted water for about 5 minutes or until just tender but still slightly crisp.

Meanwhile, heat the oil and butter in a frying pan and fry the breadcrumbs and chilli until golden. Add the mixture from the mortar and stir in the chopped parsley.

Drain the cauliflower, if necessary, and place in a warmed serving bowl. Spoon over the breadcrumb mixture.

Broad Beans in a Pot with Bacon

For broad beans late in the season, when they are large and have tough husks.

5–6 SERVINGS AS PART OF A MEAL

450 g (1 lb) shelled broad beans
3 rashers of back bacon, de-rinded
2 tablespoons olive oil
1 small onion, sliced
salt and pepper
a bunch of fresh mint or coriander, chopped

To skin the beans, make a lengthways cut in the skin of each one and squeeze the bean gently until it slips out of its skin. Cut the bacon into matchsticks and put it in a flameproof casserole or earthenware pot. Heat gently to sweat the moisture out of the bacon and to melt its fat. Add the oil and continue cooking until the bacon is just cooked but not yet beginning to brown. Add the onion and cook until golden, then add the beans, season with salt and pepper, cover with a lid and continue cooking for a few more minutes until the beans are tender, adding a splash of water if the mixture looks as if it is drying out. Add the herbs 30 seconds before you remove the dish from the heat.

Potatoes with Rosemary, Bacon and Cream

This is a very good way to cook potatoes to go with plainly baked fish or chicken breasts. There is no need to peel the potatoes as long as they are smooth and thin-skinned.

4 SERVINGS

700 g (1½ lb) potatoes, scrubbed and thinly sliced
4 rashers of streaky bacon, de-rinded and cut into thin strips
4 garlic cloves, thinly sliced
about 2 sprigs of fresh rosemary, or 1 tablespoon dried
300 ml (½ pint) single cream
about 50 g (2 oz) butter

Layer the slices of potato in a buttered or oiled baking dish or tin, scattering the bacon, garlic and fragments of rosemary between the layers. Pour the cream over and dot with the butter. Lay a piece of foil or greaseproof paper over the top and cook in the oven at 200°C (400°F, gas mark 6) for 20 minutes. Remove the foil and cook for a further 20 minutes or until the top is golden brown and the potatoes tender.

NOTE: *Depending on the type of potatoes you use, you may need to leave the covering in place for more or less time so that the potatoes cook before they dry out.*

Galette de Pommes Dauphin

A bumper sized potato cake fried till crispy on the outside but soft within, this could be the basis of a light supper with cold meat or charcuterie, or elegantly partner a straightforward meat or fish dish – Liver au Poivre (see page 151), devilled chicken legs, grilled mackerel, or your favourite sausages. The French specify lard for the frying because animal fats reach a higher temperature than oil without burning. The ideal would be lard rendered from a ham or gammon joint (see page 244) but goose fat, sold in tins, is excellent for frying though it contributes less flavour. Goose fat keeps for ever in the fridge. Don't use a commercial lard.

2–4 SERVINGS

**450–700 g (1–1½ lbs) potatoes
2–3 tablespoons ham or goose fat
sea salt and freshly ground black pepper**

Peel and quarter the potatoes, and grate through a mouli or on a standard grater. Turn the mushy result into a clean cloth, and wring to extract as much liquid as possible. Work salt and pepper into the mush with your hands.

Heat a heavy frying pan, add half the lard, continue heating till hazy, then tip in the potato, flatten it out rapidly and continue cooking over high heat for 5 minutes. Lower the heat, cover the pan, and cook for another 10 minutes. Turn the galette on to a plate, melt more lard in the pan, then cook the other side for 5 minutes uncovered.

Kedgeree

6 SERVINGS

450 g (1 lb) smoked haddock
50 g (2 oz) butter
2 onions, sliced
1 teaspoon curry powder
salt and black pepper
450 g (1 lb) 'easy-cook' long-grain rice
3 hard-boiled eggs, sliced
a large sprig of fresh parsley, finely chopped
125 ml (4 fl oz) single or whipping cream

Put the haddock in a saucepan, cover with water and simmer gently for 15–20 minutes or until the fish comes off the skin easily. Take the fish out of its simmering liquid and carefully flake the fish, removing all the skin and bones.

Melt the butter in a heavy-based saucepan and fry the onions until they have turned golden. Add the curry powder and cook for 1 minute, then remove from the heat.

Put the haddock cooking liquid in a saucepan, top it up with more water, and bring to the boil. Add salt to taste, stir in the rice and simmer for about 10 minutes or until it is just tender. Drain it well and stir it into the curried buttery onions. Gently fold in the flaked haddock and the sliced hard-boiled eggs. Season liberally with pepper and finally stir in the chopped parsley and the cream. Serve immediately.

Fish Pie

There are dozens of more or less elaborate versions of fish pie. To my mind, the simple, classic version given here, combining fish and hard-boiled egg in a creamy and faintly cheesy white sauce, is the best of all. Any firm white fish can be used: cod, bream, bass. Coley, if you can get it, is an excellent cheap substitute for cod, with a dark meat which turns white when cooked, and a good flavour. For economy's sake you can omit the shrimps.

2 SERVINGS

225 g (8 oz) white fish
1 bay leaf (optional)
40 g (1½ oz) butter
25g (1 oz) plain flour
milk
salt and pepper
50 g (2 oz) Cheddar cheese, grated
½ teaspoon mustard powder
50 g (2 oz) peeled shrimps (optional)
2 hard-boiled eggs, chopped
dried breadcrumbs or mashed potato

Put the fish in a baking dish with a little water. Add the bay leaf, if using, cover and bake in the oven at 180°C (350°F, gas mark 4) for 20–30 minutes. Drain the fish on to a plate, reserving the cooking water. Divide the fish into chunks, removing any skin and bones.

Melt 25 g (1 oz) of the butter in a saucepan and stir in the flour. Cook for 1–2 minutes, stirring, then remove from the heat. Make up the reserved fish stock to 300 ml (½ pint) with milk and stir gradually into the butter and flour mixture. Bring to the boil, stirring constantly, then simmer for a few minutes until smooth and thick. Season with salt and pepper and stir in the cheese and mustard. Remove from the heat and stir in the fish, shrimps, if using, and hard-boiled egg. Turn into an ovenproof dish. Either sprinkle the top with breadcrumbs, or spread a layer of mashed potatoes over it, dot with the remaining butter and bake in the oven at 180°C (350°F, gas mark 4) until the top is brown.

Baked Tomatoes (see page 186) go nicely with this.

Fishcakes

When nothing else appeals, one can always manage a fishcake. With cod in danger of being fished out, make them with cooked leftovers of salmon, salt cod, smoked haddock, as restaurants do. White fish need extra flavouring. The fish (skinned, boned and flaked) is extended with mashed potato plus a beaten egg to bind the mixture. Chill cakes well before cooking. Use a non-stick frying pan, if possible, and handle the fishcakes tenderly, turning them over with a metal slice to prevent them disintegrating. One mega fishcake can be easier to handle than lots of smaller ones for a family supper. Add chopped fresh herbs (chives, parsley, chervil, tarragon), finely chopped onion or shallot (briefly parboiled), a finely chopped de-seeded green chilli, according to taste and the whim of the moment. Serve with tomato ketchup, aïoli, or skordalia. Baked tomatoes, or a green vegetable, are suitable extras.

SERVES 4–6

350–450 g (¾–1 lb) cooked, flaked fish, skin & bones removed
about 600 g (1¼ lb) cold mashed potato
2 generous spoonfuls fresh herbs, finely chopped
1 small onion or 2 shallots, finely minced, steamed for a minute or two
salt and pepper
1 egg, beaten

Mix all the ingredients together in a bowl, adding the beaten egg last. Taking a spoonful at a time, shape the mixture into scone-size patties on a flat dish. Chill.

To cook, heat an oil/butter mix in a large frying pan and brown the cakes on both sides, transferring to a heated oven dish. Heat through in a moderate oven for a few minutes.

A giant fishcake is prepared the same way, but is best reversed on to a plate like a tortilla before returning to the pan to brown the other side.

NOTE: *Some cooks stir a spoonful of mayonnaise or béchamel into the mixture, as a lubricant. Fresh breadcrumbs can be added – 1–2 spoonfuls – to give a lighter texture. Some chefs dip the cakes in beaten egg and dry breadcrumbs before frying. This keeps them neat looking but makes them a little heavy.*

Fishy Chowder

Milk used to cook smoked haddock for kedgeree provides a 'stock' for this speedy version of an American fish chowder. Add chopped onion, shallot or spring onions, a diced potato or two for bulk and some fresh, tinned or frozen sweetcorn, for texture and a touch of sweetness. Any leftover haddock can of course be stirred in at the last minute, or you could substitute a spoonful of vongole (Italian tinned clams). The 'stock' can be extended with milk, water, fish stock. A little cream gives suavity to the chowder, and a sprinkle of chopped parsley looks pretty.

SERVES 2−4

haddock cooking liquid (about 1.5 litres/3 pints)
1 large or 2 medium potatoes, peeled and diced
about 2 tablespoons chopped onion, shallot or spring onions
about 300 g (11 oz) fresh, frozen or tinned sweetcorn
grated nutmeg
salt and pepper

Heat the haddock stock in a saucepan, adding diced potato and chopped onion/shallot/spring onion as it comes to the boil. Let simmer, adding milk, water or fish stock if the chowder looks too solid. Fresh corn should be boiled for 8–10 minutes separately, then sliced off the cob; frozen corn may be de-frosted or added as is; tinned corn can be tipped in with the canning liquid. Taste for seasoning, adding maybe half a teaspoon grated nutmeg, a little salt and plenty of pepper.

Once the potato is tender, the chowder is ready – this is the moment to add flaked fish, clams, cream. Let simmer a few minutes longer to merge the flavours. Sprinkle chopped parsley on top and serve in deep bowls.

Braised Herrings with Potatoes and Apple

5 SERVINGS

450 g (1 lb) herring fillets
75 g (3 oz) butter, softened
2 tablespoons prepared mustard (optional)
salt and black pepper
1 kg (2 lb) potatoes, peeled and thinly sliced
2 large, firm apples, peeled, cored and thinly sliced
2 onions, thinly sliced
300 ml (½ pint) cider or water

Lay the herring fillets skin side down and spread them with 65 g (2½ oz) of the butter and the mustard, if using. Season with black pepper and a little salt and roll them up, skin side out.

Butter a fairly deep ovenproof dish (earthenware would be ideal) and put in half the potato slices, then one of the sliced apples and one of the onions. Lay the herring rolls on top, and cover them with the rest of the onion and apple, and finally the remaining potato slices. Pour over the cider or water to come halfway up the side of the dish. Dot the top with the remaining butter and grind a little salt and pepper over it.

Cover with foil and bake in the oven at 180°C (350°F, gas mark 4) for 30 minutes, then remove the foil and turn the oven up to 200°C (400°F, gas mark 6) and cook for a further 30 minutes or until the top is golden. If it threatens to dry out before the potatoes are cooked, you can add a little more liquid.

Soft Herring Roes with Peas

This is an excellent supper dish with baked or boiled potatoes; it is also good as a starter on toast or even for a sumptuous breakfast.

4 SERVINGS

225 g (8 oz) shelled fresh or frozen peas
50 g (2 oz) butter
2 garlic cloves, crushed
450 g (1 lb) soft herring roes
salt and black pepper

Blanch the frozen peas in boiling salted water, or if you are using fresh peas boil them until they are barely cooked. 'Refresh' them under gently flowing cold water, drain and set aside.

Melt the butter with the garlic in a heavy-based frying pan until it is hot but not burned. Add the herring roes, a few at a time. (There is no need to remove the first roes from the pan, just add them gradually so that the butter stays hot and seals each roe. There is no hope of the roes all staying crisp and separate as many will be a bit smashed before they reach you, but it helps the flavour to have some which are brown on the edges.)

When they are all hot and bubbling, add the peas, heat through, season lavishly with black pepper and sparingly with salt, and serve very hot.

VARIATION: *The identical recipe can be made with chicken livers, but with the addition of some bits of crispy bacon.*

Mussel and Potato Hotpot

Mussels are still the best value in seafood, and a rare example of how farming can improve the product; I find farmed mussels need less cleaning, their flavour is unimpaired, and they are available all year round. This recipe makes a substantial and tasty meal, with a layer of mussels and bacon sandwiched between sliced potatoes and onions. The dish comes from Darina Allen, of Ballymaloe Cookery School fame, but I have adapted the original recipe a little to meet pauper requirements.

4–6 SERVINGS

4 tablespoons olive, sunflower or safflower oil
2 large onions, chopped
3 rashers of streaky bacon, de-rinded and diced
1 kg (2¼ lb) fresh mussels
300 ml (½ pint) dry white wine or dry cider
a large handful of fresh parsley, chopped
2 sprigs of fresh thyme, chopped
150 ml (5 fl oz) carton of single cream
salt and pepper
about 450 g (1 lb) cooked potatoes, peeled and sliced
25 g (1oz) butter
3–4 tablespoons dried or fresh breadcrumbs
2–3 tablespoons grated cheese (a good Cheddar or Parmesan)
2 garlic cloves, chopped

Heat the oil in a heavy-based saucepan, add the onion and bacon, cover and sweat over a low heat until the onion is soft and transparent.

Meanwhile, pick over the mussels, checking that they are all tightly closed. Scrub them well and pull off any beards with a knife. Put the wine or cider in a stainless steel or enamel pan, add half the parsley and the thyme and heat until bubbling. Tip in the mussels, clap the lid on the pan and cook over a moderate heat for about 3 minutes, then check to see if they have opened. As soon as all the mussels have opened, spoon them on to a plate and leave to cool. (Discard any mussels that do not open.) Strain the cooking liquor, add the cream and season with salt and pepper.

Layer half the sliced potatoes with half the onion and bacon mixture in a gratin dish. Take the mussels from their shells (I use a small knife; they can be quite tricky to remove whole) and spread them over the vegetables, then finish up with more layers of onion and potato. Pour over the creamy liquor.

Melt the butter in a saucepan, add the breadcrumbs and turn them in the butter over a low heat for a moment, until golden, then mix them with the remaining parsley, the grated cheese and the chopped garlic. Spread this mixture over the top of the dish and bake in the oven at 180°C (350°F, gas mark 4) until the top is crisp and the contents bubbling hot. Serve with steamed broccoli or a crunchy green salad made with frisée, chicory or a mixture.

Jannsens Frestelsee

Something of a classic in Sweden, this is one of those dishes based on the simplest ingredients – anchovies, potatoes, onions, cream – which everyone should know about because it can be knocked up quickly, using ingredients to hand, and is well nigh foolproof. The quantities given here are for two, because it is such an ideal supper dish. Double the quantities could serve five, because it is surprisingly rich and filling.

2 SERVINGS

5–6 small potatoes, peeled and cut into matchsticks
1–2 onions or shallots, peeled and finely shredded
8 anchovy fillets, in jars or tins
300 ml (½ pint) double cream or
150 ml (5 fl oz) each crème fraîche and single cream
25 g (1 oz) butter
black pepper

Layer the matchstick potatoes, shredded onions or shallots, and anchovies in a shallow ovenproof dish, ending with a spiky layer of potato, and grinding black pepper on to each layer. Pour over the cream, shaking to distribute evenly. Dot with butter. Bake in moderate oven for 45–60 minutes, or till the potatoes are tender. If the dish seems to be browning before the potatoes are quite cooked, cover with foil and cook on at a slightly reduced heat for 10–15 minutes. Serve with a characterful vegetable – cauliflower, 'hot' greens, green beans.

Stuffed Cabbage

One of the most succulent stuffed vegetable dishes, juicy cabbage counterpointing a meat and rice stuffing, sharpened by garlic and herbs, all sitting in a thin tomato sauce. A bit fussy to prepare, like many beloved old dishes, but always popular, even with children. A good way to stretch leftover cooked sausages and rice to encompass a family meal.

4–6 SERVINGS

1 large Savoy cabbage
knob of butter
2 onions, peeled and chopped
2 cloves garlic
about 300–400 g (11–15 oz) quality sausages, cooked or raw
roughly equal quantity or a bit more of cooked rice
splash soy or Worcestershire sauce
salt and pepper
handful chopped fresh herbs – thyme, parsley, oregano, fennel

SAUCE
1 tin peeled tomatoes
small glass red or white wine, and/or stock
2 cloves garlic

Steam or boil the whole cabbage for 8–10 minutes, till just tender. Drain, refresh under the cold tap and set aside. In a heavy pan heat the butter, with a little oil to stop it burning, and gently fry the onion for 5 minutes. Add the chopped garlic, raw or cooked sausage meat (slit casings and extract meat) and rice, stir well to mix, breaking up the meat with a fork, splash on soy or Worcestershire sauce, season with salt and pepper, remove from heat and stir in chopped herbs. Let cool while you prepare the cabbage and sauce. Turn the tinned tomatoes into a pan with wine and garlic (more herbs too if you have them) and reduce over moderate heat, crushing the tomatoes with a potato masher. Start defoliating the cabbage, peeling back the leaves and cutting them off the stem or core with a sharp knife. To make up cabbage leaf parcels, lay a leaf flat (cut out the hard stem if necessary) drop a spoonful of stuffing in the middle, then fold the sides over and roll up from the stem towards the tip, to make a neat little parcel.

Repeat till you run out of stuffing. Lay the parcels on a flat oven dish, pour the thin tomato sauce around and cook for around 30 minutes in a moderate oven, basting occasionally with the sauce. Add water or wine if the sauce begins to dry up before the parcels are hot and cooked through, or reduce oven heat, or cover with foil.

NOTE: *A speeded up version can be made by scooping the heart out of the pre-cooked cabbage, leaving a leafy container of outer leaves. Chop cabbage heart, add to stuffing, fill the hollowed cabbage with this, folding leaves over, then cook as above but in a smaller, deeper dish with a lid.*

Baked Stuffed Vegetable Marrow

Large vegetable marrows are very cheap in season and make a handy receptacle for a highly seasoned minced meat stuffing, the bland flavour of the marrow providing just enough contrast. It is a less solid and indigestible dish than stuffed green peppers or aubergines, and I think rather nicer. Add a few raisins, sultanas or currants to the stuffing, if liked.

4–6 SERVINGS

1 medium-sized marrow (about 30 cm/12 inches long)
a knob of butter
2–3 rashers of bacon, de-rinded and cut into small squares
2 onions, chopped
2–4 garlic cloves, chopped
225 g (8 oz) minced beef or lamb
400 g (14 oz) can of tomatoes
a sprig of fresh thyme, marjoram or fennel, chopped,
or 1 teaspoon dried
salt and pepper
25 g (1 oz) long-grain rice, cooked
a little sugar

Bring a large saucepan of water to the boil, plunge in the marrow and cook for 3 minutes. Remove. Slice off the top of the marrow, lengthways, about one third from the top so you have one deeper marrow receptacle and one shallow lid. Scoop out the seeds and membrane, and a little pulp if the space looks too shallow.

Melt the butter in a frying pan and fry the bacon, the onions and garlic. Add the minced meat and fry gently until lightly browned. Drain the can of tomatoes and add a little of the juice to the meat mixture to moisten it. Add the herbs and season well with salt and pepper. Stir in the cooked rice. If the mixture seems very dry, add more tomato liquid. Fill the scooped-out marrow with the mixture, put on the lid and secure with string or a couple of skewers. Put the canned tomatoes in a saucepan with salt and pepper and a littlesugar and cook gently until they can be mashed to a pulp. Dilute with water if too thick. Put the marrow in a roasting tin or baking dish and pour the tomato pulp around it. Bake in the oven at 180°C (350°F, gas mark 4) for 1 hour or until the marrow is tender, basting from time to time with the tomato sauce.

Serve with plain boiled rice, and the juice from the pan.

Shepherd's Pie

Revising this book, I was amazed to find no recipe for shepherd's pie, made with minced lamb or mutton, or cottage pie, made with beef. Perhaps I thought it was too familiar to be worth including. Anyway, I'm grateful for the chance to repair the omission because this is the friendliest of our native dishes. Originally, shepherd's pie was a made-up dish, an ideal way to stretch leftover cooked meat. Today, I tend to make it with fresh minced lamb from a halal butcher, for preference, because (a) their lamb verges on mutton, and so is tastier, and (b) the quality is consistently high, due to rapid turnover.

6−8 SERVINGS

700 g (1½ lb) 'floury' potatoes
salt and black pepper
700 g (1½ lb) fresh minced lamb or mutton
225 g (8 oz) carrots, sliced
2 medium-sized onions, chopped
Worcestershire or soy sauce
tomato purée (optional)
25 g (1 oz) butter
25 ml (1 fl oz) milk

Put the unpeeled potatoes in a large saucepan of salted water and bring to the boil. Reduce the heat and leave to simmer while preparing the pie filling.

Put the minced meat in a heavy-based saucepan, cover and set over a gentle heat to render off some fat. It will need an occasional stir, with a wooden fork if possible, to ensure the meat heats thoroughly and to break up lumps.

Meanwhile, bring a saucepan of salted water to the boil and add the carrots. Bring back to the boil and, after 3 minutes, add the onions and cook for 1–2 minutes longer. (This is a softening procedure, *not* meant to cook the vegetables through.) Drain the vegetables, reserving the liquid. Chop the carrots even smaller.

By now, the meat should have yielded quite a bit of fat. Pour this off – I tend to chuck it, though in the old days people swore by mutton fat for chapped hands or cracked leather! Mix the minced meat with the carrots and onions, season generously with salt and black pepper and moisten with a little of the reserved vegetable water plus a good splash of Worcestershire or soy sauce, or both. I sometimes add a squeeze of tomato purée, more for colour than anything else. Spread this mixture in a shallow oval or round ovenproof dish, with sloping sides, if possible – the classic British shape.

The potatoes should now feel soft when prodded with a fork, but not so soft that they disintegrate. Drain the potatoes, peel when cool enough to handle, and mash while still hot, adding half the butter and the milk, and salt and pepper to taste. The mash should be more solid than the usual purée, to make a decent topping for the pie. Spoon the potato over the meat mixture, smoothing it out with a fork, then roughing up the surface to help it brown. Dot with the remaining butter and cook in the oven at 190°C (375°F, gas mark 5) for 30–40 minutes or until the top is lightly browned.

Serve with buttered greens, cabbage or sprouts, and more carrots. Hand round Worcestershire sauce and ketchup, too.

Rillons

Much modern pork is improved by steeping it in salt for a few hours; wash it off and dry the meat before cooking.

6–8 SERVINGS

1 kg (2 lb) belly of pork
a sprig of fresh thyme
1 bay leaf
salt and black pepper

Cut the belly of pork into 5 cm (2 inch) cubes and put them in a heavy-based saucepan or flameproof casserole with 175–250 ml (6–8 fl oz) water, the thyme and bay leaf. Cover and cook over a gentle heat or in the oven at 140°C (275°F, gas mark 1) for 4 hours.

Drain off the fat and reserve to use for cooking on another occasion. Put the *rillons* back in the pan and continue to cook, uncovered, over a higher heat or in the oven at 190°C (375°F, gas mark 5) until brown. Season with salt and pepper and eat with mashed potatoes and baked apples.

Pork and Beans

This recipe is a classic of American domestic cookery and the inspiration, I imagine, of the ubiquitous baked beans. It is easy to make.

4–6 SERVINGS

450 g (1 lb) dried haricot beans, soaked overnight
2 tablespoons black treacle (molasses)
a dash of Worcestershire sauce
2 teaspoons mustard powder
2 teaspoons brown sugar
salt and pepper
225 g (8 oz) belly of pork or streaky bacon, de-rinded
and roughly chopped
1 large onion, sliced

Drain the haricot beans, reserving the soaking water. Heat the bean water and stir into it the treacle, Worcestershire sauce, mustard, sugar, salt and pepper. Mix up the beans, pork and onion in a casserole, pour over the bean water and add more hot water if necessary to come just over the top of the beans. Cover and bake in the oven at 180°C (350°F, gas mark 4) for 2½–3 hours, or until the beans are soft. Look at it once or twice during this time, and, if the beans seem to be getting too dry, add more hot water.

Onion, Bacon and Potato Hotpot

If I were restricted to cooking the same three recipes for the rest of my life, this would definitely be on the list. I got it from my mother, who can't remember where she got it from, and friends and acquaintances have been copying it ever since. It is very cheap, makes use of ingredients generally to hand, and tastes – I think – particularly delicious.

The bacon need not be rashers – scraps of cooked bacon left over from a boiled joint will do just as well. You can use more or less bacon, as convenient. About 2 tablespoons grated cheese can be added to the white sauce.

4 SERVINGS

50 g (2 oz) butter
50 g (2 oz) plain flour
600 ml (1 pint) milk
salt and pepper
freshly grated nutmeg (optional)
4 large onions, very thinly sliced
4 large potatoes, peeled and very thinly sliced
125–225 g (4–8 oz) bacon rashers, de-rinded and cut into small strips

Melt the butter in a saucepan and stir in the flour. Remove from the heat and gradually stir in the milk. Bring to the boil, stirring constantly until smooth and thick, then reduce the heat. Add salt and pepper, and nutmeg if you like, and leave the sauce simmering gently on a very low heat while you prepare the rest of the dish.

Grease a casserole and fill it with alternate layers of sliced onions, sliced potatoes and bacon strips, ending with a layer of potato. Pour over the white sauce. Give the casserole a good shake to distribute the sauce throughout. Cover, and bake in the oven at 200°C (400°F, gas mark 6) for 1 hour, then reduce the heat to 180°C (350°F, gas mark 4), uncover the casserole and cook for a further hour.

This is really a winter dish, and goes best with winter vegetables like Brussels sprouts and cabbage.

Keema Matar

This is authentic Indian home cooking; useful for the pauper who only has a couple of rings and a couple of pans. You will need a pan which will fry food and also has a lid – a sauté pan or a fairly wide-bottomed saucepan with a lid, or a cast-iron casserole.

6–8 SERVINGS

2 teaspoons coriander seeds
2 teaspoons cumin seeds
3 tablespoons vegetable oil
2 onions, finely chopped
6 garlic cloves, crushed
2.5 cm (1 inch) piece of fresh root ginger, peeled and finely chopped
fresh or dried chilli, de-seeded and finely chopped
700 g (1½ lb) minced lamb
75 ml (3 fl oz) water
450 g (1 lb) shelled fresh or frozen peas
salt
1 teaspoon garam masala
a large sprig of fresh mint or coriander, finely chopped

Pound the coriander and cumin seeds in a mortar, or in a strong bowl with the end of a rolling pin, or grind them in a (cleaned) coffee grinder. Heat the oil in a wide-bottomed pan and fry the onions until golden. Add the garlic and fry for 1 minute, then add the crushed seeds, ginger and chilli, stir for a minute and add the mince. Brown the mince, stirring it round for 5 minutes, then pour over the water. Bring to the boil, then reduce the heat, cover and simmer for 20 minutes.

Add the peas – if they are frozen they will cook very quickly but fresh peas may need a little more water added with them. Taste the mince and add salt at this stage. Stir in the garam masala, replace the lid and continue to cook for a few minutes. Add the mint or coriander about 2 minutes before serving with basmati or long-grain rice.

Gingered Pork Balls with Peas

6 SERVINGS

4 garlic cloves
450 g (1 lb) minced pork
5 cm (2 inch) piece of fresh root ginger, peeled and finely chopped
a bunch of fresh coriander, finely chopped
salt and pepper
1 egg
2 tablespoons plain flour
sunflower oil
225 g (8 oz) mushrooms
2 tablespoons sesame oil
450 g (1 lb) frozen peas, thawed
3–4 tablespoons dry sherry
2 tablespoons soy sauce

Finely chop two of the garlic cloves and stir them into the minced pork with the ginger and coriander. Season with salt and pepper and stir in the egg. Make the pork into small balls about 2.5 cm (1 inch) in diameter, rolling them lightly in flour seasoned with salt and pepper. Heat a little sunflower oil in a heavy-based frying pan (use the minimum you need to prevent the balls from sticking) and fry the pork balls until golden. Remove the balls to a warm dish.

Chop the mushrooms fairly coarsely so that the pieces will retain some bite, and finely chop the remaining garlic cloves. When all the balls are done, pour away any oil that is still in the pan, leaving just a tablespoonful. Add about 1 tablespoon sesame oil, the garlic and the mushrooms and fry over a moderate heat until cooked. Pour over the balls. Add the remaining tablespoon of sesame oil to the pan and tip in the peas. When these are hot, pour them over the balls and mushrooms. Pour the sherry into the pan, cook for a few seconds until reduced slightly and then pour over the pork balls. Season with soy sauce and serve with rice or noodles.

Spiced Beef Loaf

6–8 SERVINGS

3 garlic cloves
1 teaspoon juniper berries
1 tablespoon peppercorns
1 teaspoon allspice (berries or ground)
1 heaped teaspoon salt
5 rashers of streaky bacon, de-rinded and finely chopped
1 kg (2 lb) minced beef
1 glass of red wine

Chop the garlic very finely and lightly crush it in a mortar with the juniper berries, peppercorns, allspice and salt. Mix the bacon and spices into the minced beef with the wine, and leave for a few hours in a cold place.

Pack the meat mixture tightly into a loaf tin and stand it in a baking tin full of water. Cook in the oven at 170°C (325°F, gas mark 3) for 1½ hours, only covering it with foil if it seems to be burning on the top. Leave to cool and, when it is quite cold, turn the loaf out with the help of a knife. Cut thinly and eat with baked potatoes, pickles and salad.

Braised Red Cabbage and Frankfurters

2 GENEROUS SERVINGS

1 small red cabbage
1 large onion
1 large cooking apple (optional)
55 g (2 oz) butter
1 tablespoon brown sugar
1 tablespoon vinegar
salt and pepper
6–8 frankfurters

Remove outside cabbage leaves and slice and chop the cabbage including the core. Peel and roughly chop the onion and cored apple. Put a lump of butter in a heavy pan over gentle heat, add vegetables and spoon them around for a minute till the butter is distributed throughout. Mix vinegar and brown sugar and pour over the cabbage.

Cover tightly and cook over very low heat until the cabbage is tender, about 1½ hours. Add salt and pepper to taste. Ten minutes or so before dishing up bury the frankfurters well down among the cabbage, cover, and leave them to heat up.

This dish can be cooked equally well in the oven at 170°C (325°F, gas mark 3) but you will have to leave it for rather longer – 3½ hours would not be excessive. Unlike most vegetable dishes this improves with keeping. Some people like small twists of orange peel cooked with it. I usually serve it up with plain boiled potatoes and lots of mustard.

Meat Balls in Tomato Sauce

6 SERVINGS

FOR THE MEAT BALLS
1 large onion, finely chopped
6 garlic cloves, finely chopped
a bunch of fresh parsley or coriander, finely chopped
450 g (1 lb) minced lamb or beef
salt and black pepper
2 teaspoons ground cumin (if using lamb)
1 egg
sunflower oil, for frying

FOR THE TOMATO SAUCE
2 x 400 g (14 oz) can of tomatoes
2–6 garlic cloves
2 tablespoons olive oil
a splash of wine (optional)
1 teaspoon sugar
1 sprig of fresh thyme or basil, chopped
salt and pepper

To make the sauce, simmer all the ingredients together in a heavy-based saucepan or flameproof casserole for about 1 hour or until the garlic melts. Season with salt and pepper.

Mix the onion, garlic and herbs into the minced meat (best done with your hands), seasoning the mixture with salt and pepper, and cumin if you are using lamb. Lastly, mix in the egg. Flour your hands and start to form the mixture into small golf balls, leaving them on a floured surface.

Heat plenty of sunflower oil (about 0.5 cm/¼ inch deep) in a large, heavy-based frying pan and begin to fry the balls in batches until they are browned all over. As you remove them from the pan they can be placed in a casserole. When they are all in the casserole, pour over the tomato sauce. The dish can be kept warm in the oven for up to 1 hour until you need it – the balls will not disintegrate – or left to cool and reheated later. Serve with plenty of pasta, rice or potatoes.

Slow-Cooked Chickpeas and Kidneys

This dish is quite different from the more usual bean and pork combinations. It is rich and warming and very inexpensive. Beef kidney makes a good gravy which marries curiously with the nuttiness of the chickpeas. To make a meatier dish, gently melt the 'suet' from around the kidney to fry the onions in instead of the olive oil. However, only a real butcher will sell you this – you never see fresh suet in the supermarket.

8 SERVINGS

450 g (1 lb) dried chickpeas, soaked overnight
5 tablespoons olive oil or melted beef suet
2 onions, finely sliced
3 garlic cloves, finely sliced
450 g (1 lb) beef kidney, cored and roughly chopped
salt and black pepper
a sprig of fresh thyme
2 bay leaves
a sprig of fresh parsley
1 litre (2 pints) water
1 teaspoon wholegrain mustard

Drain the chickpeas and put them in a large saucepan. Cover with fresh water, bring to the boil and boil quite hard for about 40 minutes, then drain.

Meanwhile, heat the oil or melted suet in a flameproof casserole or frying pan and fry the onions and garlic until soft. Add the kidney and cook until just sealed. Remove from the heat. If you are using a casserole, remove the kidney mixture and put half the chickpeas in the bottom of the casserole. Season with salt and pepper, cover with the kidney, season again – I think it's hard to overdo the pepper – and put the rest of the chickpeas on top. Tie the herbs together with string to make a bouquet garni and bury it in the chickpeas, then pour over the water.

Put the lid on and cook in the oven at 150°C (300°F, gas mark 2) for 5–6 hours. Alternatively, cook at 170°C (325°F, gas mark 3) for 3 hours. It is important that the lid should be tight fitting: if you suspect it, you may either seal it stylishly with a flour and water paste, or easier (and probably safer until you have tried this recipe in your oven, with your particular pans, etc.), use an extra seal of kitchen foil under the lid. A few minutes before serving, remove the bouquet garni and stir in the mustard.

This dish needs only something green to go with it, raw or plainly cooked.

Oxtail Stew

Oxtail makes a rich, thick stew with a good meaty flavour. The pieces of tail should be washed, dipped in boiling water and dried before frying with the onions.

4–6 SERVINGS

1 medium-sized oxtail, jointed
1 tablespoon plain flour
salt and pepper
25 g (1 oz) butter
2 onions, sliced
2 carrots, sliced
1 celery stick, sliced
1 turnip, sliced
2 cloves
a pinch of ground mace
juice of ½ lemon

Separate the jointed pieces of oxtail, if necessary. Wash them, dip them in boiling water for 1 minute, then dry them carefully. Roll the pieces in the flour seasoned with salt and pepper.

Melt the butter in a large, heavy-based saucepan or flameproof casserole and put in the pieces of meat and sliced onions when it is sizzling. Turn them over so that the meat browns on all sides. Add the remaining vegetables, the cloves, mace and enough water to cover the lot. Bring to the boil, skimming off any froth which rises to the top. Reduce the heat to simmering, and cover the pan with a piece of kitchen foil or greaseproof paper and the lid. Simmer very slowly for 3 hours, or longer if you are not in a hurry, or until the meat is falling off the bone.

Taste the stock and add salt and pepper, if needed. Should you feel up to it, the appearance of the dish will be improved if you pick out the pieces of meat and put the stock and vegetables through a sieve, returning the thickened stock and meat to the pan for a few minutes to heat up again. Either way, add the lemon juice just before serving.

Plainly cooked, homely vegetables go best with oxtail – boiled potatoes, carrots, cabbage.

Liver in the Venetian Manner

Fried liver and onions is a well-known combination. The Venetian way of preparing it is the nicest of all, the onions stewed slowly and gently in a little oil, with the liver – cut into small, thin strips – stirred in towards the end.

2 SERVINGS

vegetable oil for frying
225 g (8 oz) onions, very finely sliced
salt and pepper
125 g (4 oz) calves' or lamb's liver

Cover the bottom of a heavy-based frying pan with a thin layer of oil. Add the onions, season with salt and pepper, cover and cook gently for 30–40 minutes.

Meanwhile, with a very sharp knife, shave thinnest possible slices off the liver. If it is calves' liver, it will only need 2–3 minutes cooking with the onions, but if it is lamb's liver you will need to add it to the onions after about 30 minutes and cook for another 15 minutes.

You can serve this just as it is, or with plain boiled rice. It is a particularly warming dish in winter.

Sweet and Sour Liver and Onions

Unglamorous ingredients, stylishly turned out. Pig's liver is the cheapest type of liver, if you like its rather strong flavour.

4–6 SERVINGS

2 onions, finely sliced
sunflower oil, for frying
700 g (1½ lb) liver
salt and pepper
3 garlic cloves, chopped
1 tablespoon brown sugar
3 tablespoons vinegar (wine, sherry or balsamic)
1 sprig of fresh coriander or mint, chopped (optional)

Fry the onions quickly in oil until just turning colour. Remove and keep hot. Slice the liver very finely, trimming it of any veinous bits, and season with salt and pepper. Fry it very quickly in the pan the onions were in, adding another tablespoon or so of oil if necessary, until crisp on the outside. Remove to the warm dish.

Heat the garlic in the oil, adding the sugar after a second (before the garlic begins to cook). Heat them together gently until the sugar is melted and golden. Pour in the vinegar and let it sizzle for a minute, then pour the sauce over the liver. Season liberally with pepper and, if you have it, sprinkle with a little chopped fresh coriander or mint.

Beef Casserole Nicoise

This recipe is based on one of those aromatic Mediterranean dishes which smell almost better than they taste. Ideally it should be made with red wine, but thick tomato sauce with a little wine vinegar will do. Don't skip the olives unless you hate them: they give a salty, smoky flavour all their own. Salt belly of pork is better than bacon if you can get it.

1 kg (2 lb) shin of beef
125 g (4 oz) bacon
3 onions
3 carrots
3 cloves of garlic
10–12 black olives
1 medium tin peeled tomatoes
wine vinegar
herbs (bay leaf, parsley, thyme, a little rosemary)
salt and pepper

Cut the beef into thick slices. Cut the bacon into small strips. Chop the onions coarsely, and slice the carrots thinly. Heat some oil in a casserole which can be heated over a hotplate; alternatively the fried ingredients can be transferred to a casserole before going into the oven. Put the bacon strips in, then the meat and onions. Turn the meat slices till brown all over. Add the tinned tomatoes, and a dash of wine vinegar. Also the chopped garlic and carrots, herbs, salt and pepper. Heat together till the stew simmers, then transfer to a moderate oven, 180°C (350°F, gas mark 4) and cook, covered, for 2½ hours. Add the stoned olives and cook, covered, half an hour longer. If the casserole liquid seems scanty you can add a little boiling water thickened with tomato purée. But the sauce should be thick.

Braised Hearts

2 SERVINGS

2 sheep hearts
1 large onion
2 tablespoons fresh breadcrumbs
1 handful chopped sage (1 tablespoon dried)
50 g (2 oz) butter
flour
a little stock or water
3 chopped and skinned tomatoes
salt and pepper
1 bay leaf

Wash the hearts well and cut out the gristle in the middle and the large vein, with a pair of scissors. Chop the onion very fine and mix with the breadcrumbs, sage and a little butter. Push the stuffing into the wide hole at the top of the hearts and sew up the edges with a large needle and thick cotton – a thimble helps, as the needle gets very slippery.

Roll the hearts in a little flour, brown lightly in butter or dripping in a small casserole. Add a little water or stock, stirring to mix it with the brown deposit on the bottom of the pan. Add the chopped peeled tomatoes, salt, pepper, the bay leaf, and cook in a moderate oven 150°C (300°F, gas mark 2), covered, for at least 2 hours.

Serve with boiled potatoes or rice and buttered carrots or any green vegetable except cabbage.

Spare Ribs

Little jars of sun-dried tomatoes in olive oil are exorbitantly expensive. Buy them dry when you can from a delicatessen or Italian shop and preserve them in oil and herbs yourself.

The quantities given in this recipe are enough for six if you will all be contented with one rib each. Serve a hearty rice dish to go with it.

6 SERVINGS

6 meaty spare ribs
1 tablespoon soy sauce
6 garlic cloves, finely chopped
vegetable oil, for frying
2 green peppers, de-seeded and cut into chunks
1 tablespoon chopped sun-dried tomatoes
1 sprig of fresh coriander, chopped
black pepper

When you bring the pork home, or at least 30 minutes before cooking, put the spare ribs into the earthenware pot or casserole in which you are going to cook them and sprinkle them with the soy sauce and three of the finely chopped garlic cloves.

Cook the spare ribs, uncovered, in the oven at 180°C (350°F, gas mark 4). They do not need any extra fat or moisture as they produce their own. When they seem just cooked but not brown, heat a little oil in a heavy-based frying pan and sear the peppers and remaining garlic. Remove the peppers to the ribs pot and put the ribs (without their juice) in the frying pan. Pour the hot pork juices into a bowl.

Cook the ribs until brown, then sprinkle the tomato pieces over them. Stir it around a bit, then put the ribs back in the pot with the peppers. Pour the juices which came from their first cooking into the frying pan and let them sizzle. Pour back over the meat and peppers, sprinkle on the coriander, season with black pepper and return to the oven for a further 5–10 minutes for the flavours to marry.

Chinese Chicken Hotpot

4–6 SERVINGS

1 kg (2 lb) chicken portions (thighs and breasts would be best –
a whole chicken is too fatty for this dish)

FOR THE MARINADE
½ glass sherry
½ glass soy sauce
2 garlic cloves, finely chopped
2.5 cm (1 inch) piece of fresh root ginger, peeled and finely chopped
2 tablespoons sesame oil
1 teaspoon Szechuan peppercorns, toasted and ground (see Note)
(you could substitute black pepper)

FOR THE HOTPOT
125 g (4 oz) dried mushrooms (black Chinese mushrooms are the
cheapest)
sunflower oil, if needed
6 garlic cloves
7.5 cm (3 inch) piece of fresh root ginger, peeled and finely chopped
225 g (8 oz) fresh chestnuts, peeled (see page 254), or dried chestnuts,
soaked overnight and drained
4 star anise
1 tablespoon Szechuan peppercorns, toasted and ground (see Note)
1 wine glass sherry
1 wine glass soy sauce
2 tablespoons sesame oil

Mix together all the marinade ingredients in a bowl, add the chicken pieces and stir to coat. Leave to marinate for at least 1 hour (though a day and night in the fridge will give even better results).

Soak the dried mushrooms in warm water for 30–60 minutes, then drain, reserving the water. Cut the mushrooms into bite-sized pieces. Strain the soaking water to remove any grit, and set aside.

Drain the chicken from the marinade, reserving the marinade, and put it in the bottom of a flameproof casserole. Heat gently until browned, adding a very small dash of sunflower oil if you need it to keep the pieces from sticking. When the chicken is nearly brown enough, put in the garlic cloves and let them turn a little golden. Add the ginger and the chestnuts and turn them until they are covered in the fat. Put in the spices and let them fry for a few seconds, then add the mushrooms. When all is hot, pour over the sherry, let it sizzle for a few seconds, then add the marinade, the soy sauce and the water the mushrooms were soaked in.

Put on a tight-fitting lid and cook in the oven at 150°C (300°F, gas mark 2) for 5 hours or at 180°C (350°F, gas mark 4) for 2 hours. Add the sesame oil about 5 minutes before the end of the cooking time.

NOTE: *To toast the Szechuan peppercorns, put them in a dry pan and heat gently, stirring, until they begin to give off their aroma. Remove from the heat, leave to cool, then grind in a mortar or strong bowl.*

Gulyas (Hungarian casserole)

Slowly cooked casseroles of various meats and vegetables are truly pan-European; each country has its own take on the basic story of cheaper cuts of meat simmered till tender with seasonal vegetables, to which regional ingredients lend a special character. Where the Flemish use beer, the English onion and potatoes, Mediterranean countries garlic and tomato, the Hungarians insist on paprika and caraway seeds. The meat used is frequently pork, in both fresh and sausage form, to which the anis flavour of caraway adds welcome astringency, and paprika a rich warmth, depth, and colour. A gulyas – goulash to you and me – is a fine, warming winter dish needing only boiled or baked potatoes as accompaniment. Pork is the best buy meat, currently, in supermarkets (or family butchers) and there is a wide choice of spicy boiling sausages, or chicken pieces, to add if you fancy a richer stew. Caraway seeds and paprika are essential, inexpensive and widely available, and make an exciting change from your standard casserole flavouring.

6–8 SERVINGS

1 kg (2 lb) pork shoulder, cut into 2.5 cm (1 inch) cubes
1 large, or two medium, onions, peeled and chopped
2 teaspoons Hungarian paprika
1 teaspoon caraway seeds, crushed to release flavour
250 g (9 oz) gammon (preferably on the bone) and/or 2 chicken legs
1–2 green peppers, cut into strips
½ tin (200 g/7 oz) peeled tomatoes
1 spicy cooking sausage (Polish, Spanish, or English blood pudding)
salt and pepper
sour cream or crème fraîche (optional)

Heat a little oil (or goose fat) in a large, heavy casserole dish, and fry the cubed pork shoulder, stirring the meat about to brown on all sides. Set aside while you soften the chopped onion in the same dish, taking care not to burn it. Transfer the onion to the pork dish.

Pour a cupful of water into the casserole, scraping up all the meat/onion juices and stir in paprika and caraway seeds. Simmer till fragrant and coloured, return the meat and onion to the pot, push the gammon (or chicken pieces) into the middle of the dish, add water to just cover and simmer, with the lid on, for 30–45 minutes. Now add strips of pepper, and tomatoes, and continue cooking over low heat for 1 hour.

Now add cooking sausage, pricked to stop it bursting, and cook on slowly, adding more water if the contents lack juiciness, for another half to one hour. Taste, and adjust seasoning. The meat should be perfectly tender by now, in a rich and aromatic stock.

Serve on hot plates with a slice or two of sausage and a morsel of gammon and plenty of gravy. A dollop of sour cream per person is a pleasant addition.

Kotopoulo Lemonato (Chicken with Lemon)

Lemons are a standby of Greek cooking, and they do wonders to chicken dishes, tenderizing as well as adding a brilliant sharpness, combined with fruity olive oil, herbs and seasoning. The simplest version is to roast your bird, whole, rubbed with olive oil and basted with lemon juice now and then, the squeezed lemon skins stuffed, with suitable herbs (oregano, basil, rosemary, thyme) into the cavity, to perfume the meat. Start cooking the bird breast downwards; when it takes colour turn on to one side, then the other, and finish breast uppermost, for the last twenty minutes or so. The idea of this is to help prevent the breast meat from drying out. A good way to roast chicken anytime.

The recipe that follows is a quickie. Chicken cut into pieces can be spread out across a large heavy frying pan to cook rapidly. But the lemony/herb flavour remains, pungent and summery. Good with a rice or millet salad.

4–6 SERVINGS

1 free-range chicken of about 1.5 kg (3–3½ lbs)
olive oil
2–3 lemons
a handful of mixed herbs – thyme, rosemary, oregano – fresh or dried
salt and pepper
a small glass of white wine or retsina (optional)

Use a sharp knife or cleaver to cut the chicken into pieces – legs, wings, and breasts. The breasts are removed by cutting down from the breastbone, loosening the flesh as you go. The breasts divide naturally into two sections each. Retain the skin as it helps keep the flesh juicy while cooking. The carcass can be simmered to make stock (see page 31). Rub olive oil into all the chicken pieces. Heat 2–3 tablespoons oil in a large pan and fry the pieces skin side down for about 10 minutes, lowering the heat once the skin is browned. Squeeze one lemon over the pieces before turning them over. Add chopped herbs, pushing them about the pan. Squeeze the second lemon over the pan contents, shaking it vigorously, over moderate heat.

Have a hot serving dish ready to take the breast pieces, and wings, which cook faster than the legs. These will need 5 minutes or so longer, turning once or twice. Add them to the serving dish, sprinkling salt and pepper over them, and use white wine, retsina, and/or stock to de-glaze the pan, scraping with a wooden spoon. Pour the pan juices through a strainer over the chicken pieces and serve at once.

NOTE: *If the lemons are small you may need more than two.*

Pork, Apple and Onion Hotpot

The secret of this excellent dish is slow cooking. This melts the pork fat which mingles with the apple and onion juices to make a rustic but highly savoury mélange.

4–6 SERVINGS

700 g (1½ lb) belly of pork rashers
700 g (1½ lb) large onions, sliced
700 g (1½ lb) firm but juicy apples (e.g. Bramleys or Cox's),
peeled, cored and sliced
salt and pepper
450 g (1 lb) 'floury' potatoes, peeled and thinly sliced (optional)
butter (optional)

Cut the skin off the pork rashers, and cut them in half. Layer the onions, apple slices and pork pieces, in that order, in an ovenproof casserole. Sprinkle with salt and pepper as you go. Continue until all the ingredients are used up, ending with a layer of onion or apple. You can cap the dish with a layer of overlapping potato slices dotted with butter, if you like.

Cover the dish with foil and bake in the oven at 180°C (350°F, gas mark 4) for 1 hour, then remove the foil and turn the heat down to 170°C (325°F, gas mark 3) for another hour.

Serve with buttered carrots, more potatoes, or crisp-cooked buttered cabbage.

VARIATION: *This is pretty good as it is, but you can add a little fresh thyme or savory, or a few slightly bruised juniper berries, for variety.*

Farmhouse Rabbit

A very English way of cooking rabbit, particularly suited to the delicate flavour of fresh, wild rabbit, if you can get hold of it. Rabbit is often compared with chicken in point of flavour and texture, but I think it unfair to both, because rabbit, especially wild rabbit, has a flavour all its own, slightly sharp and herb-scented. This recipe steam-bakes the rabbit, which comes out very white and tender with a layer of crunchy stuffing on top.

4 SERVINGS

1 rabbit
5 large onions
hunk of stale white bread
1 tablespoon sage (fresh or dried)
a pinch of thyme
half lemon rind, grated
salt and pepper
bacon fat
dripping or butter

Ask the butcher to joint the rabbit for you. Leave the pieces of rabbit in salted water while you make the stuffng. For the stuffing, chop onions roughly, cover with water in a pan and bring to the boil. Strain off the water. Soak a thick round of stale bread (7–10 cm, 3–4 inches) in cold water for a minute and squeeze dry. Tear the bread into small pieces and mix with the parboiled onions, herbs, grated lemon rind, salt and pepper and a little bacon fat, dripping or butter. Stir the ingredients thoroughly together.

Grease a baking tin. Take the rabbit joints out of the water, shake but do not dry them. Spread the stuffing thickly over all the pieces of rabbit. If your baking tin has a lid, put this on for the first hour of cooking – another baking tin inverted would do. Otherwise, cover with a piece of greased paper or foil, pressing it well down to keep the steam in. Cook at 230°C (450°F, gas mark 8). After 1 hour, remove the lid or paper and cook for another hour till the stuffing is crisp and brown on top.

Boiled potatoes and carrots, with a little butter and sugar, are particularly good with this.

Rabbit Flamande

If you can get hold of a whole rabbit, ask the butcher to draw and joint it for you. The chances are you may have to settle for frozen imported rabbit, which is usually sold cut up in joints. One saddle – the body part – should be enough for two people, or one leg each. In either case this is an excellent way of giving succulence to a meat which tends to be a little dry and insipid. (When using frozen rabbit, be sure to leave it to thaw out for a few hours at room temperature first. In emergencies, steeping in tepid water will speed thawing.)

25 g (1 oz) butter
125 g (4 oz) breast of pork or fat bacon
4 rabbit joints
24 pickling onions or 8 small onions
1 tablespoon flour
600 ml (1 pint) cider
salt and pepper
thyme
125 g (4 oz) sultanas and raisins
a few prunes
3 tablespoons sugar
1 tablespoon vinegar

Ideally you should use a heavy iron casserole. If you haven't got one, do the preliminary frying in a frying pan and transfer the ingredients after that into a heavy saucepan. Melt 25 g (1 oz) butter in the pan, cut the pork or bacon into thin strips, and brown lightly. Transfer them to a plate and brown the rabbit all over in the same butter, adding more if it seems inadequate. Put the rabbit on the plate and brown the onions. Now return the pork, rabbit and onions to the pot (or into a saucepan, adding fat from the pan if you are using two utensils), sprinkle 1 level tablespoon flour over them, stir to mix the flour well in and pour on the cider. Add salt, pepper, thyme (in moderation) and simmer over low heat for 1 hour. Now add washed raisins, sultanas and prunes, and simmer for 1 hour more.

Just before serving, melt 3 tablespoons sugar in a small pan over low heat with 1 tablespoon vinegar. When it starts to colour, or carameliz Perhaose, add it to the rabbit sauce and stir it well in.

This is such a rich, heavy dish it needs nothing but plain boiled rice with it. The cider is not essential, though it helps. Plain water will do.

Cocido Estremeno

Another hearty one-pot dish, this time from the Spanish province of Estremadura, a harsh region both climatically and geographically, so it is unsurprising that *garbanzos* – chickpeas – are an important ingredient, bulking out – together with both potatoes and rice – quite small amounts of various meats. Shredded cabbage adds vitamins and juiciness to the dish. In Estremadura it is traditional to serve the meats and vegetables separately from the broth but I prefer to dish it all up together on a mound of mashed potato, barley or rice.

4–6 SERVINGS

450 g (1 lb) chickpeas, soaked overnight
100–200 g (4–7 oz) beef shin, on the bone if possible
a bacon knuckle or thick rasher bacon or pork belly
2–3 chicken pieces (optional)
1 large onion stuck with 3 cloves
sprigs of thyme or rosemary
1 fresh or dried red chilli, de-seeded
3 potatoes
2 large tablespoons pudding or arborio rice
1 small green or Savoy cabbage, shredded
2 tablespoons of tomato purée, or half a tin of peeled tomatoes, drained
chunks of chorizo sausage or black pudding
salt and pepper

Put the chickpeas and meats (except sausage) in a deep casserole, cover with cold water, bring to the boil and simmer – skimming occasionally – for 1–2 hours. Add the whole onion, herbs, chilli, potatoes peeled and chunked, rice, cabbage, tomato and sausage and season with salt and pepper. Cook on gently for another half an hour, till meat, vegetables and rice are tender.

Valencianos use the remains of a *cocido* (it would be a Valencian *cocido*, but the principle still holds) to make a dish of Oven Rice, or Arroz al Forn (see opposite).

Arroz al Forn (oven-cooked rice)

Valencianos consider this dish a jewel of their traditional home cooking and it occupies a specific place in a weekly household menu, making use of the rich leftovers from the weekend's meat stew or *cocido*, to which chunks of chorizo, cooked dried beans, and sundry fresh vegetables and seasonings can be added. But the essential, and typical ingredient, is the rice, which must be round-grain pudding or Carolina rice, absorbent enough to soak up all the juices and flavours during the oven cooking, to emerge *seco* (dry) or *meloso* (moist), the grains distinct and full of flavour.

Valencia grows rice, eaten daily by the locals, who wax passionate about the subtleties of dishes like this. Brits will find it a savoury way to make a second, delicious, dish from the leftovers of, say, Cocido Estremeno, adding what is available from the listed ingredients. What is critical is the proportion of stock to rice – one and a half times the volume of rice, calculated as 250 ml (9 fl oz) for two people. Add water (or wine) to make it up to the right quantity. Needless to say, it stretches leftovers substantially.

4 SERVINGS

leftover stock, meat, cooked beans (chickpeas, haricots)

NEW INGREDIENTS
1–2 slices pork belly, or streaky bacon rashers
1 black pudding or chorizo (less will do), sliced or chunked
1–2 teaspoons paprika or pimenton
1 beef tomato or 2 standard size tomatoes
1 whole head garlic
pudding rice (500 ml/18 fl oz)
saffron
1 turnip, peeled and thinly sliced
1 potato, peeled and quartered
olive oil
salt and pepper

In Valencia Arroz al Forn is cooked in a round earthenware ovenproof dish, about 20 cm (8 in) across and 5 cm (2 in) deep. Preheat the oven to 200°C (400°F, gas mark 6). Set the dish on the hob, add the oil and fry the pork/bacon and black pudding, with the paprika/pimenton, sliced tomato and garlic head, setting it aside as it colours. Add the rice and stir around for 2–3 minutes, any leftover beans and meat (trimmed and diced) from the *cocido*, and the stock, to which you add saffron (Valencians often use cheaper *colorante*, instead, for its golden colour). Mix in the turnip slices and potato, push the head of garlic into the centre, lay the bacon/pork on top, with the sliced tomato, and cook for 20–30 minutes or till the stock is absorbed and the rice *seco* or *meloso*, according to preference.

Arroz al Forn has all the hallmarks of an old, beloved and much repeated regional dish – a tight list of ingredients, detailed procedure, exact proportions of liquid to rice, precise oven heat and timing.

It may take one or two trial runs to master it, but if you enjoy an honest dish, lustily flavoured, it should become a pauper standby. I think you can play around with the ingredients to some extent, using chicken stock, different vegetables, meats, but keep to the ground rules – ratio of stock to rice – and it will be good and satisfying. Just don't get into arguments with a Valencian!

Brisket of Beef

Brisket is a humble cut of beef, inexpensive and fatty but, like many such, it rewards thoughtful cooking with a beefiness that makes much more expensive cuts taste pallid by comparison. It's the fat that does it; in this recipe it is slowly rendered out of the joint (you can pour it off, for dripping), leaving it succulent and full of flavour. This is one of my mother's recipes – plain English country food of the sort that is creeping back on to menus. She has a good, helpful butcher, and cooks the brisket in a tall brown pottery casserole with a lid.

8 SERVINGS

vegetable oil, for frying
salt and pepper
mustard powder
900 g–1.4 kg (2–3 lb) rolled and boned brisket
1–2 sprigs of fresh thyme (optional)
1 garlic clove, slivered (optional)
1–2 tablespoons wine, cider or water

Heat a little oil in a frying pan large enough to take the joint. Meanwhile, heat a deep pottery casserole in the oven at 170°C (325°F, gas mark 3). Mix salt, pepper and mustard powder together, and rub it into the meat firmly, pushing it down into the cracks. You can insert a sprig of thyme or two, or slivers of garlic, if you want. Put the brisket in the pan and turn until browned on all sides, top and bottom included. Stand the joint on its end in the casserole. Put the wine, cider or water into the pan, stir to scrape up residual bits of meat, and pour over the joint. Cover the casserole with foil or greaseproof paper to make a tighter seal, put on the lid and cook in the oven for 2–2½ hours, depending on weight.

After cooking, the meat will have shrunk, but be very tender and sitting in a pool of meat juices and hot fat. Pour this off into a cold bowl, let it settle for a few minutes (you can return the meat to the bottom of the oven), then spoon off the clear fat – keep it, naturally – and bubble up the remaining meat juices with a little more water, cider or wine, for a rich gravy, which needs no flour or other ingredients. Serve with baked potatoes, boiled carrots or spring greens and lots more freshly made mustard. Use the dripping to sauté leftover potatoes, or add a sprig of rosemary to it, leave it to solidify, then spread it on hot toast for a rustic snack.

Rice Pudding

It is surprising how few rice puddings taste the way they should – neither stodgy nor gritty, but tender, creamy and mellow. There is no mystery to making a successful rice pudding – it depends on using the right proportions of rice to milk, and long, slow cooking. The proportions given in this recipe are the same for all milk and cereal puddings.

4 SERVINGS

600 ml (1 pint) milk
2 tablespoons short-grain (pudding) rice
2–3 tablespoons sugar
a few drops of vanilla essence, or
1 vanilla pod
15 g (½ oz) butter

Butter a shallow ovenproof dish lightly. Pour in the milk, add the rice and sugar and stir to distribute them evenly. Add the vanilla essence or a vanilla pod and dot a few little pieces of butter on top. Cook in the oven at 170°C (325°F, gas mark 3).

After about 30 minutes, when a skin has formed on top, stir the skin into the pudding. Repeat this about an hour later. The pudding will be cooked in 2½ hours. If you are cooking something else in the oven at the same time, put the pudding on a lower shelf, the bottom shelf if the oven is hot.

VARIATION: *An alternative way of cooking rice is to use the top of a double saucepan, cooking it for 3–4 hours over barely simmering water, until all the milk is absorbed. Use the same ingredients and proportions as for the method above. In the Middle East, rice cooked like this is mixed with thick, or whipped, cream and served very cold with a powdering of cinnamon.*

Caramel Custard

**600 ml (1 pint) milk (preferably organic and full cream; if not add a
little cream – 3–4 tablespoons – to the heated milk)
4 eggs
4 tablespoons sugar
½ teaspoon vanilla essence**

FOR THE CARAMEL
**2 tablespoons sugar
water**

First caramelize your pudding mould, which can be a mixing bowl, in which case remember to warm it before putting in the caramel or it may crack. Melt 2 tablespoons of sugar over a very low heat, and then add 1–2 teaspoons cold water. Pour the caramel quickly into your mould and twist it around and around to spread the caramel over as much of the surface as possible.

Heat the milk with the 4 tablespoons sugar, stirring till the sugar has melted. Set aside to cool. Beat up the eggs till frothy and stir into the milk. Add half a teaspoon of vanilla essence (or, better still, make the custard with vanilla sugar). Pour the custard into the mould and set the mould in a pan of hot water reaching about half the height of the mould. Cook in the preheated oven at 180°C (350°F, gas mark 4) for 40 minutes.

The custard is cooked when a knife stuck into it comes out clean. Remove it and leave it to cool before turning out.

Bread and Butter Pudding

Like most simple dishes, bread and butter pudding needs to be made with care. The slices of bread should be really thin, with the crusts removed – but don't give in to the temptation to use packed sliced bread unless you want the pudding to taste like wet flannel! This nursery favourite becomes haute cuisine when made with Italian panettone instead of plain bread. Shades of Anton Mosimann.

4–6 SERVINGS

6 thin slices of stale white bread, buttered
a handful of raisins or sultanas
5–6 tablespoons sugar
450 ml (¾ pint) milk
½ teaspoon vanilla essence
2 eggs, plus 1 extra yolk
a knob of butter

Cut the bread and butter into quarters or triangles. Arrange them in layers in an ovenproof dish, with a sprinkling of raisins or sultanas and sugar on each layer.

Put the milk and vanilla essence in a saucepan and heat gently until almost boiling. Beat the eggs and egg yolk in a bowl and mix with the heated milk. Pour this over the bread and butter. Some people believe in letting the pudding stand for 30 minutes or so before baking. Otherwise, sprinkle sugar over the top, dot with a little butter and bake in the oven at 170°C (325°F, gas mark 3) for 45–60 minutes.

Equally good hot or cold, served plain or with cream.

Junket and Cream

Junket is such a simple, unpretentious pudding that it tends to be overlooked. Dressed up with banana purée (see below), it is quite nice enough to produce at a dinner party.

600 ml (1 pint) whole milk
about 2 teaspoons sugar
1 small teaspoon rennet
150 ml (¼ pint) double cream
freshly grated nutmeg or ground cinnamon, to taste

Heat the milk over a low heat until just tepid. Add the sugar (according to taste), stir well, pour into a shallow dish, stir in the rennet and leave to set. Pour on the cream and sprinkle with a little cinnamon or nutmeg before serving.

For a slightly more elaborate version, mash two ripe bananas until very soft and frothy, adding a little sugar. Put them in the bottom of the dish, pour the junket over and leave to set as before.

Summer Pudding

A dream of a pudding when everything is just right – soft fruit running with juice, bread just stale and dry enough to soak it up. It must be *proper* bread – sliced white goes soggy and disintegrates. In my Dorset pauper days I stuck rigorously to free, found, hedgerow blackberries, picked at the juicy height of early autumn. But of course any soft fruit works as well, or better – raspberries, black and red currants, blueberries. The perfect summer pudding is evenly purple with juice, turns out firm, dark and a little shiny, like a summer version of Christmas pudding. Juiciness can be helped by warming the fruit for a few minutes, with sugar, in a pan over low heat – but *warm*, don't cook the fruit. Eat with a dollop of crème fraîche, or, most sumptuously, organic clotted or Jersey cream.

SERVES 4–6

½–1 kg (1–2 lb) soft fruit, stalks, hulls and leaves removed
about ½ loaf white bread, crusts removed
3–4 tablespoons sugar

Line a pudding basin (two if they are small) with slices of bread, tailored to fit neatly, leaving some extra for the top. Pack in fruit, adding a sprinkle of sugar as you go. Cover with more sliced bread. Some people add layers of bread *between* fruit layers.

Stand a saucer or small plate on top, that fits within the bowl, and weight with stones, tins, whatever. Let stand overnight – a Pyrex bowl allows you to gauge whether the pudding has reached perfection. Turn out on to a plain round dish. Any spare fruit can be arranged on top, or round the dish.

Apple Pie

Serve hot, with cream, for pudding, or cold for tea.

6–8 SERVINGS

4 large cooking or firm eating apples
juice of 1 lemon
10 tablespoons self-raising flour
6 tablespoons caster sugar
4 tablespoons oil
a drop of vanilla essence
125 ml (4 fl oz) milk
2 eggs
a pinch of salt
1 teaspoon ground cinnamon (more if you like)
sugar, for dusting
50 g (2 oz) butter
25 g (1 oz) walnuts, almonds or hazelnuts, roughly chopped (optional)

Peel, core and slice the apples and pour the lemon juice over them to stop them browning. Grease a medium-sized flan dish or cake tin.

Put the flour and sugar in a bowl, make a well in the centre and add the oil, vanilla essence, milk, eggs, salt and cinnamon to taste. Beat well to incorporate all the flour and form a smooth, thick batter. Alternatively, put all the ingredients in a food mixer and mix to a batter. Pour the batter into the prepared flan dish or cake tin.

Arrange the slices of apple on top of the batter, in a haphazard way or with pâtisserie smartness, as you like. Scatter a little more sugar, little lumps of butter and the broken nuts, if using, all over the pie and bake it in the oven at 200–220°C (400–425°F, gas mark 6–7) for almost 1 hour or until the pie is twice the size and golden.

Spiced Apple Purée

Most apple purées are plain stewed apples given a hopeful and vigorous stir with a wooden spoon. The result is a watery mush. It takes a minute longer to convert this into the proper velvet-smooth consistency, but this minute is crucial.

4 SERVINGS

1 kg (2 lb) cooking apples
4 cloves
a pinch of ground cinnamon
sugar, to taste
25 g (1 oz) butter

Peel, core and slice the apples. Put them in a saucepan with the cloves, cinnamon and enough water to cover. Cook gently until the apples are soft, then add sugar to taste. Press the apple mixture through a fine sieve, removing the cloves. (The sieving is vital because it removes the little fibres and gives a smooth purée. Use a plastic sieve if possible.) Stir in the butter and leave to cool. Serve with cream.

Polish Apple Charlotte

6–8 SERVINGS

1 kg (2 lb) cooking apples
sugar, to taste
1 teaspoon grated lemon rind
a knob of butter
4 macaroons, crushed
about 2 tablespoons marmalade

Core, peel and slice the apples. Put them in a saucepan with a little water, sugar to taste and the lemon rind. Cook gently until soft, then sieve them into a baking dish and stir in the butter. Mix the crushed macaroons with enough marmalade to bind them together and spread over the apples. Bake in the oven at 180°C (350°F, gas mark 4) for 20 minutes. Serve with cream.

Peach Upside-Down Pudding

4–6 SERVINGS

1 large tin peach slices
75 g (3 oz) butter
175 g (6 oz) brown sugar

FOR THE BATTER
110 g (4 oz) sifted plain flour
1½ teaspoons baking powder
a pinch of salt
2 eggs
175 g (6 oz) sugar
90 ml (4 fl oz) hot water
1 teaspoon vanilla essence

Drain the peach slices. Melt the butter and brown sugar over a moderate heat in the cake pan or baking tin. Remove from heat and arrange peach slices in rows on top of the butter/sugar mixture in the bottom of the pan.

Sift the flour, baking powder and salt together. Beat the egg yolks in a large bowl till pale yellow and fluffy. Add the sugar gradually, beating well after each addition. Then add hot water, a little at a time, still beating, and finally the flour, by degrees. Beat all well, till thoroughly mixed. Then fold in the stiffly beaten egg whites and pour the batter over the peaches. Bake in a hottish oven, 200°C (400°F, gas mark 6), for 40 minutes. Let the pudding stand for 5 minutes, then invert it on to a large plate but leave the tin over it for 10–15 minutes longer so that the caramel can drip over the cake.

This is even better made with fresh fruit – apples, apricots as well as peaches.

Apricot Fool

Apricots are quite a reasonable price towards the end of the summer, and they make excellent fool. If you can't run to 300 ml (10 fl oz) cream, use the smaller amount and add the beaten white of an egg.

4 SERVINGS

450 g (1 lb) apricots
3–4 tablespoons sugar
200–300 ml (7–10 fl oz) double cream, whipped

Cut the apricots in half and take out the stones. Crack open four or five of the stones with a hammer and extract the kernels. (The kernels add an extra something to the flavour so this little effort is worth making.)

Put the apricot halves, kernels and sugar into an ovenproof dish, add just enough water to cover them and bake in the oven at 180°C (350°F, gas mark 4) until the apricots are soft. Remove the kernels and rub the apricots through a sieve into a bowl. Fold in the whipped cream. Taste to see if the fool is sweet enough and add a little more sugar if necessary. Set aside to cool.

Batter Pudding

6–8 SERVINGS

3 eggs
200 g (7 oz) plain flour
a pinch of salt
300 ml (½ pint) milk
15g (½ oz) butter
4 tablespoons golden syrup
a dash of rum or brandy (optional)

Beat the eggs lightly, then sift in the flour and salt and stir together. Gradually add the milk, stirring all the time. Leave to stand for 1–2 hours.

Butter a baking tin and pour in the batter. Dot with butter and bake in the oven at 230°C (450°F, gas mark 8) for 15 minutes, then turn the oven down to 200°C (400°F, gas mark 6) and cook for a further 15–30 minutes or until the batter is risen and golden. In a small but heavy-based saucepan over a gentle heat, stir the golden syrup with a little water and a dash of rum or brandy, if using. When this is melted and thin, pour it over each person's slice of hot pudding.

Cheesecake

Cheesecake is quite simple to make, and inexpensive compared with the ready-made sort on sale in most delicatessens.

4–6 SERVINGS

125 g (4 oz) butter
225 g (4 oz) cream cheese
1 tablespoon sugar
4 eggs
1 tablespoon sultanas
vanilla essence

Beat the butter to a soft cream. Work in the cheese, crumbled small, then the sugar, preferably caster sugar, and lastly the well-beaten egg yolks. Whip the whites stiff and fold into the mixture. Sprinkle in the sultanas and a little vanilla essence.

Line a cake tin with shortcrust pastry and fill with the cheese mixture. Brush the top with a little egg yolk to give it a good colour and bake in a moderate oven, 180°C (350°F, gas mark 4) for approximately 1 hour or until the pastry is golden and the filling firm.

Leave to cool before eating.

Padding

This chapter deals with the art (or science) of stretching small quantities of food (and money) a bit further. Leftovers are part of the story, but the emphasis here is not so much on what bits and pieces you have to work with as on various ways of expanding them into a solid meal. This is where the idea of padding comes in. Rice and pasta are two examples of padding which need little introduction from me. But there are other less familiar ones – batters, pastry, suetcrust, pulses, polenta, pizza bases – which paupers ought to know about. The reason being, of course, that they are dazzlingly cheap and versatile. A shortcrust pastry flan case, for instance. This costs next to nothing to make. Onions, butter, flour and a little cream turn it into a savoury meal for two, or first course for four. Similarly, a trifling outlay on batter makes a few sausages into a meal for three or four people. A lot of suetcrust and a little jam gives you a roly-poly pudding to silence a party of hungry schoolboys. 450 g (1 lb) haricot beans, some belly of pork and a few other odds and ends add up to a hearty dish of Pork and Beans (see page 61) which will feed six comfortably.

No Victorian housewife would have needed reminding of these basic principles of economical cookery. But, with the current craze for high-protein, low-calorie diets, I think many of these padding foods have fallen into disrepute, as being fattening, indigestible and somehow unwholesome. And yet about a quarter of the nation's grocery bills goes on biscuits, and the same people who quail at the sight of a suet pudding will cheerfully consume mountains of crisps, cereals and chocolate bars. The point to remember, I think, is that a normal diet should strike a balance between starch, protein and vitamin foods. The padding foods in this chapter are high in carbohydrates, but this only becomes a bad thing, dietetically speaking, if you eat nothing else. A thick lentil soup, followed by steak and kidney pudding and mashed potatoes and a fruit pie, would be too much. Solid dishes need to be balanced by salads, green vegetables, light fruit puddings, thin soups.

Another point I would like to make about the padding foods mentioned in this chapter is that they are not tediously slow and complicated, or difficult, to make. A lot of people are put off attempting pastry, for instance, by the mystique which has grown up round the subject – all that talk about 'light hands', correct temperatures, proportions – which is a pity because pastry-making is a simple process and only requires a few trial runs to be reasonably foolproof. (Shortcrust and suetcrust, that is. I have deliberately excluded the more elaborate varieties like puff and flaky pastry.) Once you are familiar with the procedure you will find it takes about five minutes to make pastry, or batters, a couple of minutes with a rolling pin to produce home-made breadcrumbs.

Rice

It is astonishing how much disagreement reigns over the best way of boiling rice. This may be because it has only comparatively recently been grown in Europe, and a certain mystery still clings to its preparation. Having tried some of the more complicated methods, I am pleased to say that the easiest and quickest also gives the best results.

The best rice for boiling is the long-grain or Patna variety. Short-grain rice is suitable for puddings where the grains need to be highly absorbent. I generally use rather more rice than specified – just under 225 g (8 oz) for two people. Leftovers can be used up in salads, or combined with other ingredients in stuffings.

Bring a large pan of salted water to the boil and tip in the rice. Boil fast for about 12 minutes, though you should try the rice before this time as it may cook more quickly. When cooked, rice should be tender, but not too soft. Packaged rice will give an approximate cooking time on the packet. Drain in a colander or sieve and rinse with boiling water to wash off any glutinous starch. Alternatively, boil the rice for only 6–7 minutes, then to dry off and separate the grains, you can either return the rice to the pan after draining it, and leave it covered over a very low heat for 5–10 minutes, stirring once or twice with a fork to loosen the grains, or (which is marginally easier) you can pour it into a shallow ovenproof dish, cover it and put it in the oven for 10 minutes or so.

Rice Salad

Cold rice can be mixed with a great variety of bits and pieces and turned into a successful salad. Any of the following suggestions can be used in varying combinations, according to what is available: canned or fresh crab, shrimps, cooked mussels, cooked chicken, ham, garlic sausage, hard-boiled egg, cucumber, tomatoes (skinned), raw onion, cooked peas, spring onions, raw mushrooms, green pepper, green beans, beetroot, raisins, sultanas, capers, raw apple, carrot, mild cheese. You will probably be able to think of many more. The main thing is to try and balance the textures and flavours pleasantly – something crisp, something soft, something sharp, something sweet, etc. And dice or chop the ingredients quite small; rice with large lumps of stuff buried in it looks sloppy and faintly sinister.

When you have combined your chosen ingredients with the rice, season it well with salt and pepper or paprika, moisten liberally with a mild vinaigrette – more oily than vinegary – or thin mayonnaise, and, if possible, sprinkle some chopped parsley, or other herbs, on top.

Hot Savoury Rice

There are two ways of preparing dishes of savoury rice. The easiest, and I think safest for non-Italians, is to boil the rice and cook up the other ingredients separately, giving them a few minutes together in the pan or oven to merge the flavours just at the end. The other way, more properly the risotto or paella method, is to cook all the ingredients together, first frying the rice, and then adding boiling liquid (stock, water, wine or a mixture of the three) gradually, together with scraps of meat, fish, chicken, vegetables or whatever, until the rice is tender. The second method does produce a richer dish, with a moist creamy texture, when correctly cooked. But it requires more judgement and concentration on the part of the cook if it is not to turn into an unappetizing sludge, or worse still, a mass of gritty, undercooked rice. You do also need a really good heavy cast-iron or flameproof earthenware dish to cook it in.

My advice is, practise making risottos or paellas in small quantities, for private consumption, but avoid the common mistake of serving them up as a cheap omnibus meal for dinner guests until you are confident of getting the right results. In the meantime, the other method, or the method used in making Suleiman's Pilaff, a compromise between the two, will save a lot of nervous strain.

Suleiman's Pilaff

An excellent way of using up small bits and pieces of cooked ham left over from a joint. The rice is fried before boiling to make it richer.

4–6 SERVINGS

dripping or olive oil, for frying
450g (1 lb) long-grain rice
1 litre (2 pints) boiling water
2–3 onions, chopped
2 garlic cloves, chopped
4 fresh tomatoes, chopped, or 230g (8 oz) can of chopped tomatoes
1 tablespoon currants
1 tablespoon sultanas
a pinch of dried thyme or rosemary
salt and pepper
125–175 g (4–6 oz) lean cooked lamb, diced

Melt a good lump of dripping, or heat 3 tablespoons olive oil in a heavy-based saucepan and fry the rice gently, stirring, until it begins to look transparent. Pour the boiling water over the rice and boil fast, uncovered, for about 12 minutes or until the rice is tender. Strain and return to the pan, cover and leave over a very low heat.

Meanwhile, fry the other ingredients in oil or dripping, starting with the onions and garlic and adding the tomatoes, dried fruit and herbs when these are golden. Season generously and simmer gently until thick. Add the diced meat towards the end – too much cooking is liable to toughen it.

Stir the meat mixture into the rice, adding more dripping if you think it needs it. Cook over a gentle heat for a few minutes longer and serve.

In the Middle East a savoury pilaff would be served with yoghurt or soured cream stirred into it. If that idea does not appeal to you, try serving a salad of thinly sliced cucumber dressed with a little yoghurt or soured cream and a few finely chopped mint leaves, along with the pilaff. Alternatively, a salad made with oranges and onions would be a refreshing combination.

Risi e Bisi

This is a beloved first course in Italy, served wetter than most risottos, though the method holds good for any risotto. I think this is really so wonderful with fresh new peas you may as well cook something else when they are not in season.

4 SERVINGS

1 kg (2 lb) young peas
1.5 litres (3 pints) thin chicken stock
50 g (2 oz) butter
2 tablespoons olive oil
1 onion, sliced
2 rashers of bacon, de-rinded and sliced
450g (1 lb) easy-cook long-grain or arborio rice
salt and pepper
grated Parmesan cheese, to serve

Pod the peas and put the pods in a saucepan with the stock. Bring to the boil, then reduce the heat and simmer over a very low heat.

Meanwhile, heat the butter and oil in a deep, heavy-based frying pan large enough to hold the finished risotto, and add the onion and bacon. Heat gently until the fat runs out of the bacon, then fry until the onions are translucent and tender, but not brown. Stir in the rice and when it becomes translucent, stir in the peas. After a second, pour in some of the hot stock (without pods) and season with salt and pepper. Cook until the stock has been absorbed, then add a little more stock and cook again. Continue adding the stock, a cupful at a time, so that the rice and peas remain surrounded by moisture, but never invisible under the stock. Stir the mixture occasionally with a wooden spoon, so that it cannot burn on the bottom, but try not to mash it with constant stirring. When the rice is tender, taste and season again if it needs it. Serve with grated Parmesan.

Stir-Fried Rice with Beef

The rice must be cooked (see page 93), drained and cold. Yesterday's rice is best.

4–6 SERVINGS

4 tablespoons soy sauce
8 tablespoons peanut (groundnut) oil
salt and pepper
a pinch of Chinese five-spice powder (optional)
450 g (1 lb) minced beef
6 spring onions
2 large eggs
6 garlic cloves, chopped
1 cm (½ inch) piece of fresh root ginger, peeled and chopped
1 kg (2 lb) cooked long-grain rice
1 tablespoon sesame oil

Mix the soy sauce, 1 tablespoon peanut oil, a pinch of salt, plenty of pepper and the five-spice powder (if using) in a bowl. Add the mince, stir to coat, then leave to marinate for about 1 hour, stirring quite vigorously from time to time.

Slice the spring onions, including the green parts, and arrange the green and white pieces in two separate piles. Beat the eggs with ½ tablespoon peanut oil.

Heat a wok or large frying pan gradually until it begins to smoke. Pour in 5–6 tablespoons of the peanut oil and swirl it around in the pan. Put in the garlic, stir it about and, after a moment, add the ginger and the white parts of the spring onions. Stir again, then put in the beef, stirring all the time. When it is browned, pour in the beaten egg, then the rice and toss for 1–2 minutes or until the rice is hot and the meat mixture dispersed evenly through it. Pour the sesame oil down the side of the pan into the mixture. Add the green parts of the spring onions, stir again and serve.

Oats

It is quite a good idea to have a packet of rolled oats around, even if you do not eat porridge. They are useful for coating herring and mackerel before frying, as the Scots do. A spoonful or two can be used to thicken soups and stews.

Porridge

Porridge oats – not the instant type – are greatly improved by steeping overnight in milk before cooking. This brings out all their flavour and gives a creamy texture. The Scots name for this used to be Crowdie-Mowdie. They also used to steam the oats for two hours, but I think that is a refinement which can be disregarded.

1 SERVING

25 g (1 oz) porridge oats
175 ml (6 fl oz) milk
a pinch of salt

Mix all the ingredients together and leave overnight. To cook, bring the milk and oats slowly to simmering point and cook gently for 5–8 minutes, or until the porridge thickens.

Scots Fried Herrings

Herrings are very good rolled in oats, and fried. They can be cooked whole, or split, boned and flattened.

2 SERVINGS

2 large or 4 small herrings
salt and pepper
25g (1 oz) porridge oats
25g (1 oz) dripping or butter and ½ tablespoon oil
lemon wedges, to serve

Wipe the fish carefully, then season them with salt and pepper. Sprinkle the oats on a sheet of kitchen paper and toss the fish in them until well coated. Heat the dripping or butter and oil in a frying pan and, when smoking hot, put in the herrings and fry until brown on both sides. Whole herrings will take 7–10 minutes; split herrings will take 5 minutes.

Serve with lemon wedges and boiled potatoes.

Millet

A staple food in Africa, this is a notably pretty cereal with tiny white grains, fluffy and mild tasting, which makes a pleasant change from rice, barley, couscous, etc. It can be substituted for any of the foregoing, but makes an especially attractive salad, dressed with fresh herbs and a lemony vinaigrette and mixed with peas, chopped peppers and spring onions or shallots, and – maybe – toasted pine nuts.

To cook millet, cover measured grains with two and a half times their volume of cold water, bring to the boil and simmer till tender, about 20 minutes. Drain. For a salad, dress while still hot with a vinaigrette where lemon juice substitutes for vinegar. Season well.

Burghul with Raisins and Nuts

Both the raisins and nuts are optional, since burghul alone has a sweetish, mealy taste which is quite addictive. However, they dress up the bowl for party purposes. I prefer the texture of burghul after steaming anyway, though swelling with cold water is supposed to be adequate for salads like tabbouleh, since the cracked wheat is pre-cooked.

6 SERVINGS

450 g (1 lb) burghul
a good handful of raisins, currants or sultanas
a squeeze of orange or lemon juice (optional)
50 g (2 oz) butter
1 tablespoon oil
salt and pepper
50 g (2 oz) flaked almonds or pine nuts, lightly toasted

Put the burghul in a bowl, cover with cold water and leave to soak for 30 minutes. Soak the dried fruit in a little warm water, with a squeeze of orange or lemon juice added, if used.

Tip the soaked burghul into a round sieve that fits over a saucepan. Bring about 2.5 cm (1 inch) of water to the boil in the saucepan and place the sieve over the top. Loosely cover with a lid and cook for 10 minutes. Fork up the burghul to aerate it, then steam for another 10–15 minutes, making sure the water does not boil dry.

Turn the burghul into a warmed serving dish and stir in the soaked fruit. Heat the butter and oil together in a saucepan and pour over the burghul, fluffing it up with a fork. Season to taste with a little salt and pepper. Finally, scatter toasted nuts on top and serve.

Buckwheat Kasha

4–6 SERVINGS

450g (1 lb) husked buckwheat grain
1 litre (2 pints) boiling water
salt

Wash the buckwheat, removing any husks or unhusked grains. Put the buckwheat in a frying pan without any fat, and heat gently, stirring and shaking all the time, until it begins to pop and is roasted. Transfer to an ovenproof dish large enough to allow plenty of space for the kasha to swell. Add the water, season with salt, stir well, cover and cook in the oven at 180°C (350°F, gas mark 4), with the dish standing in a deep baking tray or roasting tin full of water, for about 45 minutes or until the grains are soft.

Serve with meat, game or sausages.

Barley

Barley is commonly used in small quantities to provide a nutty taste and pleasant texture in soups and stews.

Barley Kail Soup

An old Scots cottage recipe, and highly economical.

4–6 SERVINGS

50g (2 oz) pearl barley
1 litre (2 pints) Simple Stock (see page 31)
450g (1 lb) kale, trimmed of coarse stalks and finely shredded
3 leeks, sliced
salt and pepper

Put the barley and stock in a large saucepan and simmer for about 45 minutes or until the barley is tender, skimming off any scum which rises to the surface. Add the kale and leeks, and simmer until the vegetables are tender, adding salt and pepper as necessary.

Pulses

A whole range of dried vegetables comes under this heading – haricot beans, lentils, split peas, chickpeas, butter beans, etc. They are all cheap, can be usefully alternated with fresh vegetables, especially in winter, and form the basis of several good dishes in their own right. Incidentally, even dried vegetables deteriorate with time, so if you are stuck with a pan of beans which refuse to soften after hours of boiling, the chances are that they are antiques and have been kept too long.

All these vegetables should be soaked before cooking, unless specific instructions to the contrary are given on the packet. This cuts down the cooking time considerably and makes them more tender. Soaking overnight in tepid water will be enough for all of them.

To cook pulses, drain off the water they were soaked in. Pick out any blackened-looking vegetables, and any grit which may have found its way in, and put them in a large saucepan. Add cold water to more than cover, a sliced onion, a carrot, a clove of garlic, and pepper to taste, and bring slowly to the boil. Boil rapidly for 10 minutes (especially important for kidney beans, red and black, and soya beans), then reduce the heat, cover and simmer until tender. The initial fast boiling destroys toxins present in some dried pulses. Most pulses need 1–2 hours cooking, depending on quality and age. Split peas and lentils take less time than the others, chickpeas may need up to 6 hours. Never add salt until the pulses are tender because it tends to toughen them.

If you want to serve the pulses as they come, they are now ready to be drained and dished up with a dash of oil, a lump of butter and a sprinkling of parsley or grated cheese stirred in. For other ideas, see the following recipes.

Hummus

A blender or food processor makes this recipe an easy task. It's possible to do it with a food mill or even in a mortar, but not unless you have plenty of time on your hands. Chickpeas take such a long time to soak and cook (and a pauper must remember fuel costs), it would seem sensible to boil more than you need for this recipe (most packets contain 450 g/1 lb) and use the rest for something else – the soup on page 176, for example, or Pasta and Chickpea Salad (see page 161). Tahini (sesame seed paste) is always included in an authentic hummus, but it is expensive so if you don't want to pay for it or can't find it in your shops, the chickpeas will manage deliciously on their own.

8 SERVINGS

200 g (7 oz) chickpeas
salt
4 garlic cloves
juice of 1 lemon
75 ml (3 fl oz) olive oil
1–2 tablespoons tahini (optional)
cayenne pepper

Soak the chickpeas in cold water overnight. Drain the chickpeas, put them in a large saucepan, cover them with fresh cold water and bring to the boil. Boil rapidly for 20 minutes, then reduce the heat, cover and simmer for 2 hours or until the chickpeas are tender, seasoning with salt towards the end of cooking. Drain the chickpeas, reserving the cooking water.

Put the whole garlic cloves in a mixing bowl or blender with a cupful of the chickpeas. Mash or purée the chickpeas, a cupful at a time, pouring in the lemon juice and some of the cooking liquor and a dribble or so of olive oil as you go. Mix in the tahini.

When the whole is smooth and creamy, pour it into a bowl, sprinkle with cayenne pepper and dribble over a little olive oil. Hummus is usually served with pitta bread, but hot toast is just as good.

Split Pea Soup

This is real pauper's food.

4–6 SERVINGS

1 onion, studded with 2 cloves
1 bay leaf
1 sprig of fresh thyme, or a pinch of dried
1 ham or gammon bone
225 g (8 oz) split peas
1 litre (2 pints) water
salt and black pepper

Put the onion and cloves, the bay leaf and thyme in a large saucepan with the ham or gammon bone and split peas. Pour over the water and simmer for about 1 hour or until the peas are soft enough to mash. Remove the bone, onion and herbs, season with salt and pepper and serve the soup piping hot.

Haricot Bean Salad

Boiled haricot beans make a pleasant salad which can be eaten on its own, as an hors d'oeuvre, or with cold meat, salami, ham, etc. This is a handy way of using up any leftover boiled beans.

2 SERVINGS

125g (4 oz) dried haricot beans, soaked and cooked (see page 101)
French Dressing (see page 259)
salt and black pepper
1 onion, finely chopped
1 tablespoon finely chopped fresh parsley

Drain the beans, preferably while still warm, and season to taste with French dressing, salt and black pepper. Stir in the onion and parsley.

VARIATIONS: *Lentils and chickpeas are also good served like this. Add some garlic to the chickpeas, and a little pounded anchovy to the lentils.*

Lentils and Anchovies

An oddly successful mixture, this, with an elusive, smoky flavour, not in the least fishy. Well worth trying when you want a cheap but nourishing dish. It can be eaten on its own, with a crisp green salad and lots of black pepper, or with a halved hard-boiled egg added to each helping. The lentils must be the brown variety, which can be bought at most healthfood stores and good supermarkets.

4 SERVINGS

225 g (8 oz) brown lentils
1 onion, roughly chopped
50 g (2 oz) can of anchovy fillets, drained
75 g (3 oz) butter
2 garlic cloves, crushed
salt and black pepper
4 hard-boiled eggs, halved (optional)

Soak the lentils in cold water for 1–2 hours. Remove any lentils and tiny stalks which float to the top. Drain the lentils and transfer them to a large saucepan, add the onion and cover with fresh cold water. Bring to the boil slowly and simmer for 1–1½ hours or until the lentils are tender but not cooked to a mush. Drain in a colander.

Meanwhile, mash the anchovy fillets to a pulp with a wooden spoon. Melt 25 g (1 oz) butter over a low heat in a heavy-based saucepan or flameproof serving dish and stir in the lentil and onion mixture, together with the garlic. After a few minutes, when the lentils are heated through, stir in the pounded anchovies. Cook gently for a few minutes longer, stirring in the rest of the butter, a knob at a time. Add salt and pepper to taste. Serve, with or without the hard-boiled eggs.

NOTE: *This dish can be reheated by adding a little more butter and warming it, covered, in the oven at 170°C (325°F, gas mark 3) for 30 minutes.*

Pease Pudding

4–6 SERVINGS

450 g (1 lb) dried peas or split peas
50 g (2 oz) butter
1 egg, beaten
salt and pepper

If they are likely to be a bit old, soak the peas for 1–2 hours in plenty of cold water, then drain them and put them in a large saucepan with fresh water. Bring to the boil, then reduce the heat, cover and simmer for 1–2 hours or until tender. Drain the peas and purée them by passing them through a sieve or food mill, or by processing them in a blender or food processor. Stir in the butter and egg, season generously with salt and pepper and pour the mixture into a buttered pudding basin or fairly high-sided gratin dish. Cover with foil, or greaseproof paper and foil, and stand in a saucepan of water. Cover the pan and steam for 1 hour.

Turn the pudding out of the basin and serve with pork or poultry, or on its own with chips. Any leftover pease pudding can be sliced when cold and fried or grilled rather like polenta (see page 121).

Slow-Cooked Spiced Beans

The best equipment for this would be a deep, narrow earthenware pot with a tight-fitting lid. Failing that, any heavy casserole will do that is not too broad-based.

8 SERVINGS

a large bunch of fresh parsley, finely chopped
4 garlic cloves, finely chopped
1 teaspoon ground cinnamon
1 teaspoon ground cloves
1 teaspoon ground mace
1 teaspoon ground black pepper
a piece of pork rind (perhaps from a hand of pork), cut into strips
450 g (1 lb) white haricot beans, soaked overnight

Put the parsley, garlic and spices in a mortar or strong bowl and pound together with a pestle or the end of a rolling pin until they form a paste. Spread the pieces of pork rind with this mixture, roll them up and put them in the bottom of a deep, narrow casserole. Drain the beans and put them on top. Pour in enough water to cover the ingredients by 5 cm (2 inches), put the lid on and cook in the bottom oven of an Aga/Rayburn-type of oven overnight, or at 140–150°C (275–300°F, gas mark 1–2) for 5–6 hours.

Butter Beans

An excellent dish to serve with roast lamb.

4 SERVINGS

450g (1 lb) dried butter beans
a pinch of salt
150 ml (¼ pint) olive oil
2 garlic cloves, crushed
2 teaspoons tomato purée
plenty of black pepper
2 leaves of fresh sage or a sprig of fresh rosemary, or a pinch of dried
4 sun-dried tomatoes, chopped small (optional)

Soak the beans overnight, or for at least 4 hours, in cold water. Drain the beans and put them in a large saucepan. Cover with fresh cold water and bring to the boil. Boil rapidly for 10 minutes, then reduce the heat, cover and simmer until just tender. This may take anything from 30 minutes to 2 hours, depending on the youth of the beans. Salt the water and cook for 1 minute more, then drain.

Meanwhile, mix the olive oil, garlic, tomato purée, pepper, herbs and sun-dried tomatoes, if using, in a screw-topped jar. Screw the lid on and shake hard. Pour over the hot beans and serve immediately. It is the cold olive oil hitting the hot beans that makes this so good.

If you want to prepare the beans beforehand, cook them until they are just ready, then leave them in their water. When the time comes to eat them, heat them up, drain and dress them.

Shortcrust Pastry

Making pastry is one of those things which seems dishearteningly complicated if you have never tried it, and childishly simple once you have. Shortcrust pastry, particularly, is quick and easy to make, versatile and reasonably foolproof – no pastry, as expert cooks will tell you, is 100 per cent foolproof. However, if you stick to the directions, it will always be edible even if it falls short of crisp perfection.

Many cookbook recipes for pastry-making are bogged down in theory. The more confidently you tackle it, I find, the better it turns out (your hands are likely to be cooler for one thing) so I shall give the instructions first and diagnose briefly a few of the things that can go wrong afterwards.

MAKES ENOUGH TO LINE ONE 20–23 CM (8–9 IN)
FLAN DISH, OR COVER AN AVERAGE-SIZED PIE

175 g (6 oz) plain flour
a pinch of salt
1 tablespoon sugar (for a sweet pie)
100 g (3½ oz) butter
1 egg yolk
1–2 tablespoons water
a squeeze of lemon juice

Sift the flour, salt and sugar, if using, together into a large mixing bowl. Make a well in the centre. Put in the butter and start cutting it into the flour with a knife. The idea is to break the butter into tiny pieces while working in as much flour as possible. When the knife seems to have done what it can, use your fingertips to rub the mixture together until the butter has absorbed all the loose flour and the particles are the size of breadcrumbs (fresh not dried crumbs). *Don't* overdo this stage to be on the safe side – pastry is better handled too little than too much.

Beat the egg yolk with the water and stir it into the crumbs with your knife. Add a squeeze of lemon juice to make the dough more pliable. Gather the sticky mess together with your fingertips and work lightly until it sticks together in a lump and some of the stickiness has gone.

Put the pastry dough on a plate in a cool place, or in the fridge, to rest for 1–2 hours before use. The point of this is to make the dough less tough and less liable to shrink in cooking.

To roll out the dough, flour the table top and the rolling pin, and dust a little flour over the lump of pastry itself if it still feels very sticky. Roll out lightly but firmly until it is just under 5 mm (¼ inch) thick. If holes appear, tear off a patch, moisten the edges with milk, and iron over the hole with your rolling pin, sprinkling on a little more flour.

Lift the pastry sheet gently off the work surface – I usually slide a long knife blade underneath because it often sticks in places. Lay it over the flan tin and ease it in to fit the tin with your fingertips, taking care not to stretch it. Press it firmly down once it is in place – if you grease the tin lightly first the pastry will stick more obediently. Prick the bottom here and there with a fork. Roll the rolling pin over the top of the tin to trim off the extra pastry.

The next stage depends on whether your pastry is to cook with the filling, or separately. If the former, it is ready for the filling. If the latter (this is called baking 'blind'), cut a circle or strips of greaseproof paper to cover the bottom, then put in a cupful of uncooked dried beans. (Rice or crusts will do if you have no beans.) Put the flan in the top part of an oven preheated to 200°C (400°F, gas mark 6) and bake for 20 minutes. Remove the paper and beans and return to the oven for another 5–7 minutes. The pastry shell will now be golden brown, crisp and ready either to take a hot filling or to be left to cool and stored in an airtight container.

Some recipes only require the pastry to be partly pre-baked, in which case there is no need to use the beans and paper.

If you are using the pastry to cover a pie, roll it out a little thicker, and put an eggcup in the pie dish to support the pastry (if the area is fairly large). The pie will look more elegant if you cut a long strip of pastry, moisten it on both sides with milk or water, and press it round the rim of the pie dish, before laying on the pastry cover. You can then go round the edge with a fork, dipped in milk, to give a ribbed effect and press the two layers firmly together. Make a few cuts in the pastry to let out steam. Odd bits of pastry can be cut into flower and leaf shapes and stuck over the pie with a spot of milk. Brush over the whole surface with milk or beaten egg yolk to colour it attractively and bake as directed.

NOTES:

1 *The recipe given above is for a rich shortcrust. For greater economy, you can use half butter, half margarine; all margarine; or half butter, half lard. Some people swear by the one, some by the other, but I think butter tastes nicer and the extra cost is negligible. For eating cold, however, margarine makes a lighter-textured pastry. You can dispense with the egg yolk, in which case use a little more water.*

2 *If the pastry comes out hard and tough, you used too much water. If it is crumbly, too much fat. If soggy, it has had too much handling or been cooked initially at too low a temperature. Preheating the oven is important.*

3 *If things still go wrong, check that you are making pastry under the right conditions – everything, from room temperature to your hands, should be as cool as possible. Cool your hands by rinsing under a cold tap and drying, and make the pastry if possible in the morning before the kitchen heats up. Above all, don't worry – try it a couple more times and it will come right.*

Alsatian Onion Tart

An excellent recipe for the end of the week, when you are running out of cash and/or ideas. All you need is lots of onions, butter, shortcrust pastry and a couple of eggs. The filling is very tasty and the tart can be eaten hot, lukewarm or cold.

2−4 SERVINGS

one quantity Shortcrust Pastry (see page 107)
1 kg (2 lb) onions, chopped
a large knob of butter
1–2 tablespoons plain flour
salt and black pepper
2 eggs, beaten
2 tablespoons single cream (optional)
2 tablespoons grated Cheddar cheese (optional)

Roll out the pastry and use to line a 20–23 cm (8–9 inch) flan tin (see page 108). Put the onions in a saucepan with a little water, and cook over a low heat until soft and tender. Add the butter and leave to stew for a few minutes longer, then take them off the heat and add just enough flour to bind them. Season with salt and pepper, and add the eggs and 1 tablespoon cream, if using, to make a thick mush. Spread this mixture in the flan tin, spoon the remaining cream or the grated cheese over the top and bake in the oven at 220°C (425°F, gas mark 7) for 20 minutes, then lower the heat to 190°C (375°F, gas mark 5) and continue cooking for 45–60 minutes or until the pastry is crisp and the top nicely browned.

A plain green salad goes well with this. No other vegetables.

Suetcrust Pastry

Suetcrust is made in much the same way as shortcrust, using beef suet instead of butter or margarine. One useful point about it is that it can be used either for steamed puddings, like steak and kidney pudding, or baked as in jam roly-poly. Properly made, it is light and melting, and is associated with some of the best traditional English dishes.

MAKES ENOUGH TO LINE A 900 ML (1½ PINT)
PUDDING BASIN

**225 g (8 oz) self-raising flour, or plain flour and 1 teaspoon
baking powder
a pinch of salt
½ tablespoon sugar (for a sweet pudding)
125 g (4 oz) shredded beef suet**

Sift the flour, salt and sugar, if using, together. Add the suet, rubbing it in lightly with the fingertips for 1 minute. Gradually add enough water to make a light, spongy dough. Knead this lightly into a smooth ball on a floured board, roll out and use at once.

VARIATION: *For an extra light, spongy dough, replace 50g (2 oz) flour with 50g (2 oz) fresh white breadcrumbs.*

Baked Apple Pudding

4–5 SERVINGS

**50 g (2 oz) butter, softened
juice of 2 lemons and a little grated lemon rind
125 g (4 oz) soft brown sugar
1 quantity Suetcrust Pastry (see above)
550 g (1¼ lb) apples, peeled, cored and sliced**

Cream the butter, lemon juice and brown sugar together and put it in the bottom of a greased 900 ml (1½ pint) pudding basin. Roll out the suetcrust pastry and use it to line the bottom and sides of the pudding basin, covering the butter/sugar mixture and leaving an overhang round the sides. Lay the apples together with the grated lemon rind and 2 tablespoons water on the crust. Fold over the edges to cover, and seal. Bake the pudding in the oven at 190°C (375°F, gas mark 5) until brown, then lower the heat to 150°C (300°F, gas mark 2) to finish cooking, which will take about 2 hours in all.

To serve, turn the pudding out on to a plate. The sugar and butter mixture will have turned to a lemony sauce which will run out over the top of the pudding. Serve with more sugar and cream.

Plough Pudding

Suetcrust pastry, steamed or baked, is, I believe, one of the great English inventions, a homely native alternative to the more elegant pastries and yeast doughs of European culinary tradition. Though hardly suitable for a low-cholesterol diet, I find the resulting crust more digestible and less cloyingly rich than butter-based alternatives.

Interestingly, suetcrust is creeping back on to metropolitan menus. This savoury roly-poly is a true peasant dish, with many variants, like green hawthorn buds instead of sage. What all the variations have in common is a thrifty proportion of tasty filling to substantial roly-poly crust. It is not the suet dish I would try out on visiting foreigners, but it makes hearty family eating. Get the best quality sausagemeat by stripping pure meat sausages of their skins. The pink pappy stuff offered by some butchers is revolting.

4–6 SERVINGS

225 g (8 oz) plain flour
125 g (4 oz) shredded beef suet
salt and black pepper
2 onions, chopped
125 g (4 oz) streaky bacon, de-rinded and chopped
1 tablespoon chopped fresh sage and/or parsley
2 tablespoons soft brown sugar
125–225 g (4–8 oz) pure pork sausagemeat

Mix the flour, suet and a little salt and pepper in a bowl, and add enough cold water to make a firm dough. Roll out on a floured surface to make a rectangle about 1 cm (½ inch) thick. Mix the onion, bacon, herbs and sugar with the sausagemeat and spread evenly over the suetcrust. Season well, then roll up into a sausage shape. Roll this securely in a well-floured tea towel, tying the ends with string, and plunge into a large pan of boiling water. Cook over a moderate heat for just over 2 hours. Unroll the pudding, put it in a baking dish and bake in the oven at 190°C (375°F, gas mark 5) for about 30 minutes or until lightly browned.

Serve with mustard, a sharp fruit jelly, and cabbage, greens or carrots.

Batter

Batter is one of the small miracles of cookery – how that pallid liquid is metamorphosed into a puffy golden pillow-crust is a mystery I hope never to have explained to me. As sheer padding, batter is unbeatable value. Try the Toad-in-the-Hole recipe (below) and see.

As I have given the batter-making procedure in some detail in the recipe for Toad-in-the-Hole I will not go into it here. A point to keep in mind when making batter, though, is always to bring it into contact with high heat – whether you are baking it in the oven, or frying it in deep fat. (Fritters can be fried in shallow fat but not so successfully.) This makes it light and ungreasy. In the case of fritters, drain them on crumpled absorbent kitchen paper for a minute before eating. If you wish, you may leave the batter to stand for an hour or so before using.

Toad-in-the-Hole

Not a dish for sophisticates, but an excellent way of stretching half a pound of chipolatas into a solid meal for four people. Children, especially, love it. If you have time, I suggest braising the sausages in the oven at 180°C (350°F, gas mark 4) for 45 minutes with a little stock, gravy or butter and a dash of Worcestershire sauce, to encourage them to sweat out some of their lye, and remove that raw pink appearance. Drain them on absorbent kitchen paper to remove excess fat.

4 SERVINGS

**125 g (4 oz) plain flour
a pinch of salt
2 eggs
300 ml (½ pint) milk
a little butter or dripping
225 g (8 oz) skinless pork chipolatas**

To make the batter, sift the flour and a pinch of salt into a large mixing bowl. Make a well in the middle, so that the bottom of the bowl is exposed. Break the eggs into this well and stir a little milk into them with a wooden spoon, delicately at first to avoid mixing in the flour, then gradually begin incorporating the flour, adding a little more milk as you go along. Go on stirring in the flour and adding small quantities of milk until the mixture is the consistency of cream. At this point you can beat the mixture thoroughly with an egg whisk. After a minute or two, if you wish, put the batter aside to stand for 1 hour.

Heat the butter or dripping in a baking tin, pour in the batter, drop the sausages in and bake in the oven at 220°C (425°F, gas mark 7) for 35 minutes.

An unsophisticated vegetable should accompany this dish – boiled, buttered cabbage or sprouts.

NOTE: *It is important to have the baking tin and oven well heated. A warm tin, or cool oven, will stop the batter rising.*

If you have not experimented with batters before, you will be agreeably surprised by the transformation of the anaemic-looking raw batter into a billowing golden puff reminiscent of the best Yorkshire puddings.

Pancakes

Pancakes sprinkled with brown sugar and lemon juice, or filled with apricot jam, are an almost irresistible pudding. They are not difficult to make unless you are aiming for perfect circles, in which case you will need a cast-iron pan made specially for the purpose, straight-sided, like the ones used in Brittany, where pancakes are a local speciality. An ordinary medium-sized heavy-based frying pan gives less immaculate results, but the taste, after all, is the same.

Pancake batter is made like ordinary batter except that you add a little melted butter.

MAKES 8

125 g (4 oz) plain flour
a pinch of salt
2 teaspoons caster sugar
1 egg and 1 egg yolk
about 300 ml (½ pint) milk
25 g (1 oz) butter, melted
vegetable oil

Sift the flour, salt and sugar into a bowl and proceed as for Toad-in-the-Hole (see opposite) until you have stirred in about half the milk and the batter is a thickish cream. Now stir in the butter and more milk until the batter is a thin cream. If you wish, leave it to stand in a cool place for an hour.

Heat the pan slowly until it is good and hot. With a pad of kitchen paper sprinkled with vegetable oil (you can use melted butter but oil is better because it doesn't burn and is tasteless) wipe a film of oil over the pan. The idea of greasing the pan is to prevent the batter sticking, not in any sense to fry the pancake. Drop a generous tablespoon of batter into the pan and immediately shake the pan gently with a clockwise turn of the wrist to spread the batter thinly over the bottom. Cook gently. As soon as the pancake edges can be easily detached, the pancake is ready to be turned over. Traditionally, you should toss it, which needs a strong wrist and an accurate eye. If tennis was not your strong suit, work a metal slice or spatula under the pancake and flip it over rapidly to brown the other side. As they are done, stack them on a plate in the oven, which should be warm, not hot.

NOTE: *For a change, you can try folding the whisked leftover egg white into your batter. This gives a fluffier-textured pancake. You can also vary the flavour of the batter itself by adding a little vanilla, grated lemon rind, or even a spoonful of brandy or rum if you happen to have such a thing. And the choice of fillings is enormous: apple purée, sultanas soaked in lemon juice and beaten into sweetened cream cheese, chopped walnuts and brown sugar, redcurrant jelly, to suggest only a few.*

Breton Buckwheat Pancakes

Checking on my friends' current food preferences, one of them, Heather, explained that since her chef-son had married a Breton girl they had been eating a lot of buckwheat pancakes, now so popular with the family that they make them with a variety of fillings, sweet as well as savoury. Pancakes are ideal poor food in any case, wrapping up leftovers gracefully, or simply spread with jam or sprinkled with lemon juice and sugar. The buckwheat adds a nutty something which is addictive. Try them.

MAKES 12 LARGE PANCAKES

250 g (9 oz) buckwheat flour
60 g (2½ oz) plain flour
a pinch of salt
2 eggs
about 900 ml (1½ pints) water and milk,
mixed in equal proportions

Mix the dry ingredients together in a large bowl. Make a well in the centre and break in the eggs. Stir with a wooden spoon, gradually beating in the water and milk until you have a light batter. Leave to stand for 2 hours, if possible.

Grease a heavy-based frying pan with a piece of absorbent kitchen paper dipped in cooking oil. Heat the pan over a moderate heat and tip in a little batter, swirling it around in the pan to spread it in an even layer. After 1–2 minutes, by which time the underside should be lightly browned, flip the pancake over with a spatula, or toss it if you prefer! Cook for another 1–2 minutes. Remove the pan and keep warm while making the rest of the pancakes.

The pancakes can be filled immediately, for a gratin dish (see Note). Heather suggests cooked spinach with grated cheese; chopped ham and scrambled eggs; chopped ham or bacon with mushrooms. Or they can be prepared ahead, stacked with a piece of greaseproof paper between them to prevent sticking, and reheated by steaming over just bubbling water in a large pan. If you don't have a steamer, stand a plate on an inverted cup, in a large enough pan.

Suggested sweet fillings include: sultanas, honey and lemon; ice cream and maple syrup; soft fruits; home-made jam.

NOTE: *To make a dish of filled savoury pancakes more substantial, cover with a little cheesy béchamel sauce and a sprinkling of grated cheese, and heat through in the oven at 180°C (350°F, gas mark 4) for 20 minutes or so, flashing the top under the grill before serving to brown it.*

Brain Fritters

Brains are not easy to find these days, but if you have a trustworthy source they are worth trying, for their delicate flavour. Brain fritters like these figure in the Italian *fritto misto*.

2 SERVINGS

1 pair calf or ox brains
1 onion, chopped
a sprig of parsley
1 bay leaf
1 teaspoon vinegar
salt and pepper

FOR THE FRITTER BATTER
125 g (4 oz) flour
3 tablespoons olive oil
a pinch of salt
150 ml (¼ pint) tepid water
1 stiffly beaten egg white

The batter should be prepared first (see page 114) and left to stand for 2 hours or longer, the beaten egg white being added just before frying.

The brains should be soaked in tepid water with a little vinegar for an hour or so. The water should be changed from time to time, and any little clots of blood adhering to the brains carefully removed – brains need gentle handling or they are apt to disintegrate.

When the soaking water looks clear heat 600 ml (1 pint) water with the onion, parsley, bay leaf, 1 teaspoon vinegar, salt and pepper. When this is simmering gently, lower the brains into the water and simmer for half an hour. Remove, drain and leave to cool.

To cook the fritters, heat a lot of oil in a deep-frying pan. Divide the brains into pieces about the size of a walnut, dip them into the batter and then drop into the hot oil. They are cooked when they float to the top, about 3 minutes. Drain on kitchen paper.

Eat with a squeeze of lemon juice.

Yorkshire Pudding

Almost everyone likes a good Yorkshire pudding, and it is easier to make than those flabby slices served up with institutional meals might lead you to expect. From the economy point of view, a generous helping of Yorkshire pudding will make people less greedy for roast beef.

4 SERVINGS

125 g (4 oz) plain flour
a pinch of salt
300 ml (½ pint) milk
2 eggs

Sift the flour and salt into a bowl, make a well in the centre and add the milk gradually, beating hard. Add the eggs, beating hard after each one. Put the batter into the fridge, or in a cool place, until 35 minutes before the roast has finished cooking. Pour half the fat from the roasting tin into another baking tin (or cake tin). Put the baking tin back into the oven until the fat is smoking hot, then pour in the batter. Cook the pudding at the top of the oven at 200°C (400°F, gas mark 6) for 30–35 minutes or until puffy and golden on top. (The roast has to be moved down to a lower shelf to finish cooking.)

Barley Risotto / Orzotto

I lit upon orzotto or barley risotto by accident, mistaking those firm grains in a glass jar for risotto rice, and pouring in a bowlful of stock (made from a pheasant carcass) before I realized something was oddly different. The stock was insufficient to soften the grains – I added boiling water and a splash of white wine. We all thought the result was excellent eating, chewier than risotto made with arborio rice, but with a nutty flavour that went well with the stock and shreds of leftover bird I added at the last minute. Now, I observe, barley risotto is everywhere, dead trendy. The charm of it for anyone who finds rice risotto a worry (to stir or not to stir, how 'soupy' is correct?) is that barley stays firm, the grains distinct, though it absorbs stock as eagerly. I note Sophie Grigson soaks her barley overnight first. This would mean less stock was needed, but I use unsoaked barley with good results. Suit yourself. I think barley risotto lends itself best to gamey flavourings, fungi (fresh or dried) as well as game birds or indeed chicken, less suited to delicate vegetable flavours like asparagus, peas, broad beans. Plus barley is good for you!

4 SERVINGS

1 tablespoon olive oil
1 large onion, finely chopped
1 carrot, peeled and grated
1 large stick celery, finely chopped
3 garlic cloves, peeled and minced
900 ml (1½ pints) stock, game or chicken (see page 31)
or dried fungi soaking water
300 g (about 11 oz) pearl barley
salt and pepper
50 g (2 oz) butter
a small handful of grated Parmesan

A heavyweight pan or cast-iron pot is best for cooking risotto or orzotto. Heat oil and a little butter in this, add the chopped vegetables and garlic (Italians call this a *soffrito*) and sweat over low heat for a few minutes, while you heat the stock separately. Add the pearl barley, soaked or unsoaked, and stir it about for another couple of minutes, to absorb flavours, then pour in a good splash of stock, perhaps a third. Stir briefly and leave over medium heat till the stock is absorbed. Add another third of the hot stock, stir to distribute it, leave for 5–8 minutes, then pour in the remainder of the stock. If the barley still seems too chewy once the stock is absorbed, a bit gritty, add boiling water and perhaps a glass of white wine (red will alter the colour) or a splash of vermouth.

Once the barley is tender remove from heat, add salt and pepper to taste, plus butter cut into small bits, and a sprinkle of Parmesan. If you have any shreds of meat – chicken, duck, pheasant – to go with the stock, add these now, forking them into the barley. Cover the pan with a folded tea towel, then the lid, and let stand for a few minutes.

Serve on hot plates with more grated Parmesan to add separately.

NOTE: *The mushroom/porcini variant uses a mix of fresh mushrooms chopped and softened in butter together with the soaked porcini as flavourings. The porcini soaking water substitutes for stock, but you will need to make it up with boiling water and white wine, and be generous with shavings of butter at the resting period. Porcini (any other dried fungi can substitute) are not cheap, but they give a depth of flavour which fresh mushrooms cannot reach.*

Breadcrumbs

Two sorts of breadcrumbs are extensively used in cooking – dried crumbs for coating food for frying (see Note) or sprinkling on top of various dishes cooked uncovered in the oven, and fresh crumbs for making various stuffings, dumpling mixtures, bread sauce, etc.

Dried crumbs are made by putting ends of loaves, crusts, leftover slices, etc., in a baking tin at the bottom of the oven to dry out while you are cooking other dishes. When they are dry, they are crushed. The easiest way is to wrap them in a cloth and to roll them with a rolling pin, then put them through a coarse sieve, and store them in a screw-topped jar. They will keep for several weeks, if you remember to put the lid back at once after use. You *can* buy dry crumbs ready-made, but these look and taste odd, and the extra expense hardly seems justified when you can make your own easily and economically.

Fresh or soft breadcrumbs are made by rubbing white bread through a sieve or a grater or whizzing it briefly in a food processor. The bread should be a day old at least, and you should not use the crusts. If you are making a stuffing in a tremendous hurry, you can tear the bread up with your fingertips, but the result will be lumpier. Incidentally, fresh crumbs will not keep – they go mouldy in a trice – so you have to make them afresh each time.

NOTE: *In case you were wondering why foods are coated with crumbs, this is done for a reason, not merely for decoration. The breadcrumbs form a protective coating over the food which seals in the flavour and juices, and, in the case of fried food, is lighter and less greasy than batter.*

Baked Polenta

8 SERVINGS

1.5 litres (3 pints) water
salt and pepper
450 g (1 lb) coarsely ground cornmeal or polenta
125 g (4 oz) butter
50 g (2 oz) plain flour
600 ml (1 pint) warm milk (or a mixture of milk and cream)
125 g (4 oz) Edam cheese, grated
freshly grated Parmesan or Pecorino cheese

Put the water in a large saucepan, add salt and bring to the boil. Reduce the heat and begin to pour in the cornmeal in a slow, steady stream, stirring all the time with a wooden spoon. When all the cornmeal has been added, simmer, stirring constantly, for 30 minutes or until the mixture starts to peel away from the sides of the pan.

Pour the polenta on to a clean surface (a wooden table or formica work top will do), and spread it until it is about 1 cm (½ inch) thick. It will begin to harden as it cools.

Melt half the butter in a large heavy-based saucepan and stir in the flour. Cook, stirring, for 2 minutes, then remove from the heat and gradually add the warm milk, stirring all the time. Bring to the boil, stirring, then simmer until the sauce is thick and smooth. Remove from the heat and stir in the grated Edam cheese until melted.

With a knife or pastry cutter, cut the polenta into small circles, and arrange these, slightly overlapping each other in layers in a shallow ovenproof dish or flan dish, dotting them here and there with fragments of the remaining butter. Pour over the cheese sauce, scatter the top with grated Parmesan or Pecorino and more fragments of butter and put in the oven at 200°C (400°F, gas mark 6) for about 20 minutes to heat up, bubble and go golden brown on the top.

Pizza

Everybody loves pizza and really nothing could be easier or more economical. You don't have to use expensive mozzarella, olives, smoked sausages and anchovies. Pizza should be peasant food and some of the most successful combinations are not only less expensive but more original than classic pizzeria fare. The only English variant which would be a mistake, to my mind, is grated Cheddar. Your one really essential extravagance must be extra-virgin olive oil.

4–6 SERVINGS

700 g (1½ lb) strong white flour
1 teaspoon salt
1 sachet fast action dried yeast
2 tablespoons olive oil
1 egg
warm water

Combine the flour, salt and yeast in a large mixing bowl, pour in the oil and break in the egg. Make a well in the centre and begin to pour in the warm water, mixing all the time to make a dough. Go very gently with the water – as you knead the dough it will take in more flour than you expect. (If you do get it too wet, put it to rise in a very warm place and it should dry out a bit, before you knead it.)

Turn the dough on to a lightly floured surface and knead it for about 10 minutes or until it is smooth and elastic. (You can test this elasticity by pushing the dough ball with a finger; it should quickly spring back out to fill the identation.) Put the dough in a bowl, cover with a clean, damp cloth and leave it to rise in a warm place for about 1 hour.

When the dough has doubled in size, knock it back, knead it again, then pull or roll it out into two pizza bases. These can be any shape which will fit your baking sheets. Brush with oil and then put on your chosen topping (see opposite). Bake in the oven at 220°C (425°F, gas mark 7) for 15–20 minutes.

TOPPINGS:

- Stew some finely sliced onions very gently in olive oil. Spread these on the pizza base and sprinkle with salt and pepper.

- Tomato Sauce (see page 66), simply spread over the pizza base, makes Pizza Rosso.

- Dribble olive oil over the pizza base and sprinkle with salt to make Pizza Bianca, Rome's favourite mid-morning snack. A sprinkling of dried sage or rosemary is an optional addition.

- Fry tiny matchsticks of bacon in their own fat and scatter them over the pizza with some crumbled herby sausage and some chopped fresh marjoram or oregano (the traditional pizza herb). Break an egg on top and dribble with olive oil before baking.

VARIATION: *Calzone is a pizza which has been wrapped around its filling, an Italian Cornish pasty. The filling can be southern, perhaps ricotta cheese and a couple of sun-dried tomatoes, or northern sausagemeat and finely shredded cabbage.*

Fast Work

This is the chapter for evenings when you get back late from work, with two people expected for supper, or when a long car journey leaves everyone clamouring for immediate sustenance, or when you want a rapid but not skimpy meal after a late show – in fact for any of the occasions when a meal has to be prepared at the double, with materials to hand. Many of the recipes make use of canned foods, for convenience, but not too obviously – presumably no one needs advice on how to prepare baked beans on toast, and besides this is probably not what hungry people would consider a meal. Maximum preparation and cooking time is never more than an hour and in most cases considerably less. I have given the stages of preparation in some detail, to avoid fuss and fluster, and if you follow them carefully you should be able to produce a very presentable meal for two to four people – soup, main dish and even a pudding – in an hour, without becoming dishevelled, tired and irritable in the process.

This sort of cooking does require some forethought. You should keep a selection of tins to hand, as well as quite a few spices and herbs to ginger them up, and you will need the usual standbys – milk, eggs, butter, bread. For real emergencies, when the cupboard is practically bare, I have included one or two snack ideas.

Quick Onion Soup

The touch of inspiration in this recipe, given to me by a French friend, is the caramelizing of the onions which gives the soup colour, body and a rich but delicate flavour all at once.

4 SERVINGS

25 g (1 oz) butter
4 large onions, thinly sliced
½ tablespoon sugar
1 litre (2 pints) hot water
1 vegetable stock cube
a dash of wine vinegar
salt and pepper (optional)

Melt the butter in a large frying pan and put in the onions. Stir them around until they begin to go soft, then put in the sugar. Keep stirring until the sugar browns – brown *not* black – and then pour in the hot water and stock cube with the vinegar. Simmer for 15 minutes, taste and add salt and pepper if necessary. Serve plain with buttered toast.

Chinese Egg Drop Soup

2 SERVINGS

125 g (4 oz) mushrooms, roughly chopped
a handful of watercress or spring onions, roughly chopped
600 ml (1 pint) Simple Stock (see page 31)
2 teaspoons soy sauce
1 egg

Simmer the mushrooms and cress or spring onions in the stock until tender. Add the soy sauce. Beat the egg and stir it rapidly through the bubbling soup until it forms yellow strands. Serve at once.

Spinach Soup

225 g (8 oz) spinach
300 ml (½ pint) stock
1 onion, finely chopped
300 ml (½ pint) milk, heated
pepper and salt
nutmeg

Wash the spinach thoroughly, pulling off the largest stalks. Bring the stock to the boil and add the spinach and onion. Simmer till quite soft. Put through a sieve, and return to the pan. Now add the hot milk, pepper, salt and a grating of nutmeg, and simmer for a few minutes.

I have given soup recipes elsewhere which can be adapted to diet requirements, if you cook them as above instead of frying up the vegetables in butter first. Celery Soup (see page 35), for instance, would be suitable.

In all these recipes hot water plus bouillon cubes can be substituted for stock, though the result will not be so good. Remember to use less salt as the cubes are very salty.

Miso Broth

Made from fermented soybean paste, miso is sold in jars in healthfood stores and most supermarkets. Boiling water, a few sliced spring onions and a few tablespoons of cooked rice turn a heaped spoonful of miso into a saltily refreshing broth in – literally – minutes. The taste is not unlike Bovril, but nuttier. Excellent sustenance for the morning after, or an upset stomach when only the purest dish is acceptable.

1 SERVING

1 heaped tablespoon miso
boiling water (one bowlful)
2 spring onions, topped, tailed and cut lengthways into fine strips
2 tablespoons cooked rice

Combine miso, water and spring onion shreds in a small pan and cook for a minute or two, stirring to dissolve the miso paste. Add rice, cook a minute longer, then transfer to a deep soup bowl. Eat with dry crackers.

Chasse

I am including this recipe, originally a country-house breakfast dish, because it is an excellent way of combining the sort of odds and ends you can usually scrape together in the most depleted larder into a comforting little meal. The quantities I have given can be varied according to what is available – canned tomatoes can be used instead of fresh, or even a generous tablespoon of tomato purée, at a pinch.

2 SERVINGS

1 onion, chopped
a knob of butter
5 tomatoes, skinned and chopped
1 slice of cooked ham, or 2–3 rashers of bacon, de-rinded
and chopped
3 cooked potatoes, diced
a dash of Worcestershire sauce
50–75 g (2–3 oz) Cheddar cheese, grated
a good pinch of paprika
2 eggs, poached

Fry the onion lightly in the butter, then add the tomatoes and ham or bacon. When these are hot, add the potatoes and a little water. Cook slowly for 5 minutes. Just before serving, add a dash of Worcestershire sauce and stir in the grated cheese and paprika. Serve with a poached egg on each helping.

Quick Welsh Rarebit

When you are in a tearing hurry, or faced with the job of concocting a meal out of a lump of stale cheese and some dry bread, Welsh Rarebit seems the obvious answer. The best cheese for this, I think, is Caerphilly, which gives a sharper, lighter texture than Cheddar, but I realize that this is a counsel of perfection.

2 SERVINGS

125–225 g (4–8 oz) cheese
1 teaspoon mustard powder
salt and pepper
a dash of Worcestershire sauce
1 egg, beaten
a knob of butter (optional)
2 slices of bread

Grate the cheese and mix it with the mustard, salt, pepper and Worcestershire sauce. Bind with the beaten egg. If you can spare it, a knob of butter worked in helps. Toast the bread on one side only. Spread the other side thickly with the mixture and stick it under the grill until the cheese topping is puffy and lightly browned. Eat at once.

VARIATIONS: *Should you not have so much as an egg, you can thicken your cheese mixture (and make it go a bit further too) by stirring in a little cornflour, or flour, mixed with a little milk, water or beer. In that case you should really cook the Rarebit mixture in a saucepan for a few minutes to give the flour a chance to thicken. Then brown under the grill.*

A couple of poached eggs on top, should you be well supplied with eggs, turns this into a Buck Rarebit.

Steamed Eggs

This is a handy way of cooking eggs, as a change from frying, baking or poaching them. For some reason, they taste better like this.

2 SERVINGS

a knob of butter
2–4 eggs
salt and pepper

Put a heatproof plate over a saucepan of boiling water (you could be cooking potatoes or a vegetable in the pan at the same time). Place a few scraps of butter on the plate. When they melt, crack the eggs carefully and slide them on to the plate. Sprinkle a little salt and pepper over them and cover with another inverted plate. Look at them after 3–4 minutes. They are ready when the whites are firm.

Eggs in Nests

A cute, intriguing starter to a dinner party. Also appealing to children. It can be cooked in ramekins, in hollowed out bread rolls, or on rounds of bread (rubbed with garlic or tapenade) lightly toasted in the oven.

4 SERVINGS

4 eggs
4 rolls or bread rounds
garlic or tapenade (optional)
butter
salt and pepper

Break the egg yolks into separate cups, put the egg whites into a bowl and whisk them with a pinch of salt till firm. Rub the garlic or tapenade on to bread rounds, if using. Butter the ramekins. Spoon beaten egg white into the chosen receptacle to make a nest. Make a little hollow in the centre, slip in a shaving of butter, then an egg yolk. Bake in a moderate oven till the yolk is just set, season lightly and serve immediately.

The bread roll version, the most amusing, should have the lids (also hollowed out) crisped at the same time, but only clapped on to the egg nest just before serving.

NOTE: *A thirties country-house invention, this invites tweaking – for example, with a dusting of chopped chives, tarragon or grated cheese.*

Tortilla

There is a knack to making a good tortilla, so that it emerges golden brown, compact and juicy without being undercooked. I once watched a chef in Seville cook tortillas, one after another, all perfect, and this is what he did. He used a small (20 cm/8 inch) well-seasoned cast-iron pan. In this he fried diced potato in olive oil until it was tender but not browned. In a bowl he rapidly whisked up some eggs with a pinch of coarse salt. He then tipped the potato into the egg mixture and let it sit while he wiped out the pan with more salt and kitchen paper. He put the pan back on the heat with a splash more olive oil, tipped the contents of the bowl into it all at once, gave the pan a quick shake and pressed the contents down with a metal slice, to compact them. After 2–3 minutes over a high flame he judged the tortilla was cooked underneath. With a practised flip of a muscular right arm, he tossed this substantial but small omelette into the air and caught it as it descended, cooked side uppermost. After a minute more over the heat the tortilla was ready to slide on to a plate and serve – and excellent eating it was too.

I suggest you follow his method, using a non-stick pan, over lower heat and reversing the tortilla on to a plate before returning it to brown the base. If the potatoes, olive oil and eggs are all fresh and good quality, a tortilla needs nothing more. But you can pad out the basic mixture with various cooked leftovers – peas, chopped onions, cubes of chorizo, diced peppers, even pasta – to make it go further.

2 SERVINGS

2 biggish potatoes, weighing about 300 g (11 oz), peeled and diced
4 eggs
200 ml (8 fl oz) olive oil

Follow the method above, remembering that most of the olive oil is used to fry the diced potato, with a splash reserved for the tortilla.

NOTE: *Pan size is critical to a perfect tortilla, which should be around 2 cm (1 inch) thick, well cooked but moist in the centre, like a solid cake rather than an omelette. Using a larger pan, so the tortilla is barely 1 cm (½ inch) thick, and finishing the top under the grill (frequently recommended in UK recipes) makes for a dry, leathery pancake instead of a juicy tortilla. Tossing a tortilla needs serious muscle and practice, but reversing on to a plate and sliding back into the pan is easy enough. My Sevillan chef cooked over a high-powered professional gas ring; allow a bit longer cooking time over a domestic gas ring or electric hotplate.*

Frittata Verde

Frittata, eggah, tortilla – basically these are the same thing spoken with different accents: a solid cake-like omelette where beaten eggs have been used to bind a tasty filling, usually cooked vegetables. I have suggested broad beans, peas and spring onions because these are usually to hand. A non-stick frying pan really comes into its own for the cooking.

4–6 SERVINGS

1 small packet of frozen broad beans, thawed
1 small packet of frozen *petits pois*, thawed
5 eggs
1 bunch of spring onions, chopped
salt and pepper
a little chopped parsley
3 tablespoons olive oil

The broad beans need to be cooked for about 3 minutes. If you have time to slip the greyish skins off, well and good; if not, don't worry – it will still taste good. The peas do not need cooking, but they should be completely thawed.

In a bowl, break the eggs, whisk lightly, then add all the vegetables, seasoning and parsley, if using. Heat the oil in the non-stick pan then tip in all the eggy mixture at once, stir once or twice to distribute the vegetables, then turn the heat right down and cook for about 12–15 minutes, by which time the bottom should be solid and the top just runny. Lay a plate over the pan (wear rubber gloves), flip over so the frittata is on the plate, cooked side up, then slide it back into the pan for a few more minutes. You may find the flipping easier if you loosen the frittata from the pan first with a flexible spatula or slice.

Lay the cooked frittata on a board on a sheet of kitchen paper, and cool, if you can wait (it is more flavoursome at room temperature), or devour at once, with ratatouille or a salad.

VARIATION: *Alternative filling suggestions: leftover pasta, grilled peppers, cooked mussels, cubed fried potatoes, leftover cooked broccoli.*

Toasted Cheese and Onion Sandwiches

Melted cheese and raw onion make a deliciously crude combination, clapped between slices of toasted bread. Toast one side of bread only, smear other side with mustard, pile on grated cheese and put in a hot oven, or under a grill till the cheese starts to melt. Then lay a few thin slices of onion on to the cheese, clap the bread slices together and eat hot.

Roasted Red Peppers with Garlic and Anchovy (Bagna Cauda)

A dazzlingly simple dish to make when capsicums (sweet peppers) are at their best and cheapest, in high summer. The speediest way to prepare them is the one given here, which has the rich sweetness of red peppers grilled over a gas flame, without the hassle of scraping off charred skin. Serve it as a first course, warm, or along with grilled meat, fish, or meat balls. A lusty, colourful dish closely related to the Sicilian *bagna cauda*. Garlic quantities can be reduced to two cloves if you are not garlic fiends.

4 SERVINGS

6–8 large red peppers
olive oil
6 cloves garlic
6 tinned anchovy fillets
salt and pepper

Halve the peppers, scraping out the seeds and white membrane, and slice each half lengthwise into three strips. Lay the strips skin down on a roasting pan, sprinkle generously with olive oil, and cook in a medium oven for about half and hour till limp and tender.

Crush the garlic and anchovy fillets in a pestle and mortar, stir in enough olive oil to make a thick purée. Arrange the pepper strips, skin side up, on a flat dish, spoon over the garlic and anchovy mixture, season to taste, and leave for the flavours to mingle for 10–20 minutes.

Tomato and Red Pepper Sauce

Red peppers roasted (see opposite) and added to a simple tomato sauce, made with fresh or tinned tomatoes, lend the sauce colour, density and a sweetness that usefully counteracts tomato acidity. I prefer this ruse to sun-dried tomatoes. Process the roasted peppers to a purée, skins included, before stirring in to the tomato sauce. A fresh or dried red chilli, seeds removed, and chopped, can be cooked with the peppers, and puréed at the same time, to add an edge of fieriness to the sauce. Good with plainly boiled pasta, or grilled fish.

Tunisian Salad

This makes a terrific accompaniment to grilled fish, like the red mullet often served with it in Tunisia. It's a colourful mélange of chopped raw vegetables, crisp but juicy, spiked with fresh chilli and seasoned with an elusive whiff of cumin. Serve with vinaigrette dressing to taste.

4 SERVINGS

1 cucumber, peeled, de-seeded and diced small
1 green pepper, de-seeded and chopped
450 g (1 lb) ripe tomatoes, skinned, de-seeded and chopped
1 bunch of spring onions, chopped with some of their green shoots
1 fresh green chilli, de-seeded and very finely chopped
½ teaspoon ground cumin
juice of ½ lemon
2 tablespoons olive oil
salt and pepper

Combine all the ingredients in a bowl, squeezing over the lemon juice. Add oil, salt and pepper, turn well and chill for about 30 minutes.

NOTE: *If you like chilli, you'll love it like this. If you find it too fiery, omit the chilli and instead add 1 tablespoon of chopped fresh coriander.*

Caesar Salad

Figure-conscious women invariably head for Caesar Salad on a restaurant menu because it is light but somehow filling. Properly made – which is rare – it is a delicious combination of crisp and crunchy, mild yet piquant. This version hails from San Francisco where thin equals beautiful. I think you can get away with using less cheese, but it must be freshly grated, likewise tinned anchovies but the lettuce must be hearts of Romaine not crackly, tasteless Webbs Wonder. Ideal as a light lunch.

4 SERVINGS

4 anchovy fillets, chopped to a mush
4 cloves garlic, finely minced
1 tablespoon red wine vinegar
salt and pepper
5 tablespoons olive oil
one thick slice 'rustic' type bread, cut into 1 cm (½ inch) cubes
juice of 1 lemon
2 eggs, beaten
2 hearts of Romaine, leaves separated and chilled
125 g (4 oz) freshly grated Parmesan

Combine half the anchovy and garlic with the vinegar, salt, pepper and 4 tablespoons olive oil in a bowl and let stand while you prepare the salad. Toss the bread cubes with the remaining tablespoon of olive oil, salt lightly, spread on a baking sheet and bake in a moderate oven for about 10 minutes, till golden.

Just before serving add the remaining anchovy, garlic and half the cheese to the prepared dressing, with lemon juice, salt and freshly ground pepper to taste. Whisk in well-beaten eggs to make a smooth runny mix. Toss dressing lightly but thoroughly with lettuce leaves, then divide among four plates, sprinkling over the croûtons and a dusting of grated cheese.

Potato, Apple and Caper Salad

4 SERVINGS

**4 potatoes, scrubbed
2 small eating apples
3 celery sticks
1 tablespoon capers, drained
French Dressing (see page 259)
a squeeze of lemon juice
salt and pepper**

Cook the potatoes in boiling water for about 20 minutes or until tender. Drain the potatoes, peel them and leave to cool.

Core and peel the apples. Slice the apples, potatoes and celery thinly and combine with the capers and dressing. Squeeze lemon juice over and season with salt and pepper.

This is good with most cold meat, particularly ham.

Raw Mushroom Salad

It may sound odd, but raw mushrooms are very good, with a delicacy of flavour often lost in cooking.

**125 g (4 oz) button mushrooms
lemon juice
salt and pepper
1 teaspoon oil
thyme, chives or parsley, chopped
garlic**

Wipe the mushrooms and cut the bottom off the stalks. Slice thinly, cover with a dressing made from the lemon juice, seasoned with salt and pepper, and the oil, and leave for a little time before eating, if possible. Add the herbs and a small amount of garlic. A very little single cream can be added too.

Excellent with grilled meat.

Poached Sausage and Hot Potato Salad

A hot potato salad, if you have never tried it, combines very pleasantly with those smoked sausage rings stocked by most supermarkets and delicatessens.

2–3 SERVINGS

2 large potatoes, scrubbed
1 smoked sausage
1 teaspoon mustard powder, or 2 teaspoons French mustard
4 tablespoons oily French Dressing (see page 259)
salt and black pepper
1 tablespoon finely chopped onion
a little chopped fresh parsley (optional)
pickled onions or gherkins, to serve

Bring two pans of water to the boil. Put the potatoes in one and the sausage ring in the other. The sausage should simmer, not boil, for 5–10 minutes until hot. I think the flavour is improved by removing the polythene wrap, never mind what the makers tell you.

After about 20 minutes, test the potatoes with a fork. When they are tender, take them out and peel them, holding them in a cloth. Cut them into smallish chunks. Stir the mustard into the vinaigrette dressing and pour over the potatoes, spooning them about gently to spread the dressing evenly. Sprinkle with salt and black pepper. Add the chopped onion and parsley, if using, and spoon around a bit more.

Take the sausage out of its cooking water, cut it into chunks and serve with a few pickled gherkins or onions, which go well with this dish, and the salad.

Endives au Jambon

What we call chicory the French call endives. More often used raw in salads, they are a revelation cooked in this simple supper dish, each smooth chicon wrapped in a slice of ham and braised with a little stock, or cream. Mop up the juices with slices of baguette.

2 SERVINGS

**4 pieces chicory
1 tablespoon Dijon mustard
4 slices ham
approx 100 ml (4 fl oz) chicken stock or crème fraîche
salt and black pepper**

Steam or parboil the chicons till the outer leaves start going transparent and limp. Drain and pat dry with kitchen paper. Spread the mustard over the ham slices, then wrap each slice round a piece of chicory. Lay in a small oven dish, pour over stock or cream, season with salt and pepper and braise in a moderate oven for half an hour under a foil lid.

Kidneys en Chemise

2 SERVINGS

**2 round bread rolls
butter
salt and pepper
2 sheep's kidneys
dash of Worcestershire sauce**

Cut the tops off two rolls, remove some of the crumbs and butter thickly. Sprinkle on salt and pepper. Skin and core the kidneys and put them inside the rolls, with a dash of Worcestershire sauce. Replace the bread lids on top and bake the rolls in a medium oven for 20–30 minutes. When cooked they will have absorbed most of the juice from the kidneys.

Soufflés

Soufflés have such glamour, with their golden crust billowing out of the dish, and they are easier to make than one might imagine. Three tips towards the perfect soufflé are: 1) don't overbeat the egg whites, they should stand in soft peaks without becoming 'rocky'; 2) fold the beaten white into the basic soufflé mixture with a light hand and a palette knife, scooping down to the bottom of the bowl and rapidly incorporating the fluffy whites, aiming for lightness rather than full and thorough mixing; 3) stand the soufflé dish on a hot baking sheet in a preheated oven, so the soufflé mixture starts cooking from the bottom up. I think soufflés qualify for a pauper's cookbook because they make quite a small amount of basic flavouring look and taste important. The recipe here is for a cheese soufflé, always popular and elegant in its simplicity. Other suggestions follow.

4 SERVINGS AS A STARTER, 2 AS A MAIN DISH

25 g (1 oz) butter
25g (1 oz) plain flour
150 ml (¼ pint) milk, warmed
50 g (2 oz) strong dry cheese (Parmesan, Pecorino, mature Cheddar,
red Leicester) grated
nutmeg
a pinch of cayenne or dry mustard
salt and pepper
4 eggs

Melt the butter in a small heavy pan, stir in the flour, add the warmed milk and stir till smooth and thick. This béchamel is the foundation of a soufflé. Stir in the grated cheese, a sprinkle of nutmeg, cayenne or mustard, salt and pepper and cook over a low heat till the cheese is melted. Spoon and scrape this mixture into a good-size bowl and leave to cool slightly.

Separate the eggs, beating 3 yolks into the soufflé mix, and tipping 4 whites into a large, clean, dry bowl. Butter a 900 ml (1½ pint) straight-sided soufflé dish, set the oven to 200°C (400°F, gas mark 6) and put the baking sheet in to heat up.

Whisk the egg whites (you can add a pinch of salt) till they form soft peaks. Fold the beaten egg whites into the flavoured béchamel lightly and quickly, overarm fashion, using a palette knife or large metal spoon – a wooden spoon is too clumsy here. Tip the mixture into the prepared soufflé dish and make a shallow cut round the surface 2.5 cm (1 inch) from the rim to create a two-tier soufflé. You can sprinkle any surplus grated cheese on top. Stand on the baking sheet and cook for just over 20 minutes, by which time the soufflé will have risen impressively and be golden brown on top. Serve on hot plates immediately.

Other flavourings can be added to the basic béchamel: 125–150 g (4–5 oz) cooked spinach puréed with half a tin of anchovy fillets; tinned or fresh crab meat with a good pinch of cayenne; a small tin of tuna or salmon well mashed, adding a small spoonful of capers; 125–150 g (4–5 oz) ham or gammon leftovers, briefly processed, plus a generous spoonful of Dijon mustard; 4 red peppers, roasted with 4 shallots, peeled and puréed with 1 tablespoon chopped parsley, chives, oregano. Punchy flavours work best, I think. Any additions should be as dry as possible, cooked over low heat to evaporate moisture and concentrate the flavour before mixing with the cooked béchamel.

A sweet soufflé is made on exactly the same principle, omitting salt, pepper, etc., adding 50 g (2 oz) sugar and 125–150 g (4–5 oz) puréed fruit, or 75 g (3 oz) melted bitter chocolate and a spoonful of rum to the béchamel. Another twist on the basic soufflé is to make little individual soufflés, in buttered ramekins. These will cook faster – check after 8–10 minutes. The perfect soufflé is firm on top, a little creamy in the centre.

Salmon Soufflé

Making a soufflé is not at all difficult as long as you do it methodically, stage by stage. If you deviate from the routine you are apt to get flustered and this will spoil your appetite, if not the soufflé.

2–3 SERVINGS

1 small can of salmon
4 eggs
butter for greasing

FOR THE WHITE SAUCE
25g (1 oz) butter
2 teaspoons plain flour
150 ml (¼ pint) milk
a pinch of salt
1 teaspoon paprika

Drain the can of salmon, reserving the liquid. Pick out any bones or skin and mash the salmon with a fork. Take two mixing bowls, one large, one smaller, and carefully break 3 egg yolks into the larger bowl and 4 whites into the smaller one. Whisk the whites until firm but not too dry.

Make the white sauce base for the soufflé. Melt the butter in a saucepan, stir in the flour and cook for 1–2 minutes, stirring. Remove from the heat and gradually stir in the milk. Bring to the boil, stirring constantly, then simmer over a low heat until smooth and thick. Add the salmon liquid, salt and paprika and stir together. Stir in the mashed salmon, heating until warmed through.

Grease a 900 ml (1½ pint) soufflé dish with a little butter. Beat the egg yolks and stir in the salmon mixture thoroughly. Into this, you now fold the beaten egg whites, using a circular action. The idea is to distribute the egg white throughout the heavier salmon base, but not to labour the point to the extent of driving out all the air bubbles.

Turn the whole lot into the prepared dish and bake in the oven at 200°C (400°F, gas mark 6) for 20–25 minutes or until the soufflé is well risen and the top is firm and slightly browned. A few peas are all you need with this.

VARIATION: *Canned tuna fish makes a more substantial soufflé.*

Stir Fried Prawns and Peas

A well-stocked freezer should contain packets of peeled prawns and garden peas. Combined in a stir-fry, with garlic, ginger, and soy sauce, these make a quick and appetizing dish, served with plain rice. The prawns and peas should be defrosted first – a microwave does this in a jiffy. Otherwise, if you are in a tearing hurry, steam both in their packs (to retain the juices) for a few minutes till largely thawed.

2 SERVINGS

2–3 tablespoons soy sauce
2 teaspoons cornflour
1 tablespoon vegetable oil
2.5 cm (1 inch) knob fresh ginger root, grated
1 large clove garlic, finely minced
4–5 spring onions, topped, tailed and shredded lengthwise (optional)
1 small pack frozen peeled prawns
1 small pack frozen garden peas
salt, pepper and a pinch of sugar

Combine the soy sauce and cornflour, adding any liquid from the prawns and peas. Heat the oil in a wok (or frying pan) and briefly fry the ginger, garlic and spring onions, adding prawns after a minute, then peas, lowering the heat if anything looks like scorching. Then stir in the soy-cornflour mix, stir or toss to amalgamate, adding a little hot water if the dish looks dry – a stir-fry needs some tasty juice. As soon as the sauce thickens the dish is ready – season to taste.

Serve over plain boiled rice, which should have been cooking – 12 minutes – meantime.

Grilled Herring or Mackerel with Mustard

1 SERVING

1 herring or mackerel
English or French mustard
a little butter
a squeeze of lemon juice (optional)

Have the fish cleaned and opened out flat like a kipper. Smear both sides fairly generously with mustard. Put a little butter in the grill pan, after removing the rack. Heat gently and, when it begins to sizzle, put the fish in, skin side up. Immediately turn the fish over and continue cooking for about 5 minutes. It will not need to be turned again.

A squeeze of lemon juice heightens the flavour. Plain boiled potatoes are the best accompaniment to highly seasoned fish dishes.

Sprats/Whitebait, etc.

If you are lucky enough to come across whitebait or similar tiny fish cook them like this, a classic English dish favoured by Charles Dickens at the Trafalgar Inn in Greenwich.

Pat the fish dry with kitchen paper, shake in a plastic bag with a few tablespoons of seasoned flour – cayenne, salt and pepper. Heat the vegetable oil till smoking in a wide pan, tip the fish in in one mass, fry till crisping, then turn over with a slice to fry the other side. These tiny fish are eaten whole, like crisps.

Serve piping hot with lemon quarters and brown bread and butter.

Crab Salad

Crab meat makes an elegant variant on kedgeree mixed into hot rice (I add chopped spring onions, peas, hard-boiled eggs, a few prawns or brown shrimp, shreds of roasted peppers, chopped parsley and chives, a little cream) but it can also star as the main ingredient of a rice salad, using all the same ingredients, but dressed while hot with a vinaigrette to which you add the soft-boiled yolk of one egg. Chopped fresh herbs – chives, parsley, tarragon – make this a summery feast. Serve at room temperature.

Partan Pie

A traditional Scots recipe for making a substantial hot dish from a cooked crab, concentrating rather than smothering the flavour of the beast. You can use tinned crab, for speed, or a dressed crab, or more economically, a freshly boiled but whole crab – ask the fishmonger to remove the inedible bits, the greenish 'dead man's fingers' or lungs. See below for dealing with it. Crabs should be heavy for their size, and weighing between half to three quarters of a kilo in their shell, to feed two, generously. But crab meat is so intensely marine flavoured that a little goes a long way stretched, as here, with breadcrumbs, which absorb the juices – so don't worry too much about the weight. I have made this dish with the legs of spider crabs, a tiny amount of the sweetest meat after endless cracking and picking, and it was sublime.

2 SERVINGS

1 crab
2–3 tablespoons dry breadcrumbs
2 tablespoons wine vinegar
a pinch of dry mustard and/or cayenne
½ teaspoon grated nutmeg
salt and pepper
50 g (2 oz) butter

Combine all the ingredients except the butter in a bowl, mixing well. Spoon into the crab shell, or a small buttered oven dish. Dot with butter and heat through in a moderate oven for 10–15 minutes, then dot the surface with butter again and brown briefly under the grill.

Serve with a lightly dressed green salad. If you must have bulk – some steamed new potatoes.

NOTE: TO PREPARE A CRAB
First remove the big claws. Twist off the small claws and pull off the under-shell which lies between them. Scrape out the creamy brown substance in the big shell with a small spoon – this is edible. Pick out all the white meat from the body of the crab. Crack the big claws and remove all the white meat, likewise the small claws. Mix the white and creamy brown meat together for Partan Pie.

Fish Baked in a Salt Crust

To my mind oily fish – mackerel, herring – are disappointing unless eaten cucumber fresh, straight off the boat, or better still, line caught off a sailing boat, when they are superb. In London I choose bream, brill and hake, white fish which seem to travel better and cost less than sole, turbot, halibut, monkfish. Their flesh is fragile, however, easily overcooked to a mushy consistency. Baking in a salt crust – for which a whole fish is essential – is my favourite cooking procedure here. It seems to bring out an elusive sweetness – 'de-fishing' as the Chinese put it – and leaves the flesh flaky, firm and delicate, needing only the simplest dressing of melted butter and lemon juice.

Gros sel, the greyish coarse sea salt sold all over France, is the ideal crust, cracking off cleanly at the finish, but it is relatively expensive, imported. I have used cheaper pouring salt successfully, but it is fiddly uncovering the fish to be free of unwanted salt. Worth trying nevertheless because the fish skin shields the flesh during cooking. Thrifty French housewives are said to use cheap dishwasher salt for baking, but its purity is questionable. All the same I think the salt crust remains the ideal way to cook a small, whole, white fish. Use the smallest baking dish into which the fish fits neatly or at a pinch use baking foil to contain the fish closely.

2 SERVINGS

1 whole sea bream or other white fish weighing about 500 g (1 lb)
a small bunch of fresh dill
salt (of your choice) to cover
50 g (2 oz) unsalted butter
1 lemon

Pat the fish dry with kitchen paper and stuff the belly with dill. Lay on a thin layer of salt in a dish, then pour over more salt to cover, thinly rather than deeply. Bake in a preheated moderate oven for 20 minutes. A *gros sel* crust can be cracked off cleanly, bringing the skin with it. Pouring salt must be carefully scraped off, the fish lifted out whole (use two slices) and then peeled of its skin at table.

To make the sauce, melt the butter, add squeezed lemon juice and a grind of pepper and pour over the fish on hot plates.

Small steamed new potatoes are the best accompaniment.

Potato Latkes

This is a Jewish dish, and a very tasty one, substantial enough to serve on its own with some slices of garlic sausage and a plate of pickled gherkins. Latkes, definitely not recommended for calorie counters, are made of grated raw potato and onion, bound with egg and flour, and fried until brown on both sides.

4–6 SERVINGS

450g (1 lb) potatoes
1 tablespoon grated or finely chopped onion
2 tablespoons plain flour
2 large eggs, beaten
salt and black pepper
vegetable oil for frying

Peel and grate the potatoes into a mixing bowl. Add the onion and flour, then stir in the eggs and season with salt and pepper. The mixture should be soft enough to drop from a spoon. If it seems too dry or stiff, add another egg.

Heat some oil in a frying pan and, when it is hot, drop in spoonfuls of the mixture and fry until brown on both sides, turning the potato cakes with a spatula. Serve at once.

A Meal in a Potato

Large baked potatoes with a little something tucked inside are a god-send when you are hard pressed, or hard up. All you need is one or two (depending on how hungry you feel) large potatoes per person, some grated cheese, butter, salt and pepper. And, if you want to make a pretty solid meal of it, an egg for each potato.

1 SERVING

1–2 large potatoes, scrubbed
salt and pepper
a knob of butter
about 50 g (2 oz) cheese, grated
freshly grated nutmeg (optional)
1 egg (optional)

Dry the potatoes and rub salt into the skins. Bake in the oven at 220°C (425°F, gas mark 7) for about 1 hour or until they feel soft when pinched. Cut a cap off each potato and scoop out a little pulp. Put a knob of butter and a handful of grated cheese in the hollow, and sprinkle with salt and pepper. A little nutmeg is nice too. Return to the oven for a few minutes.

If you want an egg as well, scoop out rather more of the potato pulp, proceed as before except that you break an egg in before putting back the cap. Cook for 7 minutes or until the egg is set.

VARIATION: *A variation on this meal-in-a-potato theme is kidneys baked in potatoes. It takes longer but is very appetizing, if you like kidneys. Scrub and bake the potatoes for 1 hour as above. Cut a slice off the top and scoop out some of the inside. Skin the kidneys and rub in salt, pepper and a little mustard. Roll each kidney in a rasher of bacon and put in a potato case. Wrap the potatoes in foil with a scrap of butter and bake for 1 hour longer. The kidney gravy is soaked up by the potato.*

Pommes Roquefort

Unbelievably more-ish, this is a simple way to glorify boiled spuds
introduced to me by Jay, my son-in-law, in San Francisco. He used a
similarly pungent but local cheese, and he added a dollop of crème
fraîche but no boiling milk. It is a recipe you can play around with, I
think, subtracting cream or milk, trying different cheeses – even a
dried out chunk of Stilton. Men love this.

2–3 SERVINGS

About 500 g (1 lb) potatoes, peeled and roughly cubed
(waxy potatoes work best)
50 g (2 oz) pungent cheese
2 tablespoons cream
110 ml (4 fl oz) milk
salt and pepper

Throw cubed potatoes into a pan of boiling, salted water and cook
till just tender, but not mushy – this needs supervision as it takes less
time than you think. Drain.

Mix the cheese thoroughly with the cream. Heat the milk. Return
the potatoes to the pan, add the milk, then the cream and cheese
mixture, shaking to mix. Add salt and pepper to taste and serve hot.

Chicken Parcels with Lemon and Sesame

This was a top favourite dish with my daughter and her friends when they were teenagers. I think they were seduced by the idea of tantalizingly aromatic food to unwrap on the plate. The Japanese seasonings do a lot for supermarket chicken pieces, skinned and trimmed, but for special treats I usually make it with chicken breasts only. It usually pays to buy two or three small chickens rather than pieces because the bones and trimmings make an invaluable stock (see page 31).

4–6 SERVINGS

3 tablespoons white sesame seeds
1 teaspoon black peppercorns
1 small bunch of spring onions, finely chopped, including
some green tops
150 ml (¼ pint) light soy sauce
1 tablespoon light brown sugar
4–6 chicken breasts, skinned and cut into bite-sized pieces
1 large lemon, sliced
1 tablespoon peanut (groundnut) oil
a few drops of sesame oil (optional)

Place the sesame seeds and peppercorns in a dry pan and shake over heat until the seeds jump and smell toasty. Crush both in a mortar. Mix the crushed spice, onion, soy sauce and sugar in a bowl. Add the chicken, turn well to coat and leave for about 1 hour to absorb the flavours.

Cut four pieces of foil about 15 cm (6 inches) square, oil them, then spoon a heap of chicken with some marinade on to each square. Lay a thin slice of lemon on top, sprinkle with a little lemon juice, then wrap neatly and bake on a baking sheet in the oven at 190°C (375°F, gas mark 5) for 30 minutes or until well cooked but tender.

Serve with a small pile of Chinese egg noodles, sprinkled with soy and sesame oil, and a big green salad.

Sliced Tongue in Caper Sauce

4 SERVINGS

1 small tin tongue
150–300 ml (¼–½ pint) stock
½ tablespoon cornflour
a dash of soy or Worcestershire sauce
1 tablespoon capers

Slice up the tongue. Any jelly with it goes into the sauce. Mix the stock with the cornflour and heat in a pan till it thickens. Add a dash of soy or Worcestershire sauce, more for colour than flavour, and stir in the capers. Pour this over the tongue slices in a shallow oven dish and bake for ½ hour in a moderate oven at 180°C (350°F, gas mark 4).

Serve with plain boiled rice, with plenty of butter stirred into it, and boiled carrots finished off with butter and a little sugar.

Hash

2 SERVINGS

2 onions, roughly chopped
butter for frying
2–3 boiled potatoes, diced
some boiled cabbage or Brussels sprouts, chopped
1 small can of corned beef
salt and pepper

Fry the onions in a little butter until soft. Add the potatoes and cabbage or sprouts, and fry gently until they are warmed through. Cut the corned beef into chunks and add to the frying pan. Cook over a moderate heat, stirring from time to time, until the corned beef has mingled with the other ingredients into a sort of mush. Use a little more butter if the mixture looks dry and in danger of sticking to the pan. Add lots of pepper and a little salt if needed, though corned beef is salty enough, so don't overdo it. You can, if you like, break a couple of eggs on top of the hash, at this point, and cover the pan until they are set.

For extra vegetables, I suggest boiled or steamed carrots.

Steak Tartare

If you enjoy carpaccio (sliced raw beef) you may love the classic steak
tartare, raw beef grated to a small ruddy mound, with a raw egg yolk
in the centre, and chopped onion and other additions to taste.
Carnivore food, undoubtedly, but instantly hits the spot – both
strengthening and digestible. Famed as a hangover cure, with a dash
of Worcestershire sauce. My mother claimed lesser cuts of steak made
excellent steak tartare, because her patient scraping with a sharp knife
removed juicy flesh from any fat or gristle, and the cheaper cuts –
sirloin, rump, entrecôte – had more flavour than expensive fillet. But
avoid scarlet, shiny-wet supermarket beef – the meat should be dusky,
purplish, well hung, preferably from a family butcher.

1–2 SERVINGS

250 g (8 oz) rump or sirloin steak
salt and pepper
1 tablespoon chopped chives or parsley
olive oil
1–2 egg yolks
1 onion, finely chopped
1 tablespoon capers
a dash of Worcestershire sauce

Either scrape the meat – all fat trimmed off – along the grain with a
sharp knife, which reduces it to a soft mush (tendons, gristle, etc., left
behind) or against a grater, which has a similar effect. Season with salt
and pepper, and stir in the herbs with a thread of olive oil. Mound up
on two plates, dropping a raw egg yolk into a little dent in each centre
and serve with little heaps of chopped onion and capers alongside,
and a bottle of Worcestershire sauce, to be stirred in or not. Serve at
room temperature with grissini, or melba toast, for crunch.

Liver au Poivre

Everyone knows steak au poivre, where the raw meat is coated in crushed peppercorns before grilling or frying. Liver au poivre is my own variant and is both very good and very cheap as meat dishes go these days. Use pig's liver, which is cheaper than lamb's. The secret of palatable liver is not to overcook it. The quick-fry method here, plus the coating of peppercorns, keeps the liver tender and gives it an excellent flavour.

2–3 SERVINGS

225g (8 oz) pig's liver
2 teaspoons black peppercorns
2 tablespoons vegetable oil

With a sharp knife, slice the liver into narrow strips about 0.5 cm (¼ inch) thick. Crush the peppercorns to a gritty consistency in a grinder, or pestle and mortar, or, failing that, by folding them in a tea towel and banging them with a blunt instrument. Sprinkle over the sliced liver until well coated.

Heat the oil in a frying pan, drop in the sliced liver and fry over a high heat for about 3 minutes, turning with a spoon until lightly browned on all sides. As soon as the liver pieces have stiffened, without being hard, they are done.

Good with chips and a green salad.

Soufflé Omelette

A nice, quick pudding, which you can fill with whatever is available – apricot jam, apple purée, even marmalade.

2 SERVINGS

3 eggs, separated
2 tablespoons double cream (optional)
1 tablespoon caster sugar
50g (2 oz) butter
apricot jam, apple purée or marmalade, to fill
icing sugar, to dust

Beat the egg yolks, cream (if using) and sugar together until smooth. Whisk the egg whites until stiff and fold lightly into the yolks. Melt the butter in a frying pan over a moderate heat, pour in the egg mixture, level it off with a spoon and leave until small bubbles appear on the top. Spoon in the jam or whatever filling you are using, fold the omelette over and dust the top with icing sugar. Serve at once.

Caramel Oranges

This is a simple fruit salad of sliced oranges glorified by a sprinkling of crushed caramel, like amber chips. Use a sharp knife to prepare the oranges and take off every scrap of outer pith, which sticks in one's teeth and spoils the taste. Hold the oranges over the dish you are serving them in while preparing them so none of the juice is wasted.

2 SERVINGS

**3 oranges
juice of 1 orange
4 tablespoons sugar**

Slice the peel off the oranges, downwards rather than round and round, and trim off every bit of pith. Slice the oranges thickly, picking out the pips. Put the orange slices in a bowl with the orange juice and 1 tablespoon sugar. Alternatively, if you have time, boil up a little sugar, water and orange juice and pour it on the oranges when cooled.

To make the caramel, heat the remaining sugar in an enamelled pan with a little water, until it melts and goes brown – golden brown, not treacle coloured. Pour on to a sheet of greased paper to cool. When it is hard and brittle, shatter it by hitting it with something heavy, such as a bottle or rolling pin. Scatter the fragments over the fruit salad.

Baked, Buttered Apricots

A remarkably nice and simply made pudding.

4 SERVINGS

**1 small tin apricot halves
4 thick slices of bread
butter
sugar
cinnamon**

Drain the apricots, reserving the syrup. Cut the crusts off the bread. Fresh white bread is best for this dish. Butter thickly on both sides. Lay the slices over the bottom of a baking tin.

Press the apricot halves firmly into the buttered bread. Sprinkle sugar (preferably Demerara) generously over the top, and a dusting of cinnamon. Bake in a moderate oven 180°C (350°F, gas mark 4) till the bread is crisp and golden (about ½ hour).

You can serve these with a sauce made from the apricot syrup thickened with a little cornflour, or with plain cream. Fresh apricots, plums or peaches are even better done this way.

Baked Bananas

I think this is the nicest way of eating bananas. It is also very quick and easy to prepare.

2 SERVINGS

**4 large bananas
1 tablespoon brown sugar
juice of 1 orange
juice of ½ lemon
a little grated orange and lemon rind
butter**

Peel the bananas and slice in half lengthways. Arrange them in a shallow ovenproof dish. Sprinkle with brown sugar and pour over the orange and lemon juice. Sprinkle with a little grated orange and lemon rind. Dot fairly liberally with butter and bake, uncovered, in the oven at 180°C (350°F, gas mark 4) for about 20 minutes or until the bananas are soft and the other ingredients have turned to a thin syrup.

Serve exactly as they are – cream would be too cloying.

VARIATIONS: *A few sultanas sprinkled over the dish is a pleasant addition. And, if you have any rum around the place, a spoonful added with the other ingredients gives you Baked Bananas Creole.*

Poor Knights

This is a recipe for using up stale bread.

> 3 tablespoons brown sugar
> 150 ml (¼ pint) milk
> slices of stale bread about 1 cm (½ inch) thick
> 2 egg yolks, beaten
> oil and/or butter for shallow frying
> about ½ teaspoon ground cinnamon
> brown sugar, to sprinkle

Stir the sugar into the milk. Cut the bread into soldiers and put them in the milk and sugar for a few moments on each side, turning them over carefully. (Do not over-handle them or they will become soggy.) Dip each one into the beaten egg and then fry in hot oil or butter until golden and crispy.

Serve sprinkled with the cinnamon and more brown sugar.

Pasta Faster

The most obvious candidate for a chapter all to itself in a twenty-first-century pauper's cookbook is pasta, that staple food of Italy and South-East Asia which is rapidly becoming the world's favourite cheap and cheerful fast food. I know scarcely anyone who does not eat some form of pasta dish two or three times a week, and students, in particular, seem to eat pasta almost every day. The reasons are obvious: pasta is cheap, filling and endlessly versatile, and it enables hungry people to be fed in fifteen minutes flat. Not that all the recipes in this section are of that order; it is also possible, and desirable, to extend your repertoire to include some of the more elaborate and time-consuming pasta-based dishes, such as the variations on lasagne, the odd timballo, even home-made ravioli with various fillings, all of which have enough clout to form the main dish at a dinner party.

My own discovery where pasta is concerned is more of a rediscovery. After some years of preferring the so-called 'fresh' pasta on supermarket shelves, I have been reconverted by Italian cookery writers, like Marcella Hazan and Anna del Conte, to the superior merits of the dried variety, now available in a profusion of different shapes and sizes in any supermarket which knows its business. Fresh pasta is brilliant if you buy it from a reputable Italian grocer, or delicatessen, or if you make it yourself (a skill I recommend any serious pasta fan to acquire). You can make your own fresh pasta from nothing more than strong white flour and an egg or two, so it makes good 'emergency' food, and you might prefer to serve fresh pasta on special occasions, when you have reason to suppose that your guests will appreciate the extra lightness and subtle texture of the real hand-made article. However, for every day, a good-quality dried pasta made from durum wheat (as most of them are) is infinitely preferable to the standard 'fresh' pasta commonly available. When cooked correctly, dried pasta has the ideal 'springy' texture and a mild but inimitable flavour all its own. By comparison, most bought fresh pasta is flaccid, sticky with starch, and characterless. And it costs more. The explanation, according to the experts, is that this type of pasta is not made from the correct durum wheat flour, and so does not provide that slight bouncy chewiness that distinguishes the authentic pasta cooked al dente – in fact the term al dente is rendered almost meaningless in this context.

Another small but significant discovery I have made is that pasta should not be drained too rigorously. Italians tip out most of the cooking water, but not the last drop. A couple of tablespoons left in the pan helps prevent the pasta coagulating into a sticky lump while you are completing the sauce, seasonings and other additions. Nor, when using dried pasta, is there any need to rinse off extra starch, as there is with the 'fresh' type. Once the dried pasta is cooked al dente, tip off most but not all the cooking water, splash a little olive oil into the pan, give it a good shake and you can leave it in a warm place safely for up to five minutes, while you get on with the other preparations. It also makes an important difference if your serving dish (a big round bowl or platter is a lot more simpatico than a saucepan for presenting pasta) and plates are all piping hot. A pair of wooden forks is ideal for tossing and mixing pasta and additions, plus a large spoon for serving.

A good fruity olive oil represents real added value when used for tossing cooked pasta; a couple of spoonfuls makes it glisten appetizingly, and creates a splendid aromatic 'nose'. Keep the lesser oils for frying the sauce ingredients if you need to cut back. Ready-grated Parmesan cheese, though handy, is about as tasteless as tea-bag tea, and pricy to boot. Often, too, it is unnecessary. There are many bone-simple pasta recipes, as you can see from those in this chapter, where the cheese treatment is out of place, and these are increasingly the ones I prefer; a lot of pasta is lightly coated with a little pungent seasoning and dished up hot, shiny and fragrant. True Southern food, at once stimulating and soothing.

Finally, for the worriers among you, a word of reassurance about timing. Well, maybe it's not so reassuring, if you are the scatty type of cook. The truth is that pasta, both dried and fresh, needs watching and testing while it cooks, to determine 'doneness'. Whatever the packet instructions say, you would be wise to start checking sooner than the time given; the simplest foodstuffs need a little care to give of their best. Fork out a strand or morsel and chew it. If the centre is still chalky, uncooked, give it a minute or two longer. When it is almost tender right through but just chewy is right for any dish that will be cooked a moment or two longer, while tossing with sauces and seasonings. If, for some reason, the pasta will need to be kept warm in the oven, it can do with being slightly undercooked. If you are going to dump it straight on to hot plates, with a spoonful of sauce to be added individually, the pasta can be cooked a little longer until it is more tender, only faintly resistant.

Making Fresh Pasta

Having sifted 550 g (1¼ lb) flour and a pinch of salt on to a floured work surface, make a well in the centre and break into it 5 large eggs or, for pasta *verde* (green pasta), 4 eggs and 75 g (3 oz) of puréed cooked spinach. Using two fingers, draw the flour into the egg mix until it lumps together.

Slap the lump down and attack with the heels of both hands with a scrubbing action which stretches the dough away from you. Gather up and repeat the process for not less than 15 minutes. Then divide the dough into lumps.

Flatten each lump by rolling vigorously with a floury rolling pin, from the middle outwards in all directions. At first it will spring back but suddenly it will grow thinner, wider. Roll it thinly then lay it on a cloth over the back of a chair.

A pasta machine can save you this last step. Pass the dough through the mangle and it will stretch it finely, though not to any great width. To make pasta ribbons – or tagliatelle – set the machine with grooved rollers to slice to the width you want: 0.5 cm (¼ inch) gives slim noodles.

Pasta comes in all shapes and sizes. For ravioli, roll out a rectangle of fresh pasta. Divide one half into lightly marked squares and spoon meat filling into the centre of each square. Moisten the other half of the pasta, fold over the meat-filled squares, press down firmly with your hand and lightly edge with a pastry cutter.

Spaghetti with Lemon

If possible, use the richer and more expensive egg pasta, *al uovo*, for this dish.

6 SERVINGS

a pinch of salt
grated rind of 2 lemons and juice of 1 large lemon
175 g (6 oz) crème fraîche, or whipped or double cream
1 teaspoon freshly grated nutmeg
1 teaspoon black pepper
450 g (1 lb) spaghetti or spaghettini
freshly grated Parmesan cheese, to serve

Fill a large saucepan with slightly salted water and bring to the boil. Put the lemon rind and juice into the dish in which you'll serve the spaghetti. Add the crème fraîche or cream, nutmeg and pepper.

Cook the spaghetti in the boiling water for about 8 minutes or until just tender. Drain, and toss in the lemon mixture. Serve with plenty of freshly grated Parmesan cheese.

Spaghetti all'Arrabbiata

The 'raging' of the title refers to the 'blaze' imparted by dried chillies. This is not for the tender palate, but a fine, appetizing and fast way to serve spaghetti for those who like it hot.

4 SERVINGS

3–4 dried red chillies, de-seeded and chopped
3–4 garlic cloves, chopped
½ x 50 g (2 oz) can of anchovies, mashed
450 g (1 lb) spaghetti
6 tablespoons olive oil
salt and pepper

Prepare the red chillies and pound them roughly in a pestle and mortar with the garlic and anchovies. Put this mixture in a wide flameproof dish over a very low heat. Cook the pasta in boiling salted water for about 8 minutes or until just tender. The spaghetti should look creamy pale, and be flexible but not sticky. Drain, reserving 1 tablespoon of the cooking water. Combine the spaghetti with the other ingredients in the hot dish, adding the reserved cooking water and the oil. Season and toss well with forks, then serve immediately on hot plates.

NOTE: *The quantity of chillies is approximate. Nervous types can begin with one or two, removing the seeds, where most of the 'hotness' lies. I remove the seeds from one or two, myself, leaving them in the other chillies.*

Orechiette with Peas and Mint

A wonderful way to use the first peas – so delicate it's better without Parmesan.

6 SERVINGS

salt
1 kg (2 lb) fresh new peas
125 g (4 oz) butter
2 shallots or 1 small onion, finely chopped
450 g (1 lb) orechiette
a bunch of fresh mint, torn into small pieces

Fill a large saucepan with plenty of salted water and put it on a high heat. Shell the peas and blanch them for about 1 minute in boiling water in a separate saucepan. Strain the peas but keep the water.

Heat the butter in a heavy-based saucepan, add the shallots or onion and cook gently until softened but not browned. Put the orechiette in the boiling water and cook for about 8 minutes or until almost tender. Put the peas in with the shallots over a low heat. Add the mint, a pinch of salt and 1–2 tablespoons of the pea liquor. Drain the pasta and serve with the sauce on top.

Pasta Shells with Prawns

The prawns must be in their shells as the stock made from these gives this dish its flavour. Parmesan should not be served with fish sauces.

6 SERVINGS

sunflower or olive oil
225 g (8 oz) cooked prawns in their shells
250 ml (8 fl oz) white wine
250 ml (8 fl oz) water
350 g (12 oz) pasta shells
salt and black pepper
2 garlic cloves, crushed
150 ml (5 fl oz) single cream
a pinch of freshly grated nutmeg
a bunch of fresh parsley, finely chopped

Heat 2 teaspoons sunflower or olive oil in a small, heavy-based saucepan. Remove the prawns from their shells and put the shells and heads in the hot oil. Turn the shells round in the oil until they stop sizzling loudly, then pour over the glass of wine. Let it evaporate for a moment, then add the glass of water. Cover and simmer for at least 30 minutes to extract maximum flavour from the shells. Strain the stock through a sieve, then return it to the pan and continue to simmer until the stock has reduced to about 100–175 ml (4–6 fl oz).

Cook the pasta in plenty of boiling salted water for about 8 minutes or until just tender. Meanwhile, put the garlic in a heavy pan deep enough to hold all the pasta, and heat gently until it is just translucent, then turn up the heat and add the peeled prawns. Drain the pasta and stir it in with the prawns, then pour over the condensed prawn stock and the cream. Season with lots of black pepper and nutmeg.

Stir in the parsley and serve immediately on hot plates.

Pasta and Chickpea Salad

This is one of the best store-cupboard salads, the bland, tender pasta and firm, nutty chickpeas adding up to one of those truly irresistible pairings of texture and taste. Eat this alone, or with crisp green salad leaves, or as an accompaniment to cold meat, or hot grilled sausages or chops. I find this dish so useful and more-ish that I try to make a big bowlful every week, using up most of the chickpeas prepared as described on page 101.

6–8 SERVINGS

225 g (8 oz) chickpeas, soaked overnight
500 g (1 lb) packet of penne, farfalle or conchiglie
salt and pepper
1 bunch of spring onions, chopped
about 250 ml (8 fl oz) well seasoned vinaigrette, made with some garlic
and a dash of fresh lemon juice (see page 259)
a small handful of fresh parsley or coriander, chopped

Drain the chickpeas and put them in a large saucepan. Cover with fresh water, bring to the boil and cook for 2–3 hours (depending on the age of the chickpeas) or until they are nutty but tender. Drain well.

Meanwhile, cook the pasta in boiling salted water for about 8 minutes or until just tender. Drain and put in a big dish with the chickpeas. Add the spring onions and vinaigrette slowly, tasting and tossing while the ingredients are still hot, until you have added just enough. Add the parsley or coriander, salt and pepper, and a squeeze more lemon juice if you like. It should all glisten attractively.

Serve at room temperature, not chilled.

Japanese Cold Noodles

The advantage of these cold noodles is that they can be prepared and left in the fridge or larder for a day and a night, if it is more convenient to cook them in advance.

4–5 SERVINGS

500 ml (18 fl oz) dashi or chicken stock
200 ml (7 fl oz) dry sherry
200 ml (7 fl oz) dark soy sauce
5 cm (2 inch) piece of fresh root ginger, peeled and grated
2 spring onions, finely sliced (including green parts)
450 g (1 lb) dried Japanese or Italian noodles

Put the dashi or stock, sherry and soy sauce in a saucepan, bring to the boil, then remove from the heat and leave to cool.

Stir the ginger and onions into the cooled sauce. Cook the noodles in boiling water following packet instructions or until cooked but still firm. Drain, then rinse under cold running water and drain again. Transfer to a serving dish and pour over the sauce. Serve at once, or cover and store in the fridge until required.

Spaghetti with Red Clam Sauce

This recipe is just as good with mussels and other shellfish.

4 SERVINGS

450 g (1 lb) clams
350 g (12 oz) spaghetti (preferably egg, al uovo, spaghetti)
salt and black pepper
4 tablespoons olive oil
3 garlic cloves, crushed
a glass of white wine
1½ tablespoons tomato purée
a pinch of sugar (optional)
a bunch of fresh parsley, finely chopped

Wash the clams carefully and make sure they are all fighting to stay shut when you tap them. Any that gape must be thrown away.

Cook the pasta in plenty of boiling salted water for about 8 minutes or until just tender. Meanwhile, heat the olive oil in a heavy-based saucepan large enough to hold the drained spaghetti, add the garlic and cook until it is just beginning to take on some colour; do not let it burn. Pour in the wine and let it bubble for a couple of minutes, then stir in the tomato purée and cook for 1 minute. Season with black pepper, the sugar, if using, and a little salt. (Don't overdo the salt as there is plenty occurring naturally in the clams and the tomato purée.) Add the clams and turn them in the hot oil and wine. The moment all the clams have opened, remove the pan from the heat and stir in the parsley. Drain the spaghetti and stir it into the clams and their sauce. Serve at once on warmed plates.

Pasta with Broccoli and Anchovies

My daughter Daisy introduced me to this excellent pasta dish which has a Sicilian lustiness of flavour. If you faithfully follow the instructions, it is foolproof, and can be served as a main dish after a starter of grilled red peppers. A wide, but not too shallow, heatproof pottery bowl that can go into the oven safely, or stand on a hotplate over a heat diffuser, makes the final assembly of this (and many other pasta dishes) easier.

4–6 SERVINGS

2 heads of firm green broccoli (about 350 g/12 oz)
salt and pepper
1½ x 500 g (1 lb) packet of penne or farfalle
50 g (2 oz) can of anchovies, drained
4 garlic cloves, chopped
1 dried red chilli (optional)
4–6 tablespoons fruity olive oil

Remove any woody ends and yellowing leaves from the broccoli. Cut the stems off and chop them into chunks. Cook the stems and florets as described on page 173, then drain, reserving the cooking water. Chop the cooked broccoli to a coarse mush.

Meanwhile, bring a large saucepan of salted water to the boil, add the pasta and cook for about 8 minutes. Pound the anchovies, garlic and chilli, if you want that fiery tingle, to a pulp in a mortar with a pestle or in a strong bowl with the end of a rolling pin.

Put a shallow, flameproof dish over a very low heat and add the olive oil. When it is hot, add the anchovy mixture, stir and bubble for 1 minute, then add the chopped broccoli, mixing with forks. Let it all get thoroughly hot.

By now, the pasta should be al dente, tender but still chewy in the middle. Drain quickly and tip the pasta into the flameproof dish. Toss thoroughly, adding a little of the reserved broccoli water if it seems too dry. Heat through for 1 minute, then serve on hot plates.

Pasta with Peas, Cream, Bacon and Thyme

Made with canned *piselli* (*petits pois*) and pancetta, this will taste more authentic and Italian. However, an Anglicized version using frozen *petits pois* and diced smoked bacon or gammon is also excellent. I once ate this with pasta authority Lizzie Spender, and she added a couple of spoonfuls of vodka, which gave it a certain frisson, but this is optional.

6–8 SERVINGS

1½ × 500 g (1 lb) packet of penne, farfalle or conchiglie
salt and pepper
3 tablespoons olive oil or 50 g (2 oz) butter
2 onions, chopped
2 garlic cloves, crushed
100–150 g (4–5 oz) pancetta, chopped, or bacon, de-rinded and diced
2 cans of *petits pois*, drained, or
2 × 450 g (1 lb) packets of frozen *petits pois*
several sprigs of fresh thyme
a small carton of single cream

Cook the pasta in plenty of boiling salted water for 8 minutes or until just tender. Meanwhile, heat the oil or butter in a saucepan, add the onion and garlic, cover and cook over a low heat until softened. Add the pancetta or bacon and cook until opaque but not brown. Add the canned or frozen peas, cover and heat through. Pinch the thyme leaves from the stalks and add them to the peas.

Drain the pasta and tip it into a warmed serving dish. Add the cream to the peas, bubble up quickly, season with salt and pepper and toss with the pasta. Serve on hot plates.

Pasta with Courgettes and Cream

A light summery dish. I suggest penne as the pasta shape, as they echo the courgette sticks in size.

6 SERVINGS

6 small courgettes
salt and pepper
4 tablespoons olive oil
2 garlic cloves, finely chopped
500 g (1 lb) packet of penne
a small carton of double cream
fresh mint or basil leaves, torn into small pieces

Slice the courgettes lengthways, remove some seeds, then slice again lengthways into quarters, then into little sticks. Place these in a colander, sprinkle lightly with salt and leave to sweat for 10–15 minutes to extract some moisture.

Heat the oil in a frying pan or in a large flameproof pottery dish, and add the garlic. Fry for 1 minute, then add the courgette pieces and cook for about 10 minutes or until tender, turning to prevent them catching and burning, and reducing the heat if necessary.

Meanwhile, cook the penne in plenty of boiling salted water for about 8 minutes, or until just tender.

Add the cream to the courgettes, bring to the boil, stirring, then add the torn herb leaves. Drain the pasta, stir it into the courgettes and serve at once on hot plates.

Pasta with Borlotti Beans

Canned borlotti beans, like canned chickpeas, are a useful store cupboard standby. They look attractive, with their pink marbled skins, and this is an Italian way to serve them, contrasting with plain cooked pasta. The dish is halfway between a soup and a pasta dish.

6–8 SERVINGS

3 tablespoons olive oil
1 large onion, chopped
2 large carrots, diced
2 celery sticks, sliced
75 g (3 oz) pancetta, smoked bacon or gammon, diced
2 x 410 g (15 oz) cans of borlotti beans
salt and pepper
500 g (1 lb) packet of conchiglie or farfalle
chopped fresh rosemary
freshly grated Parmesan cheese, to serve (optional)

Heat the oil in a heavy-based saucepan, add the onion, carrot and celery, stir and fry over a low heat until soft. Add the diced pancetta, gammon or bacon, and continue cooking until thoroughly amalgamated and quite dark. Stir in the borlotti beans with some of their liquid, season with salt and pepper, and leave to heat through.

Meanwhile, cook the pasta in plenty of boiling water for about 8 minutes or until just tender. Drain quickly and add to the pan. Mix well and add more bean liquid if the mixture seems too dry. Stir in a generous amount of chopped fresh rosemary and serve. Some fresh Parmesan can be dusted over this dish, for richness.

VARIATION: *Add a can of tomatoes to the softened vegetables for colour and body.*

Pasta with Leeks and Mussels

You could replace the butter in this recipe with olive oil – which would be better for your heart – but the leeks won't caramelize in the same way, and it is the sweetness of the leeks which makes this dish. If you like the sweet flavour, you can turn this into more of a party dish by adding one or two fresh dates. Stone them, slice them lengthways into strips, and put them in when you fry the leeks.

6–8 SERVINGS

450 g (1 lb) mussels
1½ × 500 g (1 lb) packet of penne or farfalle
salt
75 g (3 oz) butter
450 g (1 lb) leeks, cut into 1 cm (½ inch) slices

Scrub the mussels clean, removing all the barnacles and hairy bits and discarding any which don't shut when tapped on the side of the sink.

Cook the pasta in plenty of boiling salted water for about 8 minutes, or until just tender. Meanwhile, heat the butter in a sauté pan or heavy-based saucepan deep enough to hold all the mussels, add the leeks and cook them until they begin to caramelize without becoming too soft. Add the mussels, cover with a lid and cook for 20 seconds. Remove the lid and lift out the mussels one by one as they open. Wearing rubber gloves, shell the mussels over the pan, so that none of the juice is lost, and remove the flesh to a warm plate. Leave some of the mussels in their shells or half shells to make the dish more attractive.

Drain the pasta and pour over the mussels, leeks and buttery juices. Serve at once on warmed plates.

Seafood Pasta

I first made this in Dorset with mussels gathered off the rocks at low tide; the briny freshness of them, in a garlicky tomato sauce, made a memorable dish eaten with a tangle of spaghetti. Better still was a steaming dish of spaghettini studded with various *frutti di mare* eaten outdoors on the Venetian island of Torcello. Seafood has an affinity with pasta; together you have one of those dishes which blows the mind while it comforts the stomach. These days I mix some clams with the mussels – tiny as they are they give intense flavour. I keep the tomato sauce thin but pungent with garlic and chilli, and use spaghettini for preference, spaghetti seeming too coarse in this company. Ditto prawns, though a few brown shrimps are delicious. Mussels and clams should be kept in the coldest part of the fridge. This stops them opening, and losing their juices, vital to the dish.

4–6 SERVINGS

1 kg (2 lb) live mussels
450 g (1 lb) live clams
4 tablespoons olive oil
4 cloves garlic, minced
450 g (1 lb) fresh tomatoes, skinned or 1 can peeled Italian plum
tomatoes, both chopped to a mush
1 fresh or 2 dried red chillies, de-seeded and chopped
a generous handful of flat-leaf parsley, chopped
salt and pepper
450 g (1 lb) spaghettini

To prepare mussels and clams see page 39. Set a large pan over medium heat, tip in the mussels, cover, cook for 2 minutes, then add clams, which cook more quickly. Once open transfer to a bowl, using a slotted spoon, taking care not to lose any precious liquid. Heat olive oil in another pan over medium heat, add minced garlic and seconds later (the garlic must not burn) the tomatoes. Stir to mix, then add the shellfish juice through a strainer to clear any grit or sand, the chopped chilli and simmer together for a few minutes. I sometimes add a splash of Italian white wine at this point. Taste, and season.

Meantime scoop most – about three quarters – of the mussels and clams from their shells, keeping some on the half shell for effect, and add the lot to the tomato mixture, along with the finely chopped parsley. Stir just long enough to warm through the shellfish, then toss with the hot cooked spaghettini in a large shallow dish (also hot) and serve immediately on heated plates. Restaurants, even Italian ones, often overlook the importance of serving pasta steaming hot, which forfeits much of the fragrance and flavour of the dish.

Fettucine with Smoked Salmon

Smoked salmon pieces, or scraps, turn up in delicatessens and on market stalls cheaply enough to make this a pauper's pasta, especially as a little goes a long way, flavour-wise.

4 SERVINGS

275 g (10 oz) fettucine
salt and black pepper
1 tablespoon olive oil
15 g (½ oz) butter
a small bunch of spring onions, finely chopped
125–175 g (4–6 oz) smoked salmon scraps, trimmed into neat shreds,
dark bits removed
a small carton of double cream
1 egg yolk
milk, to dilute
a small handful or bunch of fresh herbs, such as parsley, basil or dill

Cook the fettucine in plenty of boiling salted water for about 8 minutes or until just tender. Meanwhile, heat the oil and butter in a frying pan, add the spring onions and fry over a low heat until softened. Add the smoked salmon shreds and turn rapidly to heat rather than cook. Beat the cream and egg yolk together and dilute to a runny consistency with a little milk. Add this to the salmon mixture, stir, and season generously with black pepper and a little salt. Remove from the heat. Drain the pasta and tip it into a warmed serving dish or bowl. Tip in the salmon mixture, plus the chopped herbs, and fork vigorously to mix well. Serve at once on warmed plates.

Aubergine and Pasta Timballo

Aubergines have a rich flavour and this pie is as satisfying as many meaty dishes.

4–6 SERVINGS

450 g (1 lb) tagliatelle
4 small aubergines
salt
olive oil, for frying
450 g (1 lb) fresh tomatoes or 1 medium can of peeled tomatoes
3 garlic cloves
50 g (2 oz) butter
black pepper
a handful of fresh basil (or parsley, thyme or marjoram)
125 g (4 oz) Parmesan cheese, grated
4 tablespoons dried, home-made breadcrumbs

Cook the tagliatelle for 3 minutes so it is still firm. Drain and set aside in a warm place.

Thinly slice the unpeeled aubergines, salt lightly and leave for 10 minutes to sweat. Deep fry, a few slices at a time, in olive oil until golden brown, then drain on kitchen paper. Continue until all the aubergine is cooked.

Skin the tomatoes, remove the seeds, chop roughly and transfer to a colander to drain. Chop the garlic and lightly fry in a little oil and butter until golden, then add the tomato, salt and pepper and simmer for a few minutes. Chop the basil, minus stalks, or other herbs, quite finely. Mix the herbs, tomato mixture and grated cheese together with the cooked tagliatelle.

Butter a deep cake tin generously (it must be big enough to take pasta and aubergines) and coat it evenly all over with breadcrumbs. Fill the dish with one layer of the pasta mixture, then one layer of aubergine, and so on until all the ingredients are used up. Top with more cheese, then breadcrumbs, then dot with butter and bake in a preheated oven at 220°C (425°F, gas mark 7) for 30 minutes. Turn on to a dish to serve.

NOTE: *For grand occasions you can substitute a pastry case, with lid, for the*

crumb case. Use shortcrust pastry (see page 107) and bake blind for 15
minutes. Cook a lid of the same pastry, decorated with pastry leaves, on a sheet
of foil at the same time. Check after 10 minutes.

Spaghetti with Lumpfish Caviar and Crème Fraîche

A very quick and extravagant-seeming pasta dish. Though the roe is
quite expensive, this is one pasta dish which would be ruined by
Parmesan, so there are no hidden extras. This is a good one to start a
dinner party as there is really no work required and only one pan.

4 SERVINGS

450 g (1 lb) spaghetti (preferably egg spaghetti)
salt
a knob of butter
75 g (3 oz) crème fraîche or soured cream
50 g (2 oz) lumpfish caviar (red or black)

Cook the spaghetti in plenty of boiling salted water and have ready
a warm serving dish. Drain the spaghetti when it is al dente and toss
it with the butter. Pour into a hot serving dish and spoon the crème
fraîche and then the lumpfish roe on top. Toss again at the table, so
that everyone can see the contrasting colours before they are
blurred.

Veggies

Vegetarian food needs no apology today, with eating habits evincing such a marked drift in the green direction, for reasons of health, economy and sentiment in varying measures. My family are not vegetarians, but like most of the people I know, we eat fewer meat meals a week than we used to, and many more which are either completely vegetarian or a compromise, in that they use some meat stock, or diced bacon, or leftover morsels of roast lamb or chicken, bulked up with rice or pasta.

Perhaps the happiest outcome of our change to a new, greener diet is that we have learnt, as a nation, to cook vegetables with proper respect, and imagination. *Nouvelle cuisine* played a part in this evolution, as do the elegant assemblies of vegetables, cooked or raw, emanating from South-East Asia. Cashing in on the trend, shops, markets and supermarkets offer a profusion and variety of vegetables which would have been unthinkable thirty years ago outside Berwick Street market in Soho. In a picky mood, I might grumble that there is a certain sameness about much of the out-of-season produce – watery green peppers, floppy round lettuces, tasteless tomatoes – mostly raised in hydroponic greenhouses on Holland's light, sandy soil. And I agree with Italian cookery writer Anna del Conte that the practice of cooking vegetables until al dente (tender but still slightly crisp) only, has gone too far. She claims that certain vegetables, notably asparagus, green beans, mange-touts, cauliflower and courgettes, are positively indigestible served *croquants* or crunchy. I certainly find the restaurant presentation of microwaved but undercooked vegetables, however prettily arranged, a damper on the appetite.

At the risk of seeming contrary, however, I am increasingly coming round to the view that finesse in preparation and cooking is all-important where vegetables are concerned. By finesse, I don't mean arty presentation so much as thoughtful treatment of each particular vegetable, designed to bring out its essential flavour and texture, and to make it look appetizing. Nowadays, I always steam broccoli stalks for a few minutes ahead of the green florets, which so easily turn mushy. For years I sliced carrots and courgettes crossways, into discs; now I bother to cut them into matchsticks, because they actually taste better that way. I cook potatoes in their skins whenever possible because they retain so much more flavour. I undercook cabbage and spinach, drain and chop it, then toss quickly with butter, olive oil and chopped garlic.

The real inspiration for my own increasing interest in vegetables, and vegetable dishes, which may or may not be vegetarian, is the box of organically grown seasonal vegetables and herbs which arrives each week, ten months of the year, from a Suffolk garden. I never know what to expect – sheaves of chard, knobbly tomatoes, muddy celeriac, beetroots the size of marbles, white aubergines, purple basil, black salsify. Organic vegetables spoil fast, so it is a regular challenge to do justice to that week's delivery, but the bursting vitality of taste and texture almost straight from the soil is an unfailing reward, even if I do have to scrub off enough honest mud to plant a windowbox, and stuff the freezer with purées of this and that to prevent a surfeit of goodies going to waste. The delight of working with such excellent produce is that, after knocking oneself out trying to think of new and interesting recipes, one flops back on occasion to the simplest, most obvious solution in the world – a lick of butter and a grinding of pepper – and it's as if you are tasting them properly for the first time.

Lettuce and Pea Soup

6 SERVINGS

125 g (4 oz) butter
1 lettuce, shredded
1 kg (2 lb) peas, shelled
a sprig of fresh mint
a large pinch of salt
1 teaspoon sugar
1 litre (2 pints) water

Melt the butter in a large heavy-based saucepan, put in the lettuce, peas and mint with the salt and sugar, cover and cook gently for 10 minutes, stirring occasionally.

Add the water to the pan, turn up the heat and simmer with the lid off for 5–10 minutes or until the peas are tender. Leave the soup to cool slightly, then purée in a blender or food processor, or rub through a sieve. Return the soup to the pan and reheat gently before serving piping hot.

NOTE: *If possible, use a flavoursome type of lettuce for this soup, such as Cos or Little Gem.*

Curried Parsnip Soup

6 SERVINGS

50 g (2 oz) butter
2 onions, chopped
2 teaspoons curry powder
450 g (1 lb) parsnips, peeled and diced
1 eating apple, peeled, cored and diced
1 litre (2 pints) water
salt and pepper
6 tablespoons crème fraîche, cream or yoghurt, to serve
a sprig of fresh parsley or coriander, chopped

Melt the butter in a large heavy-based saucepan, add the onions and fry for about 5 minutes or until lightly coloured. Stir in the curry powder and fry for 1 minute. Add the parsnips and apple, cover and leave to sweat for 5–10 minutes, stirring occasionally. Add the water and simmer the soup for at least 30 minutes or until the parsnips are very tender (it won't hurt to keep them on the heat after they are ready). Leave the soup to cool slightly, then purée in a blender or food processor, or rub through a sieve. Return to the saucepan, season with salt and pepper, and reheat gently before serving with a spoonful of crème fraîche, cream or yoghurt and a sprinkling of herbs for each diner.

Carrot and Coriander Soup

This soup made my daughter Tabitha's reputation as a gastronome among her student pals. It is best made with vegetable stock, but an equal mixture of water and milk can be used instead.

4 SERVINGS

25 g (1 oz) butter
1 tablespoon vegetable oil
4 large carrots, peeled and grated
1 onion, finely chopped
1 litre (2 pints) vegetable stock
a handful of fresh coriander, finely chopped
salt and pepper
4 tablespoons single cream (optional)

Heat the butter and oil together in a large, heavy-based saucepan. Add the carrot and onion, cover, reduce the heat and leave to soften for 2–3 minutes. (This procedure considerably enriches any vegetable soup.)

Add the stock and simmer for 20–30 minutes. Add the coriander and cook for a further 2–3 minutes. Add salt and pepper to taste. Leave the soup to cool slightly, then purée in a blender or food processor. Return to the saucepan and reheat gently before serving in warmed individual bowls with a splash of cream added to each one if liked.

Serve with hot bread or crostini (see page 207) for a light meal.

Chickpea and Lemon Soup

A good soup all the year round: the ingredients are always available and it's warming enough for winter and fresh enough for summer.

6 SERVINGS

200 g (7 oz) chickpeas
salt
3 tablespoons olive oil
1 large onion, finely chopped
3 garlic cloves, crushed
½–1 teaspoon cumin seeds
½ dried red chilli or ¼ teaspoon chilli powder
1 tablespoon tomato purée
1 teaspoon brown sugar
a medium can of tomatoes
grated rind and juice of 1 lemon

Soak the chickpeas in cold water for at least 3–4 hours, or overnight, then boil them in fresh water for about 1½ hours or until tender, salting them at the very end. Drain the chickpeas but do not throw away their cooking water.

Heat the oil in a large heavy-based saucepan and fry the onion until it is transparent. Add the garlic and continue to fry for a few minutes. Crush and grind the cumin seeds and chilli in a mortar, or in a strong bowl with the end of a rolling pin, and add to the onions and garlic. Cook for 1 minute. Pour in the chickpeas, heat through, then stir in the tomato purée and sugar. Pour over the canned tomatoes and bring to the boil. Make up the chickpea cooking water to 900 ml (1½ pints) with water and pour into the pan. Bring back to the boil, then reduce the heat and simmer for 10 minutes. Stir in the lemon rind and juice.

Serve it on its own with rolls and butter for a light lunch or supper.

Broad Bean Soup

This is a useful emergency standby because it can be made from frozen broad beans. It needs to be puréed in a blender or food processor, or put through a mouli, to make a smooth soup, and you will need to add more stock, water or milk, to thin the soup after puréeing.

4 SERVINGS

2 tablespoons oil
50 g (2 oz) butter
1 large onion, chopped
100 g (½ lb) packet of frozen broad beans
a medium can of tomatoes
1 teaspoon sugar
2 garlic cloves, chopped
a sprig of fresh thyme or savory
500 ml (18 fl oz) vegetable stock
extra stock, water or milk
salt and pepper

Heat the oil and butter together in a large heavy-based saucepan, then add the onion, cover and sweat for about 5 minutes or until the onion is soft but not browned. Add the beans, tomatoes, sugar, garlic and thyme or savory, re-cover and simmer for 5–10 minutes or until the beans are thawed and tender, shaking the pan frequently.

Add the stock and simmer for a further 20–30 minutes. Leave to cool slightly, then purée by pressing through a sieve, or by processing in a blender or food processor, or put through a mouli to make a thick purée. Return to the saucepan and add more stock, milk or water to achieve the desired consistency. Reheat, season generously with salt and pepper, and serve in deep warmed bowls.

Crostini (see page 207) go well with this soup, for a light meal. Non-vegetarians might add diced unsmoked bacon with the beans. I sometimes add a soaked strand or two of saffron, for its glorious colour and aroma, but this is an extravagance.

Pappa Pomodoro (Bread and Tomato Soup)

Stale bread is never wasted in peasant cookery; the Tuscans serve it as crostini, or more nourishingly, as the thickening in this sturdy summer soup. The practice of using bread as thickening goes back to medieval times, but it must be good bread, ciabatta if you can get it, or stale white farmhouse, or best of all, Fleur Kelly's Roman Loaf (see page 275). Using sliced bread will produce a sticky, sloppy mush.

4 SERVINGS

4 slices of stale bread
600 ml (1 pint) vegetable stock
1–1½ × 400 g (14 oz) cans of tomatoes
3 tablespoons olive oil
4 garlic cloves, chopped
salt and pepper
olive oil and lemon juice, to season
a handful of fresh basil, roughly torn

Tear the bread into pieces and soak it in the stock in a large saucepan until it is very soft. Drain the canned tomatoes, and fry in the oil with the garlic, mashing the tomatoes to break them into a purée. Continue to cook over a moderate heat until reduced to a thick, tasty purée. Season well with salt and pepper. Add the tomato mixture to the bread and stock, and heat through, stirring to mix. If the flavour needs boosting, add a spoonful or two more of olive oil, and a squeeze of lemon juice. Add the basil just before serving.

Céleri Rémoulade

A classic salad starter which for me epitomizes the bistro food I first met in Paris, as a student. I like it best made from celeriac, a knobbly root tasting like celery but more so, and now widely available. It should be peeled of rough skin, and coarsely grated or, better still, processed into matchstick pieces, and sprinkled with lemon juice to stop it discolouring. Then mix with a fluid mayonnaise to which you have added a dollop of Dijon mustard, adding salt and pepper to taste.

NOTE: *Opinions vary as to whether the celeriac should be parboiled (five minutes) first or used raw. Both are good.*

Tomatoes with Tzatziki

Tzatziki is a refreshing blend of cucumber and yoghurt; it makes a pretty and complementary filling for halved, peeled tomatoes. The tomatoes should be ripe so this is best made when they are in season.

4–6 SERVINGS

1 medium cucumber
salt and pepper
150 g (5 fl oz) carton of natural yoghurt
2 garlic cloves, finely chopped
2 tablespoons chopped fresh mint or coriander
4–6 ripe tomatoes
a little sugar

Peel the cucumber, cut it in half lengthways and scoop out the seeds with a teaspoon. Chop the cucumber quite small, put it in a sieve and sprinkle it with salt. Leave to stand for 20 minutes to draw out some of the moisture, then drain and mix with the yoghurt. Add the garlic and mint or coriander, and season with salt and pepper.

Pour boiling water over the tomatoes, leave for 1 minute, or until the skins start to split, then drain, refresh under cold running water, and peel. Cut the tomatoes in half and scoop out the seeds to make cups. Sprinkle with sugar, salt and pepper, then fill each cup with the tzatziki. Serve alone, or with crisp lettuce leaves, as a starter.

Coleslaw

Coleslaw is a very useful standby in winter, when the usual salad materials are expensive. Shredded raw cabbage – the hard, white type is the best – provides the bulk of the salad, and you can vary the other ingredients according to what you have in the way of vegetables. It is a good idea to make it an hour or so ahead, mix the dressing in and leave it standing.

4 SERVINGS

¼–½ white cabbage
1–2 carrots
1 large eating apple
2 celery sticks
½ small onion (optional)
French Dressing (see page 259)

Shred the cabbage as finely as possible with a sharp knife and leave it to crisp in a bowl of cold water while you prepare the rest of the ingredients. Peel and grate the carrots; peel, core and dice the apple; wash the celery and cut it into thin strips; grate or finely slice the onion. Dry the cabbage carefully and mix all the ingredients together. Dress with a French dressing to which you have added a little lemon juice, mustard and brown sugar.

VARIATIONS: *I find a sprinkling of chopped fresh thyme – grown in a flowerpot on the windowsill – helps this salad. Dried thyme can be substituted, and you can throw in chopped walnuts, sultanas, grated cheese, shredded raw Brussels sprouts, shredded celeriac, and so on, as the fancy takes you.*

Eggs in Cheese Sauce

This is a much more sustaining dish than it sounds. If it is to be the main dish I suggest serving it on a bed of puréed spinach – the slight bitterness tones down the richness of the sauce. You can use more or less eggs according to your appetite.

SERVES 2 AS A MAIN DISH

1 tablespoon butter
1 tablespoon flour
600 ml (1 pint) milk
125 g (4 oz) Cheddar, grated
salt and pepper
nutmeg
mustard
6 eggs

Start with the sauce. Melt 1 rounded tablespoon butter, stir in 1 rounded tablespoon flour, pour on 600 ml (1 pint) cold milk and bring to boil over moderate heat. Reduce the heat to simmering point when the sauce boils. In a minute or two, it will thicken considerably. Now add the grated cheese, stirring for a minute or so till it melts. Taste the sauce and add salt, pepper, a dusting of nutmeg and ½ a teaspoon of mustard for pungency. Leave to simmer.

Meanwhile, put on a pan of water, add the eggs, bring gradually to the boil and simmer for 4 minutes. Leave in the water for a minute or two to cool, then pour off the water, run cold water over the eggs, and crack the shells to stop them cooking away in their own heat.

Peel the eggs, halve them and arrange them flat side down in a shallow heatproof dish (flan tin at a pinch). If you are using spinach, spoon the hot purée into a dish and arrange the eggs on top. Pour the sauce over the eggs and brown lightly under a hot grill.

New Potato Salad with Eggs, Peas and Mayonnaise

If you have mastered mayonnaise – and you should because even the best bottled is no substitute, as well as costing more – salads like this are splendidly tolerant and can be stretched to feed more faces by bumping up the potato and egg ratio, or adding some other ingredient to hand, such as cooked broad beans, or green beans, diced raw peppers, sliced radish and so on, not forgetting diced raw fruit, apple maybe, or a few chopped nuts. The staple ingredients are the waxy new potatoes, chopped spring onion, shallots or chives, a handful of herbs, the eggs and the mayonnaise.

4–6 SERVINGS

1 kg (2 lb) smallish new potatoes
salt and pepper
6–10 eggs
1 bunch of spring onions, or 3 shallots, or 1 bunch of chives
500 ml (18 fl oz) Mayonnaise (see page 260)
1 small packet of frozen peas (or broad beans)
fresh herbs, such as parsley, dill or a little basil, chopped
250 ml (8 fl oz) French Dressing (see page 259)

Scrub the potatoes, but do not peel them. Throw them into a large saucepan of boiling salted water and cook for 8–15 minutes, depending on size. If some are big, some tiny, add the tinies after 5 minutes, for parity.

Meanwhile, put the eggs to cook. All hard-boiled eggs in my experience are best started in cold water, brought to the boil gradually, simmered for 4–5 minutes, then left in the water just to cool a little before being drained and peeled. This avoids green shadows and rubbery yolks, and makes for a bright and tender egg.

While these are cooking, prepare and finely chop the shallots, spring onions or chives, and make the mayonnaise. When the potatoes are tender to the fork, drain and leave to cool a moment or two. Cook the frozen vegetables in a very little simmering water until just tender. Drain.

Peel the potatoes, wearing household gloves. Cooked potatoes peel quickly and cleanly, and taste better for being cooked in their skins.

Combine the potatoes, shallots, peas, etc., and herbs in a bowl and anoint while warm with vinaigrette, adding salt and pepper to taste. Peel the eggs, slice them thickly and add. Dilute the thick mayonnaise by adding warm water slowly, beating after each slurp, until it reaches a thin cream consistency. When the salad has cooled somewhat (not steaming hot), pour on the mayonnaise, stir, toss (a bit gently) and serve, with a green, crunchy salad as ballast.

VARIATIONS: *Acceptable extras include a few stoned black olives, a sprinkle of capers, one green chilli, very finely sliced, chopped walnuts or hazelnuts.*

NOTE: *If such a quantity of mayonnaise alarms you, remember that you need not use olive oil alone. Use two parts olive oil to one of cheaper safflower or grapeseed oil and expect to dilute the thick, home-made article by as much as one third its volume with tepid water. This needs to be a fluid, mild mayonnaise.*

Greek Salad or Horiatiki

Eaten with crusty bread, or pitta warmed in the oven, nothing is more quick, appetizing or refreshing on a hot summer day. I love crude food, and this is definitely it. Ingredients and their proportions can be varied at will, according to what is available, but feta cheese, crumbled, is a must, as are black olives.

SERVES 4

**4 large ripe tomatoes
half a cucumber
1 sweet onion
a handful of black olives
150 g (5 oz) feta cheese
olive oil
salt and pepper
lemon juice or vinegar**

Slice tomatoes vertically into segments. Peel the cucumber stripily, and chunk. Slice peeled onion into the thinnest rounds. Combine with black olives in a plain white dish. Crumble feta cheese into the dish and dress with a fruity olive oil, salt, pepper and the merest squeeze of lemon juice or splash of vinegar.

This is the essential horiatiki, redolent of vine-shaded meals on broiling days, but it can take such extras as diced green peppers, halved hard-boiled eggs, cubes of spiced dried sausage, and a generous sprinkle of oregano, dried or fresh.

Braised Leeks

4 SERVINGS

450 g (1 lb) leeks
50 g (2 oz) butter or 2 tablespoons olive oil
a pinch of salt
a splash of red or white wine, or water

Trim and cut the leeks in quarters lengthways. Put them in a baking dish or casserole (preferably earthenware) which has a tight-fitting lid with the butter, or the oil, on top, a pinch of salt and the wine or water (plus a bit more if the leeks are not still a bit wet from washing). Cover tightly and cook in the oven at 180°C (350°F, gas mark 4) for about 30 minutes or until soft.

Brussels Sprouts and Chestnuts

Chestnuts are a nuisance to prepare but they combine very well with sprouts. This is the perfect accompaniment to festive dishes like roast turkey or ham.

Cook the sprouts and chestnuts separately, using about half as many chestnuts as sprouts. Boil the sprouts in salted water till just tender – they should be slightly underdone. Make an incision in the pointed end of the chestnuts and boil for 12 minutes. Peel the chestnuts – shells and inner skins – a few at a time, keeping the rest hot in the water. Melt a lump of butter in a pan and put drained sprouts and chestnuts in together and shake them about till buttery. Salt and pepper them and, if you can, add a spoonful of juices from the roast. Cook together a couple of minutes longer and serve.

Potatoes Cooked in Milk

Although time-consuming (as the potatoes must be stirred constantly), this is real 'comfort' food and is enough on its own for a light supper or lunch.

4 SERVINGS

700 g (1½ lb) potatoes, peeled and diced
600 ml (1 pint) milk
salt and black pepper

Put the potatoes in a heavy-based saucepan and pour over the milk. Bring to the boil over medium heat, then turn the heat right down. Season with salt and black pepper, and simmer, stirring constantly, for 25–30 minutes or until the potatoes are cooked.

Leek and Potato Pie

4–6 SERVINGS

1 tablespoon plain flour
salt and pepper
freshly grated nutmeg
1 kg (2 lb) potatoes, peeled and thinly sliced
4 leeks, trimmed and finely sliced
50–75 g (2–3 oz) butter
450 ml (¾ pint) hot milk

Season the flour with salt, pepper and nutmeg. Grease a baking dish or small casserole and put in alternate layers of potatoes and leeks, sprinkling each layer with the seasoned flour and dotting with butter. The top layer should be potatoes. Dot the top with more butter, pour over the hot milk and bake in the oven at 190°C (375°F, gas mark 5) for about 1 hour or until the vegetables are tender.

Baked Tomatoes

This is a delicious way to cook tomatoes as a vegetable dish. It keeps all their delicate natural flavour. You should use home-made breadcrumbs (see page 120). The kind sold in packets are not suitable.

4 SERVINGS

8–10 tomatoes, thickly sliced
salt and pepper
4 teaspoons brown sugar
125–175 g (4–6 oz) butter, cut into tiny pieces
50 g (2 oz) breadcrumbs

Arrange the tomatoes in a shallow ovenproof dish. Season with salt and pepper, and sprinkle with the sugar. Dot with the butter and cover with breadcrumbs. Bake in the oven at 180°C (350°F, gas mark 4) for about 20 minutes.

'Hot' Greens

If you like chillies, try this fast way to perk up any of the rather more bitter green vegetables, such as spinach, Brussels sprouts tops, chard, land cress or spring greens. The quantities of chilli used are optional; one chilli may be as much as most people can take, but I like two, for a touch of fieriness. Remember to wash your hands well after handling chillies, and don't wipe your eyes or face until you have.

4 SERVINGS

1 kg (2 lb) greens (see above)
4 tablespoons olive oil
1–2 dried red chillies, de-seeded and chopped
2 garlic cloves, chopped
salt and pepper

Pick over the greens, removing any tired-looking leaves or coarse stalks. Wash well and shake off most of the washing water. Put the greens in a large saucepan, cover and cook over a high heat until the leaves have wilted. Tip out on to a board and chop coarsely.

Heat the oil in a shallow pan, add the chilli and garlic and turn briefly, taking care not to burn the garlic. Add the greens and mix well to distribute the garlic, chilli and oil mixture evenly. Add salt and pepper to taste, then turn into a warmed dish and serve.

Spinach Soufflé

4 SERVINGS

225 g (8 oz) spinach,
15 g (½ oz) butter, plus a small knob
1 tablespoon plain flour
150 ml (¼ pint) milk
40 g (1½ oz) Edam cheese, grated
2 large eggs, separated
salt and pepper
freshly grated nutmeg

Wash the spinach and trim off any tough-looking stalks. Put it in a pan with a small knob of butter and place a small heatproof plate or saucer upside-down on the pile of leaves to keep them near the source of the heat. Cover and cook over a high heat until the spinach has wilted. Drain and chop.

Melt the butter in a small saucepan, add the flour and cook, stirring, for 1–2 minutes. Remove from the heat and gradually add the milk, stirring constantly. Bring to the boil, stirring, and simmer until smooth and thick. Stir in the cheese until melted, then stir in the spinach and leave to cool slightly.

Beat in the egg yolks and season with salt, pepper and nutmeg. Beat the egg whites until stiff and fold them into the mixture. Turn the mixture into a buttered soufflé dish and cook in the oven at 190°C (375°F, gas mark 5) for about 20 minutes or until risen and brown on top.

Orange-Glazed Carrots

4 SERVINGS

50 g (2 oz) butter
450 g (1 lb) carrots, peeled and cut into matchsticks
1 tablespoon brown sugar
175–250 ml (6–8 fl oz) water
juice of 1 orange

Melt the butter in a wide, heavy-based saucepan, put in the carrots and the sugar, and heat gently until the sugar has begun to melt. Pour over the water and bring to the boil, then turn down the heat and simmer for about 10 minutes or until the carrots are almost tender, adding a little more water if necessary. Pour in the orange juice and simmer until the juice has reduced to a rich glaze.

Turnip Omelette

This recipe is a good example of everyday ingredients treated with sophisticated simplicity. It makes an excellent lunch or supper dish which needs only a green salad to keep it company.

2 SERVINGS

450 g (1 lb) small crisp turnips
salt and black pepper
50 g (2 oz) butter
4 eggs
a sprig of fresh parsley, finely chopped
2 tablespoons olive oil

Cut the turnips into small cubes and sprinkle with salt. Put them in an omelette pan or small frying pan, preferably one with a handle that can go in the oven, with the butter and cook, stirring, for about 15 minutes or until the turnips are tender and slightly browned. Season with salt and pepper.

In a separate bowl, beat the eggs thoroughly with the parsley and season with a pinch of salt and plenty of black pepper. Pour the turnip mixture into the beaten egg and mix well.

Clean the omelette pan, put the oil in it and heat. When the oil is hot, pour in the egg and turnip mixture, stir and flatten out the mixture in the pan. Cook for a minute over a high heat, then cook in the oven at 180°C (350°F, gas mark 4) for 5–10 minutes. If you have a pan which can't go in the oven, cook it for 5 minutes on each side under a moderate grill.

Mushroom Kasha

Kasha is a traditional dish in Russia and Poland. It can be made with buckwheat oats or pearl barley. This version uses barley.

It is a pleasant-looking and tasting dish, with an earthy, nutty flavour, a little reminiscent of wild rice. I find it goes very well with sausages, gammon and braised pigeon. The original recipe uses dried porcini, which have a pungent flavour and smell of their own, but I have substituted ordinary cultivated mushrooms with satisfactory results. The only difference in preparation is that the dried kind need preliminary soaking in warm water.

3–4 SERVINGS

1 egg
450 g (1 lb) pearl barley
25 g (1 oz) dried porcini or 125 g (4 oz) cultivated mushrooms
25–50 g (1–2 oz) butter
salt and pepper
2 tablespoons grated cheese

First beat up the egg and stir it into the barley, so that the grains are well coated, and leave to dry. Soak the mushrooms (if you are using dried mushrooms) in 600 ml (1 pint) warm salted water. Then simmer them, covered, in the same water for ¼ hour or until tender. With cultivated mushrooms, wipe and slice them, then simmer in 600 ml (1 pint) salted water, covered, for ¼ hour. In both cases pour off the mushroom liquor into a bowl, put the mushrooms aside, and return the cooking liquor to the pan. Put a lump of butter into the pan and simmer till melted. Then add the barley, cover, and simmer very slowly for 10 minutes, stirring from time to time.

Transfer the contents of the pan to a small, heavy casserole with a lid. Cast-iron pots were traditionally used for cooking Kasha, but earthenware makes a good substitute. Mix in the mushrooms, cut into small strips, a pinch of salt and a sprinkling of pepper. Put on the lid and bake in a moderate oven (180°C, 350°F, gas mark 4) for 1 hour. Before serving, stir in another lump of butter and the grated cheese.

Rice with Broad Beans, Lemon and Herbs

4–6 SERVINGS

450 g (1 lb) easy-cook long-grain rice
salt and pepper
450 g (1 lb) shelled young broad beans
2 tablespoons good olive oil
finely grated rind and juice of 1 lemon
a bunch of fresh coriander or chives, finely chopped

Cook the rice in plenty of boiling salted water for about 10 minutes or until tender. Put the beans in a steamer or colander and place on top of the boiling rice. Cover and steam for about 10 minutes or until just tender. Put the beans in a bowl and add the olive oil, lemon juice and lemon rind. Toss well to mix. Drain the rice and put it in a large serving bowl. Gently fold in the broad beans and herbs. Serve as part of a vegetarian feast.

Pumpkin Risotto

6 SERVINGS

1 medium pumpkin, peeled and de-seeded
1 tablespoon olive oil
150 g (5 oz) butter
3 small onions or 4 shallots, sliced
450 g (1 lb) easy-cook long-grain or arborio rice
900 ml (1½ pints) hot stock or water
salt and black pepper
grated Parmesan cheese

Cut the pumpkin into 2.5 cm (1 inch) cubes. Heat the oil and 125 g (4½ oz) of the butter in a heavy-based frying pan large enough to hold the finished risotto. Add the onions or shallots and cook until softened then put in the pumpkin. Cook the pumpkin and onions for 10 minutes, stirring, but don't let the onions burn. Pour in the rice. As soon as the rice is translucent, pour over a cupful of stock, cook until it has been absorbed, then pour over two more cupfuls and cook again.

Continue to add stock a cupful at a time until the rice and pumpkin are tender. Season with salt to taste and plenty of black pepper. Stir in the remaining butter and 1 tablespoon grated Parmesan.

Serve immediately with more Parmesan on the table.

Sesame Rice

6–8 SERVINGS

2 teaspoons salt
450 g (1 lb) long-grain rice
1 teaspoon fenugreek seeds
1 teaspoon ground turmeric
1 teaspoon paprika
8 cardamom pods, lightly crushed
4 teaspoons sesame seeds
2 teaspoons coriander seeds
50 g (2 oz) butter
1 teaspoon mustard seeds
2 tablespoons unsalted peanuts
juice of 1 lemon

Put the salt in a large saucepan of water and bring to the boil. Add the rice and cook for 10–12 minutes.

Meanwhile, put all the seeds and spices, except the mustard seeds, in a frying pan with a knob of butter and heat gently for about 5 minutes or until roasted. Remove them from the pan and add the mustard seeds and peanuts to the pan. Fry until golden.

Drain the rice thoroughly and stir in the remaining butter. Add all the spices, seeds and nuts, sprinkle with lemon juice and mix thoroughly. Serve hot.

Lentils with Basil

I am always curious to know what people who cook professionally like to make for themselves. This Italian recipe for lentils is a favourite with chef Sam Clark. He uses the tiny brown lentils sold in posher food stores and healthfood shops, but you can use the cheaper and more widely available green lentils also. When fresh basil is out of season, try a mixture of chopped spring onions (including some of the green part) and parsley.

4 SERVINGS

75 g (3 oz) brown or green lentils
3 large garlic cloves, crushed
juice of 1 large lemon
salt and freshly ground black pepper
4 tablespoons olive oil
a handful of fresh basil, finely chopped

Lentils do not need pre-soaking. Put them in a saucepan and cover with cold water by about 5 cm (2 inches). Add the garlic and bring gradually to the boil over a low heat. Simmer, uncovered, for 30–35 minutes or until the lentils are tender but not mushy. Check after 30 minutes.

Drain the lentils, but not too thoroughly – a little cooking water will improve the texture of the dish. Turn the lentils into a serving dish and squeeze over the lemon juice. Add salt and lots of freshly ground black pepper, then the olive oil, turning with wooden forks (less bruising than spoons) until it glistens appetizingly. Add the chopped basil, mix well and serve hot, warm or cold, as a starter or as a salad or a *contorno*, or side dish, with a frittata, or with fried or grilled fresh sardines.

Falafel

Excellent picnic food to eat with a salad dressed with yoghurt, and pitta bread. Alternatively, it makes a good party dish served with rice and a hot tomato sauce. The remarkable thing about this chickpea recipe is that the chickpeas do not need to be boiled, making it economical on fuel.

8 SERVINGS

450 g (1 lb) chickpeas
2–4 small onions
4–5 garlic cloves
a sprig of fresh parsley or coriander
1 teaspoon cumin seeds
1 teaspoon coriander seeds
salt and pepper
1 teaspoon cayenne pepper
sunflower oil, for frying

Soak the chickpeas in cold water overnight. Grind the chickpeas in a food mill, blender or food processor. If you are using a food processor, put the onions, garlic and parsley or coriander in with them. Otherwise, chop these finely and mix them into the ground chickpeas.

Grind the cumin and coriander seeds in a mill, or in a mortar, and stir them into the mixture. Season with salt, pepper and a little cayenne pepper. Continue working the mixture until it forms a rough paste, then form it into balls somewhere between the size of a walnut and a table tennis ball.

Pour about 0.5 cm (¼ inch) sunflower oil into a heavy-based frying pan and heat. When the oil is hot, add the falafel and fry them for about 15 minutes or until golden brown. Drain on absorbent kitchen paper before serving.

NOTE: *It may help to refrigerate the mixture for a while before forming it into balls.*

Daal

6 SERVINGS (OR MORE IF SERVED AS PART
OF AN INDIAN MEAL WITH OTHER DISHES)

450 g (1 lb) yellow split peas or 'Egyptian' lentils
1 tablespoon ground turmeric
5 cm (2 inch) piece of fresh root ginger, sliced but not peeled
1 small tablespoon salt
1 tablespoon garam masala
1 tablespoon coriander seeds
2 tablespoons cumin seeds
2 dried red chillies
6 tablespoons ghee or vegetable oil
3 onions, finely sliced
4 garlic cloves, sliced
1 sprig of fresh coriander, chopped (optional)

Wash the split peas or lentils and pick out any tiny stones or seeds. Put them in a large pan with about 2 litres (4 pints) water, the turmeric and ginger. Bring to the boil, then turn down the heat and simmer, partially covered, until the peas or lentils are tender (30–60 minutes). When the daal is cooked, stir in the salt and garam masala.

In a pestle and mortar (you can improvise with a strong bowl and the end of a rolling pin), crush the coriander and cumin seeds until they are at least partially ground. You could do this in a coffee grinder if you have one. (Alternatively, if you don't fancy this stage at all, it will not be the end of the world if you use ready-ground spices, provided they are fresh. In this case, reduce the quantities to 1 teaspoon ground coriander and 2 teaspoons ground cumin.) Bruise the chillies slightly but do not let them split.

In a large sauté or frying pan, heat the ghee or vegetable oil and put in the sliced onion, adding the garlic when the onion has just softened. When the onions are beginning to caramelize add the spices and chillies. Let them sizzle for a few seconds and give off their aroma, then pour this hot spicy mixture over the daal and sprinkle the top with chopped fresh coriander if wished.

Serve with brown or basmati rice and perhaps other Indian dishes.

Aubergine Toad-in-the-Hole

6 SERVINGS

2 large aubergines
salt
2–6 garlic cloves, crushed
olive oil, for frying

FOR THE BATTER
125 g (4 oz) plain flour
a pinch of salt
1 egg
200 ml (7 fl oz) milk
100 ml (3 fl oz) water

Trim the ends off the aubergines, then halve the aubergines crossways and cut each half lengthways into sections as similar in shape to sausages as possible. Put the aubergine pieces in a colander, sprinkle them with salt and leave for about 30 minutes to extract the bitter juices.

To make the batter, put the flour and salt in a bowl, make a well in the centre and add the egg and half the milk. Gradually work in the flour, stirring with a wooden spoon, then beat until smooth. Add the remaining milk and the water, and beat until well mixed and the surface is covered with tiny bubbles. Set aside.

Put the garlic and 4 tablespoons olive oil in a large heavy-based frying pan, preferably one with a handle that can go in the oven. Drain the aubergine pieces, rinse them and pat dry with absorbent kitchen paper. When the oil is hot, add the aubergine pieces and fry them for about 20 minutes or until golden. They will first absorb the oil, then melt it back into the pan as they cook. Remove the aubergine from the pan with a slotted spoon, place the pieces on a warmed plate and keep warm.

Add some more oil to the pan, if necessary, and when it is hot, remove the pan from the heat and pour in the batter. Place the aubergine pieces in the batter, arranging them evenly in the pan. Bake in the oven at 220°C (425°F, gas mark 7) for 40–45 minutes or until the pudding is risen and golden.

A Vegetable Gratin

Gratin, from the French *gratter*, to scrape or grate, defines a multitude of dishes whose sole purpose is to extend and glorify one basic, usually vegetable, ingredient. Chic thirties cooks, like Mrs Leyel, suggest serving a gratin of spinach or cauliflower, topped with cream, grated cheese and breadcrumbs, as a 'light luncheon' dish. At the other extreme a *pain* or loaf of lightly pre-cooked vegetable (carrot, cabbage, endive) bound with a soufflé mixture (white sauce beaten with eggs, maybe cream) is a classic of French bourgeois cookery. Either way, the principle involved – bulking out and transforming a vegetable into a stand-alone dish – seems ideally pauperish, and a vegetarian standby. The retro version is quicker, but the *pain* is more substantial, a pleasant supper served with a green salad.

My recipe is for cauliflower, but you could substitute spinach, carrots, leeks, spring greens, sprouting broccoli. In every case the vegetable should be lightly pre-cooked (i.e. firm, not mushy) then thoroughly drained, and chopped quite finely by hand before adding to the basic soufflé mix, to which you can add a little cream, a handful of grated cheese, or a topping of breadcrumbs. The same treatment can be usefully applied to leftover cooked vegetables though a loss of freshness might need extra grated cheese.

2 SERVINGS

1 small to medium cauliflower
300 ml (½ pint) Basic White Sauce (see page 264)
2 eggs
a handful of grated Parmesan or other strong dry cheese
2 tablespoons cream (optional)
salt and pepper
1 oz butter or a handful of breadcrumbs

Break the cauliflower into florets, chop the stalk, and steam or parboil till just tender. Drain, and chop to a coarse mush. Whisk the egg yolks and grated Parmesan into the white sauce and cream, if used. Season with salt and pepper. Combine the chopped cauliflower with the sauce, mixing well. Whisk the egg whites till just stiff, then fold into the gratin mixture.

Rub butter round a shallow serving dish, then tip in the gratin mixture, smoothing the surface flat. Top with shavings of butter or breadcrumbs and bake in a hot oven at 230°C (450°F, gas mark 8) till firm to the touch and golden brown.

Gratin of Courgettes

Leftover cooked vegetables can also be recycled as a gratin (in fact, I suspect this is how the idea originated) but make a little extra effort to trim and chop the vegetables for an appetizing effect. Cheddar cheese can be substituted for pricy Parmesan or Gruyère. Rice adds substance.

4 SERVINGS

**1 kg (2 lb) small, firm courgettes, sliced into rounds or matchsticks
salt and pepper
4 tablespoons olive oil
2 large onions, chopped
2 garlic cloves, chopped
3 eggs, plus 1 egg yolk
75g (3 oz) Parmesan, Gruyère or mature Cheddar cheese, grated
3–4 tablespoons cooked long-grain white or brown rice**

Put the courgettes in a colander, salt lightly and leave for 30 minutes to extract the juices.

Heat 1 tablespoon oil in a frying pan, add the onion and garlic, cover and cook over a low heat for about 5 minutes or until soft but not burned. Remove the onions and garlic from the pan, wipe out the pan, add 2 tablespoons oil, and, when hot, add the courgettes. Cover and cook for 10–15 minutes or until softened.

Break the eggs into a large bowl, add the extra yolk, and beat with a fork. Add 50 g (2 oz) grated cheese and the cooked rice and season with salt and pepper. Mix in the softened onions, garlic and courgettes.

Oil a shallow gratin dish and tip in the vegetable mixture. Drizzle the remaining oil on top, sprinkle with the remaining grated cheese, then bake in the oven at 180°C (350°F, gas mark 4) for about 30 minutes or until solid enough to cut with a knife, and lightly browned on top.

Serve warm, rather than hot. Excellent picnic food.

Ratatouille

This must be a cornerstone of any vegetarian diet – good to look at, good to eat, versatile and blessedly easy to make. It is not the sort of dish where quantities are critical; you can use more courgettes, less or no aubergine, various peppers, fresh or canned tomatoes. It always seems to come out right, succulent and colourful. I like mine quite juicy so I don't skimp on tomatoes.

As well as being delicious warm or cold, on its own with a slice of coarse bread, it makes a fine companion to a frittata, or a bowl of small new potatoes with aïoli. When you are getting down to the bottom of the pot, spread a layer of ratatouille over the bottom of an ovenproof dish, break in an egg or two per head, drizzle with oil, cover with foil and bake in the oven at 180°C (350°F, gas mark 4) until the eggs are just set – about 12 minutes.

5–6 SERVINGS

1 medium aubergine
salt and pepper
250 ml (8 fl oz) olive oil
700 g (1½ lb) onions, roughly chopped
450 g (1 lb) peppers, green, red or yellow, or a mélange, de-seeded and cut into strips
700 g (1½ lb) ripe tomatoes, skinned and chopped,
or 2 medium cans of peeled tomatoes
5 garlic cloves, chopped
1 sprig each of fresh thyme, rosemary and parsley
1 bay leaf
450 g (1 lb) courgettes, sliced
chopped fresh parsley, to serve

If you can cook the ratatouille in an earthenware pot, do, because it not only looks nicer but seems to taste richer. Use a heat-diffuser mat between the pot and the hotplate or gas ring. Start by preparing the aubergine. Cut it into dice and stand it in a colander. Sprinkle with salt to extract the bitterness.

Heat the oil in an earthenware pot or saucepan and cook the onion, covered, over a low heat for about 8 minutes or until softened. Add the aubergine and peppers, and cook for another 10 minutes, stirring now and then, over low heat. When these are softening, add the tomatoes, garlic, herbs, and a little salt and pepper. Canned tomatoes add more liquid than fresh, so add water in the latter case; ratatouille should start cooking with plenty of juice.

Simmer, half covered, for about 1 hour. Add the courgettes, and cook for another 30 minutes or until the courgettes are tender. If the liquid seems insufficient, stir in some warm water. Taste and adjust the seasoning. A sprinkle of fresh parsley on top is traditional.

Spanakopitta

This classic Greek pie of spinach baked with cheese in layers of papery filo pastry is so good that every vegetarian cook should know it by heart. Packets of frozen filo pastry are obtainable in most supermarkets and delicatessens, and make the preparation simplicity itself. Spinach tastes mysteriously nicer if you tear the leaves with your fingers instead of chopping them.

6 SERVINGS

1 kg (2 lb) spinach
250 g (9 oz) feta cheese, crumbled
salt and pepper
4 tablespoons melted butter or olive oil
1 packet frozen filo pastry, thawed

Wash the spinach thoroughly in cold water, drain in a colander, then tear into pieces, discarding any tough stalks. Put the spinach in a large saucepan, cover and cook over a high heat for just long enough to wilt the leaves. Drain the spinach and put it in a bowl with the cheese. Mix lightly and season with salt and pepper.

Oil or butter a shallow earthenware gratin dish. (A square dish makes laying out the filo sheets easier, but a round or oval one can be used.) Brush about six sheets of filo pastry with melted butter or oil and use to line the dish, allowing flaps of pastry to hang over all the sides. Spread this with half the spinach and cheese mixture. Butter or oil some more sheets of filo and lay these on top, then pour the rest of the spinach in. Fold all the loose flaps of filo over to make a nice neat parcel, adding another sheet or two, if necessary.

Brush the top of the pie with more butter or oil, then bake in the oven at 180–190°C (350–375°F, gas mark 4–5) for 30–40 minutes or until the pastry is golden. Cover with a loose piece of foil if the pie is browning too fast. Remove from the oven and turn the pie out on to a plate, then slide it back into the dish, upside down, and cook in the oven for another 10 minutes or until the bottom is golden.

Best served warm, good with a tomato salad.

Curried New Potatoes in their Jackets

New potatoes, cooked with spices in the Indian manner, are a treat, substantial enough for a main dish served with a daal, and *caehumbar*, the chunky Indian salad of tomato, cucumber and lettuce. Ghee (clarified butter) makes it much richer and does not catch and burn like ordinary butter.

4–6 SERVINGS

75 g (3 oz) ghee (or use vegetable oil)
1 large onion, finely chopped
1 heaped teaspoon ground turmeric
700 g (1½ lb) very small new potatoes, scrubbed
2 green chillies, de-seeded and finely chopped
salt
250 g (9 oz) packet of frozen peas, thawed
2 teaspoons garam masala

Heat the ghee or oil in a saucepan wide enough to take all the potatoes in one layer. Add the onion, cover and fry for about 5 minutes or until soft and just golden. Add the turmeric, stir and cook for 1 minute, then add the potatoes, chilli and salt. Cook for 5 minutes, shaking the pan from time to time. Turn the heat right down, cover and cook for 20 minutes or until the potatoes are almost done. Add the peas, sprinkle over the garam masala, shake again and cook for a further 10 minutes.

Potato and Pea Curry

Coconut milk can be bought in tins or as a powder to which you add
water. If you cannot find it, use dairy milk instead.

6 SERVINGS

700 g (1½ lb) potatoes, scrubbed
25 g (1 oz) butter
1 onion, chopped
5 cm (2 inch) piece of fresh root ginger, peeled and chopped
a sprig of fresh coriander, chopped
1 teaspoon ground turmeric
½ teaspoon ground coriander
½ teaspoon chilli powder
450 g (1 lb) shelled fresh or frozen peas
a pinch of salt
300 ml (½ pint) coconut milk
1 teaspoon garam masala

Cook the potatoes in boiling water for 8–10 minutes or until they are
half cooked. Drain, leave until cool, then peel and roughly chop.

Melt the butter in a frying pan and fry the onion, ginger and
coriander for 5–10 minutes or until the onion is golden. Add the dry
spices, except the garam masala, and continue to fry for a further 4
minutes. Stir in the potatoes, peas and salt. Add the coconut milk and
garam masala, cover and simmer for about 15 minutes or until the
potatoes are cooked.

Fancy Work

The food in this chapter is intended to be slightly out of the ordinary in one way or another – more extravagant, more elaborate, or more exotic. For these reasons, I think of it as food for special occasions, rather than every day. You can please yourself as to what occasions you choose to call special – dinner party, anniversary, seduction scene, peace offering or simply a break in humdrum routine for the cook. Your choice of food depends on the circumstances. Jiaozi (Peking Dumplings) would be a mistake at a rather stiff gathering of people, where your presence, all smiles and unruffled charm, is needed to keep things moving at all. A largely cold meal, which can be prepared ahead, with one hot dish needing very last-minute attention, is in order here. Crostini, Baked Gammon and perhaps Steamed Lemon Mousse would be a good choice. Greedy friends of long standing, on the other hand, will enjoy all the brouhaha of making the above-mentioned dumplings, and probably give you a hand as well. Something light and elegant seems to be indicated for romantic evenings, unless instinct tells you that you are dealing with a massive appetite. Almost all men can be appeased by platefuls of hot and fiery food – provide plenty of cold beer or lager to wash it down with.

Paupers are probably debarred by lack of cash from giving as many duty dinners (to impress the boss, rich relations, chance celebrities) as other people. Still, such occasions crop up from time to time and cause a disproportionate amount of anxious planning and brooding and fussing about what to eat, and what to drink, and what will they like and/or be impressed by. The rule in such cases is – don't over-reach yourself. Better to provide them with an unpretentious dish you know you can cook well, without agony of mind, than something untried which sounds very grand and costs so much you have to rely on the cheapest of wines to lubricate the conversation. (Rule 2 – you can offer cider or plonk to your friends, but never to the other category of guests. If you can't afford at least two bottles of a reasonable wine, it would be wiser to put the evening off.) If you wish to impress, don't try to be impressive. A pleasant soup to start off with, followed by a handsome-looking pie or Steak and Kidney Pudding (this homely classic has acquired considerable class, perhaps because so many people have forgotten how to make it) with appropriate vegetables (again for snob reasons, boiled sprouts score over frozen peas). Some frothy-looking confection to end up with (Dur Mou, Orange Jelly), quite a lot of some pleasant wine to wash it all down, and your evening of strategic socializing is off to a good start. The effect to aim for is home-made food as it was in the good old days, simple, well cooked, and a far cry from the tarted up stuff they eat at expense-account lunches.

Gazpacho

Cold, highly spiced Spanish soup. If you own an electric blender, you can whizz through the preparation in a few minutes. Otherwise, you will have to use a mouli, comforting yourself with the thought that most Spanish cooks still pound up the ingredients in a mortar or chop them interminably until they are reduced to a pulp.

4 SERVINGS

½ cucumber, peeled and chopped
1 large onion, chopped
450 g (1 lb) tomatoes, skinned, de-seeded and chopped
1 garlic clove, crushed
1 green pepper, de-seeded and chopped
540 ml (19 fl oz) can of tomato juice
cayenne pepper, to taste
2–3 tablespoons lemon juice or wine vinegar or a mixture
4–6 tablespoons olive oil
salt (optional)
ice cubes and croûtons (see page 41), to serve

Reserve a little cucumber, onion and tomato to serve with the soup. Purée all the remaining vegetables in a blender (with a little of the tomato juice) or mouli, or chop them all together very finely on a board. Mix with the tomato juice, cayenne, vinegar or lemon juice and olive oil. It is probably best to add the last two ingredients a bit at a time, tasting frequently, to make sure the soup is neither too acid nor too oily. Add a little salt if necessary. Chill well.

Serve in bowls with an ice cube floating in each one. Guests help themselves to raw diced vegetables and croûtons.

Wonton Soup

This is a favourite with children but you may want to omit the chilli and go easy on the garlic and ginger – the quantities given below are designed for adult tastes.

8 SERVINGS

6 garlic cloves, skinned
5 cm (2 inch) piece of fresh root ginger, peeled
225 g (8 oz) minced pork
a sprig of fresh coriander or parsley, finely chopped
1 fresh or dried red chilli, de-seeded and very finely chopped
soy sauce, to taste
salt and black pepper
1 small packet of wonton wrappers (about 30)
900 ml (1½ pints) chicken stock, made with a 2.5–5 cm (1–2 inch)
a piece of root ginger
a bunch of spring onions, thinly sliced
sesame oil, to taste (optional)

Chop together the garlic and ginger, and mix with the minced pork and coriander or parsley. Add the chilli and season with soy sauce, salt and pepper. Put a small amount of the mixture on each wonton wrapper and twist to close.

Put the chicken stock in a saucepan and bring to simmering point. Drop in the wontons and spring onions and simmer for about 5 minutes. Season to taste with soy sauce and sesame oil, if using, then pour into individual bowls and serve immediately.

Pumpkin and Coconut Soup

An unusual and delicious combination, mild and fragrant, which I see as a new classic. Pumpkin slices can be found in most Asian food stores, likewise tinned coconut milk. This is one soup which demands to be processed, or liquidized, because the pumpkin flesh remains fibrous even after slow cooking.

6–8 SERVINGS

2 tablespoons vegetable oil
1 slice pumpkin approx 8 cm (3 in) wide
6 shallots or 2 small onions
3 cloves garlic
1 tin coconut milk
1½–2 litres (3–4 pints) stock (vegetable or chicken)
salt and pepper

Peel the pumpkin slice, scrape off the seeds (try roasting these in the oven) and cut the pumpkin into smallish cubes. Peel and chop the shallots, onions and garlic.

Heat the oil in a large heavy pan; add first the pumpkin cubes, stirring so they don't catch, then the chopped onion/shallot, and stir again for a minute or two till they begin to soften, finally the garlic – garlic burns easily so I always add it last.

Pour on the stock, stir to mix, and leave to simmer slowly for an hour. Add the coconut milk, stir and cook a further 10 minutes. Liquidize the soup till smooth, and return to the pan. Now taste and adjust seasoning – it needs a fair bit of salt to counteract the pumpkin sweetness. If the soup is too thick – the coconut milk seems to thicken as it cooks – add water, or more stock. It should be pale gold in colour, and no thicker than single cream.

Serve in deep bowls with sliced pitta, crisped in the oven, as an extra.

Devils on Horseback

A wintry treat to serve with drinks, or as a starter or 'savoury', or as an accompaniment to roast fowl.

MAKES 12

12 prunes
hot tea or water for soaking
6 teaspoons chutney
12 rashers of streaky bacon, de-rinded and trimmed of excess fat

Soak the prunes for 30 minutes in hot tea or water. Drain them, then remove the stones and fill each cavity with ½ teaspoon chutney. Wrap a rasher of bacon around each prune and secure with wooden cocktail sticks. Place on a baking sheet and cook in the oven at 200°C (400°F, gas mark 6) for about 20 minutes or until the bacon is cooked. Serve hot.

'Seaweed'

4 SERVINGS

450 g (1 lb) spring greens or green cabbage, trimmed
peanut (groundnut) or other light oil, for deep-frying
2 teaspoons caster sugar
½ teaspoon salt
a pinch of monosodium glutamate (optional)

Wash the spring greens or cabbage leaves carefully, then cut into the thinnest possible strips. Spread them out on a clean cloth and leave to dry for a few hours, or overnight.

Heat the oil and deep-fry the strips of leaves in batches for 2 minutes or until darker green and crisp. Drain on kitchen paper and toss with the sugar, salt and monosodium glutamate, if using.

Tapenade

Tapenade is a sort of relish, salty and pungent, much eaten in Provence. You can spread it on thin slices of toast, eat it with cheese, on biscuits, even stuff hard-boiled eggs with it. If you like the taste of olives, you will love it. It would be a good appetizer before a meal, a change from taramasalata made with pounded cod's roes. You will need a pestle and mortar, or a very strong bowl and the end of a rolling pin, for the preparation.

6–8 SERVINGS

125 g (4 oz) black olives, pitted and chopped
125 g (4 oz) green olives, pitted and chopped
10 anchovy fillets, drained
1 tablespoon capers, drained and chopped
1 hard-boiled egg yolk
a little chopped fresh or dried thyme
olive oil, to moisten

Put the olives in a mortar and pound to a paste. Add the anchovy fillets and pound until smooth. Add the capers and egg yolk and pound until smooth. Add the thyme and a trickle of olive oil and mix well. The tapenade should not be liquid, just moist enough to spread easily, so add only enough oil to achieve this consistency. Pack into a small jar.

Crostini

4–6 SERVINGS

50 g (2 oz) can of anchovies, drained
milk for soaking
1 French bread stick
225 g (8 oz) chicken livers, thawed if frozen
2 tablespoons olive oil
2 garlic cloves, crushed
75–125 ml (3–4 fl oz) wine
2 tablespoons capers, drained

Put the anchovies in a bowl, cover with milk and leave to soak. Cut the bread diagonally into long slices, place on a baking sheet and bake in the oven at 190°C (375°F, gas mark 5) until golden.

Clean the chicken livers and chop into large pieces. Heat the olive oil in a heavy-based frying pan and fry the chicken livers and garlic until the livers are browned but not overcooked. Add the wine for the last minute.

Leave to cool slightly, then put in a food processor with the capers. Drain the anchovies and add them to the mixture, then process until finely chopped. Alternatively, combine everything on a board and chop finely.

Spread on the French bread slices and serve at once.

Kipper Paste

4–6 SERVINGS

1 pair of traditional undyed kippers
about 125 g (4 oz) unsalted butter, softened
1 tablespoon lemon juice
salt, cayenne pepper and ground mace, to taste

Pour boiling water over the kippers and leave for 10 minutes, then drain, skin and bone them. Weigh the flesh, then flake it and beat in an equal weight of butter. Add the lemon juice. Season with ground mace, cayenne pepper and extra salt if you think it needs it. Serve with slices of hot toast.

Leeks Vinaigrette

Serve these cold, either as an hors d'oeuvre, or with cold meat or chicken. Choose leeks as near as possible the same size.

2 SERVINGS

4 leeks
salt and pepper
freshly grated nutmeg
French Dressing (see page 259)

Wash the leeks carefully – steeping them upside down in cold water helps to loosen the mud and grit – and trim them to roughly the same length, leaving an inch or so of green on each one. Plunge them into boiling salted water, and boil, covered, until tender but not mushy. The time depends on the size of the leeks – prod them with a fork to test them.

Drain them very thoroughly in a colander, finishing off by patting them dry with absorbent kitchen paper. Sprinkle them with a little salt, pepper and nutmeg, and douse with French dressing. Leave to get cold.

Baked Chicken Liver Salad

This can be served for a light lunch or supper, or as a dinner party starter.

4 SERVINGS

225 g (8 oz) chicken livers
3 tablespoons olive oil
1 teaspoon black pepper
1 teaspoon paprika
2 garlic cloves, finely chopped
salt
2 tablespoons vinegar (wine, sherry or balsamic)
125 g (4 oz) streaky bacon, de-rinded and cut into thin strips
1 teaspoon wholegrain mustard
a salad of strong-flavoured and bitter leaves – spinach, Cos lettuce, rocket, radicchio, dandelion, chicory – any one or a combination of these would be suitable

Trim the chicken livers of any green or sinewy parts. Put them in a bowl with 2 tablespoons olive oil, the pepper, paprika and garlic, and marinate for at least 1 hour (overnight won't hurt).

Lay the oily livers on a baking sheet, sprinkle with salt and bake in the oven at 200°C (400°F, gas mark 6) for 20 minutes, pouring 1 tablespoon vinegar over them 5 minutes before the end of the cooking time.

Heat the bacon in a dry, heavy-based frying pan over a gentle heat. (Always cook streaky bacon over gentle heat with no extra fat – this allows it to shed the water which factory bacon so often has in it, and gives its fat time to melt, banishing that dreaded rubbery texture.) When the bacon is crispy, turn off the heat and stir in the remaining olive oil and vinegar, and the mustard. Pour the baked livers and crispy bacon bits over the salad.

Broad Bean, Shrimp and Dill Salad

A light, pretty starter that can be made with ingredients from the freezer. However, one bothersome step is essential to the attractiveness of the dish. The broad beans, defrosted and cooked, must be peeled to remove their pasty skins and reveal the vivid green, tender kernels. This takes around fifteen minutes. The rest takes less than five.

SERVES 4–6

700 g (1½ lb) packet frozen broad beans
1 small packet frozen peeled shrimps
1 clove garlic, peeled and minced
3 tablespoons light olive oil
1 small bunch fresh dill, finely chopped
1 lemon
salt and pepper

Defrost the beans and shrimps. Steam or boil the beans till tender. Set aside to cool. In a little oil fry the shrimps with garlic over medium heat till they go opaque pinky white. Season with a little more oil, lemon juice, salt and pepper.

Peel the beans. Combine with the shrimps in a bowl, and add the remaining oil, lemon juice and salt and pepper to taste. Stir in chopped dill and toss to mix, lightly but thoroughly. Serve at room temperature.

Smoked Mackerel, Radicchio and Hot Potato Salad

4–6 SERVINGS

450 g (1 lb) new potatoes, scrubbed
1 smoked mackerel
1 small head of radicchio
1 onion, finely chopped

FOR THE DRESSING
75 ml (3 fl oz) olive or hazelnut oil
1 tablespoon white wine vinegar
½ teaspoon mustard powder
salt and pepper

Cook the potatoes in boiling salted water for 15–20 minutes or until tender. Meanwhile, remove the skin and bones from the mackerel and cut the fish into even slices. Tear the radicchio leaves into manageable pieces. Make up the dressing by beating the ingredients together in a bowl.

When the potatoes are ready, drain them, cut them up roughly and put them back in the warm pan. Place over a high heat and very quickly throw in the onion, radicchio and dressing. After just a few seconds, turn the salad into a bowl, throw on the mackerel pieces and serve immediately.

British Rail Starter (Salad)

Give credit where it is due: British Rail was usually associated with sandwiches soggy with mayo, but I first ate this sparky starter in the dining car of a Great North Eastern Railway train en route to Edinburgh, and found it hit the spot. I have made it myself since; it is unusual, looks appetizing and tastes good. A neat, easy start to a dinner party.

SERVES 6

1 dozen quail eggs, boiled, peeled and halved
1 black pudding, skinned and cubed
1 thick slice 'rustic' bread, cut into 1 cm (½ inch) cubes
1 clove garlic, minced
2 bunches rocket, fresh and crisp, stalks removed

FOR THE VINAIGRETTE DRESSING
3 tablespoons virgin olive oil to 1 tablespoon white wine vinegar
1 teaspoon Dijon mustard
salt and pepper

Boil the quail eggs as directed: usually 2 minutes simmering, starting in cold water. Make bread croûtons by tossing the cubes in a splash of olive oil, and the garlic. Then bake in a moderate oven till crisp and golden. Pick over the rocket to remove stalky bits and tired leaves, and crisp by dunking in cold water for as long as you can manage. Drain and dry – use kitchen paper or shake in a colander.

To serve, toss the rocket with dressing (keep it scant), then make a little nest of leaves on each plate. Add 2 quail eggs, a tablespoon of black pudding cubes and a handful of croûtons per serving. A cherry tomato or two adds colour contrast.

Swedish-Style Marinated Herrings

This must be made with the freshest herrings, bright-eyed and firm as cucumbers. An obliging fishmonger will fillet them for you. Then all you need do is cut them diagonally into neat strips and marinate them in this sweet and spicy Swedish-inspired 'cure' for 48 hours or so. I find standard roll-mop marinades harshly vinegary; the Scandinavian additions of sugar, mustard and spices transform this into an elegant and unusual starter, served with half a hard-boiled egg, a slice of dark rye bread and Curry Mayonnaise (see below). A thimbleful of ice cold aquavit, or schnapps if you can afford it, is the perfect chaser.

6–8 SERVINGS

4 very fresh herrings, filleted and de-scaled

FOR THE MARINADE
about 500 ml (18 fl oz) white wine vinegar
1 tablespoon mild French mustard, e.g. Dijon
2 teaspoons fresh coriander seeds, slightly bruised in a mortar
1 tablespoon soft brown sugar
1 teaspoon salt
1 tablespoon finely chopped fresh dill (optional but nice)

Combine all the marinade ingredients in a bowl and stir to mix well and dissolve the sugar. Arrange the strips of fish, skin side out, in a glass jar, piling them up in an overlapping spiral. Pour over the 'cure', cover the jar and stand in a cool place for 2 days.

To serve, lay the strips on plates with hard-boiled egg halves and dark bread for contrast, and pass round Curry Mayonnaise separately.

Curry Mayonnaise

The chef at one of my favourite restaurants (The Spread Eagle in Greenwich) used to serve this mayonnaise with sweet-cured herring.

6–8 SERVINGS

2 egg yolks
1 tablespoon Dijon mustard
salt
a pinch of cayenne pepper
500 ml (18 fl oz) vegetable oil, preferably mild-tasting safflower or
grapeseed oil
1½ teaspoons Madras curry paste
½ tablespoon white wine vinegar
a squeeze of lemon juice (optional)

Whisk the egg yolks, mustard, salt and cayenne pepper together in a bowl. Add the oil a drop at a time, whisking constantly, until the mixture begins to come together in a glossy lump. At this point, you can add the oil in splashes, but continue whisking until the oil is all incorporated. Stir the curry paste into the vinegar and add to the mayonnaise, whisking to blend well. Taste and adjust the seasoning, adding a squeeze of lemon juice, if liked. If the mayonnaise is too thick, 1–2 tablespoons warm water can be whisked in to lighten it.

NOTE: *This mayonnaise has many other uses: as a dip for crudités; with poached fish; or in a potato salad.*

Stuffed Mussels

An appetising way of serving mussels as a light first course. You can use less garlic if you prefer.

4 SERVINGS

1 litre (2 pints) fresh mussels
50 g (2 oz) butter
about 3 tablespoons dry breadcrumbs
3 garlic cloves, finely chopped
a handful of fresh parsley, finely chopped
salt and black pepper
1 teaspoon grated lemon rind
a little white wine (optional)

First clean the mussels thoroughly. Rinse them under running water to remove grit or weed. Pull off the beards with pliers or a strong knife. Discard any mussels that refuse to close. Rinse again. Put the mussels in a saucepan large enough to take them in one layer on the bottom. Place the pan over moderate heat, with the cover on, and cook for 1–2 minutes or until the mussels have opened. Discard any mussels that do not open at all. Half open is enough. If the mussels are overcooked at this stage, they will be tough. Strain any liquid off into a bowl and remove one shell from each mussel.

Melt the butter in a frying pan and gently fry the breadcrumbs and garlic, stirring until the crumbs are soft and have absorbed the butter. Remove from the heat and mix in the parsley, a little salt, black pepper and the grated lemon rind. Arrange the mussels in a shallow ovenproof dish and spread a little stuffing over each one. Pour over the mussel liquor, and a splash of white wine, if you have any. Cook in the oven at 190°C (375°F, gas mark 5) for 5–10 minutes or until the mussels are heated through. Serve at once.

Mussels in Black Bean Sauce with Coriander

Fermented black bean sauce, from any good supermarket, is a bit like the Chinese equivalent of brown sauce, with a pungent, salty-sweet base which goes wonderfully well with seafood. The addition of ginger, garlic and coriander gives this mussel dish an authentic and mind-blowing fragrance.

4 SERVINGS

1 kg (2 lb) mussels
1 tablespoon peanut or other vegetable oil, for frying
a small knob of fresh root ginger, peeled and finely chopped
2 garlic cloves, chopped
2–3 tablespoons black bean sauce
a small handful of fresh coriander, chopped together
with 3 spring onions

Wash and scrape the mussels and pull off the beards with a small, sharp knife. Throw out any mussels that are not tightly closed. Heat the oil in a heavy-based saucepan, add the ginger, garlic and mussels, cover and cook over a brisk heat for 2 minutes, then check whether the mussels are opening. Catch them as soon as possible after they open as prolonged heat toughens them.

Meanwhile, pound the bean sauce to a smooth paste in a mortar. Add it to the mussels and give the pan a good shake to mingle the bean paste with the mussel liquor. Scatter chopped coriander and spring onions on top and serve in bowls or soup plates, with a big dish to put the shells in.

Grilled Squid with Chilli, Parsley and Garlic Sauce

This makes an elegant and colourful starter. Each diner has a few pieces of the crispy squid which he or she dips into the green or red sauce.

4–6 SERVINGS

450 g (1 lb) small squid, thawed if frozen
1 large or 2 small fresh green or red chillies, de-seeded and very finely chopped
6 garlic cloves, very finely chopped
a bunch of fresh flat leaf parsley or coriander, very finely chopped
150 ml (¼ pint) olive oil

To clean fresh squid, rinse it thoroughly, then pull on the head and tentacles until the soft contents of the body slip out. Cut the tentacles off just in front of the eyes. Discard the body contents and the head. Remove the semi-transparent quill from inside the body and rinse the body inside and out, rubbing it with your fingertips to remove any white substance and the fine, dark outer skin. Cut the body pouch into strips and the tentacles into bunches. Score the strips on one side with a knife.

Put the chilli, garlic and parsley or coriander in a mortar and crush together with the pestle, or use a very strong bowl and the end of a rolling pin. Stir in the olive oil to make a thick sauce. Put 1 tablespoon of the sauce in a bowl, stir in the squid and leave to marinate for at least 30 minutes.

Cook the squid under a medium grill for 5–10 minutes or until it turns stiff and opaque, turning once. Serve with the remaining sauce.

Seafood Dumplings (Ravioli)

This recipe is inspired by one in Frances Bissell's *The Pleasures of Cookery*. I have made it pauperish by substituting some prawns for scallops, and editing the presentation. What we end up with here is about six semi-circular pasta dumplings per person, with a delectable fishy stuffing, sitting in a pool of fragrant sauce. It is not often I embark on home-made ravioli but the excellence of this combination justifies the toil, not major in this case as your guests get only a few (though surprisingly filling) ravioli each. I used to think of this as a starter for an occasion where to please/impress is important, but by increasing quantities as I suggest you have a superb main dish. Do budget for the saffron. I know it is an extravagance, but it adds real glamour. Buy it powdered, in sachet form, from Italian delis.

6 SERVINGS

225 g (8 oz) home-made Fresh Pasta (see page 157)

FOR THE FILLING AND SAUCE
600 ml (1 pint) prawns in their shells
1 sachet powdered saffron
6 shallots, finely chopped
2 large scallops
salt and pepper
1 tablespoon finely chopped dill

Shell the prawns and put the shells in a saucepan with the saffron. Cover with cold water and simmer for 20 minutes. Strain off the debris, return the liquid to the pan, add the chopped shallots and simmer for another 5 minutes. Drain through a fine sieve into a bowl, reserving both stock and shallots. Separate the corals from the white parts of the scallops, and cut off the thin dark ring round the white meat, plus the little tough pad of muscle. Chop the raw scallops, corals and peeled prawns to a coarse mush. Season lightly with salt and pepper and mix in half the reserved blanched shallots and a pinch of chopped dill.

Roll out the pasta as thinly as possible, and stamp into rounds with a wine glass. Cover the pasta with a damp tea towel while making the ravioli. Put a heaped teaspoon of filling on each pasta circle, fold over and wet the edges with water before pressing firmly together. Lay these on a floured tea towel and cover with another dampened tea towel as you complete them. Do all this ahead, the afternoon of the party; the ravioli will be fine under a dampened cloth for a couple of hours. Continue until you have used up all the filling.

The sauce can also be prepared ahead. Boil up the prawn stock with the remaining reserved shallots until reduced by a third to a half. It should taste concentrated and look deep golden. Add the remaining chopped dill, and season to taste.

Allow 5 minutes to get the ravioli and sauce on to the table from the time the pan boils. Put serving plates in the oven to heat. Bring the sauce back to simmering. Bring a large, wide pan of water to the boil and drop in the ravioli, in two batches if necessary. Cook for 3 minutes, then remove with a slotted spoon. Spoon a little sauce on to each warmed plate and add some ravioli. Serve as quickly as possible.

It would be a mistake to clutter up such a special dish with extras; start the meal with a vivid soup, such as gazpacho or borscht, served with hot crusty bread, and finish up with a green salad and cheese, or fresh fruit and cheese.

La Crique

4 SERVINGS

**450 g (1 lb) potatoes, peeled
salt and black pepper
2 garlic cloves, chopped
1 tablespoon chopped fresh parsley
2 tablespoons olive oil**

Grate the potatoes by hand or in a food processor. Place in a bowl, sprinkle with salt and leave for 10 minutes. Squeeze the potato between your hands to extract as much water as possible, then add the garlic, parsley, salt and pepper. Heat the oil in a heavy-based frying pan and put the mixture in all at once, spreading it to fill the bottom of the pan. Cook until golden brown on both sides.

Koulibiac

This is a trusty party recipe. It looks spectacular as pies will, and it has the great virtue of being as good cold as hot, so you can prepare it a day beforehand. It also makes extravagant ingredients go a long way – so that though your guests will feel you've gone to town you won't in fact be over-paupering yourself. Though it is traditionally made with salmon, I've tried this pie with less grand kinds of fish – smoked haddock gave it a good colour and interesting flavour. Served with plenty of salad, this dish will serve 12, more as part of a buffet with another main dish.

1 2 SERVINGS

FOR THE PASTRY
700 g (1½ lb) strong white flour
2 teaspoons salt
1 packet fast-action dried yeast
2 eggs
3 tablespoons olive or sunflower oil
1 egg, beaten, to glaze

FOR THE FILLING
6 tablespoons millet, rinsed
salt and pepper
a pinch of ground turmeric
3 onions, chopped
butter, for frying
225 g (8 oz) mushrooms, chopped
450 g (1 lb) salmon fillets or a mixture of salmon and smoked haddock
4 eggs, hard-boiled and chopped
a large bundle of fresh dill, parsley or chervil, finely chopped

Make the yeast pastry by pouring the flour into a mixing bowl. Stir in the salt and the yeast, break in the eggs and pour in the oil. Add enough cold water gradually to make a smooth dough. Leave to rise in a warm place for about 45 minutes.

Toast the damp millet in a dry pan until it begins to give off a nutty smell. Put it to boil in plenty of boiling salted water, with the turmeric, until it is tender but not soggy. Drain and rinse under cold running water and leave in the sieve to drain thoroughly. Fry the onions gently in butter until they are just softened, put in the chopped mushrooms and continue to fry gently until they yield up their moisture. Turn the onions and mushrooms into a dish and leave to cool. Put another knob of butter in the pan (there is no need to wash it) and gently cook the salmon fillets (grind some black pepper and a fraction of salt over them) – just until they are firm and the colour has lightened. Remove them from the pan and put on another plate. Leave to cool.

When the dough has doubled in size, knock it back and knead it briefly. Remove a nugget for decorating the finished pie with. Flour the table, your hands and whatever you are using as a rolling pin and roll the dough out to as large a rectangle as will fit your baking sheet, or two smaller ones. The dough should be fairly elastic and you might be able to make a pie with a very fine crust, but about 0.5 cm (¼ inch) thickness is probably a safe thickness to work with for your first try.

Lay half the millet down the middle of your rectangle (or a quarter down the middle of each, and so on), leaving enough margin to fold up round the sides and at the ends. Season with salt and pepper and lay half the mushroom and onion mixture over the millet. Season again with a little salt and a grinding of black pepper.

Lay the salmon fillets over the mushrooms, season, sprinkle with the chopped eggs and herbs, then cover with the other half of the mushrooms and onions. Season and finish the sandwich with the rest of the millet. Wet the edges of the dough, draw them up and fold them over the top – provided the dough tapers rather than thickens towards the edges it should flatten down quite easily, but you may need to cut out the corners before you fold up the ends (these bits of dough can go towards the decoration). Now you will need another pair of hands, if your pie is large, to help you convey it to a greased baking sheet, without it folding or breaking.

To decorate your pie, roll out the reserved bit of dough and cut it into leaves or flowers, or whatever. Damp them on one side and lay them gently on the top of the pastry. Brush the whole of the top with beaten egg – your fingers will do – and bake in the oven at 200°C (400°F, gas mark 6) until it is golden brown.

Flammeküche

This is a recipe from Sue Style's book, *A Taste of Alsace*. A sort of northern answer to the pizza. Very simple to make and always a knock-out.

2–3 SERVINGS

FOR THE DOUGH
700 g (1½ lb) strong white flour
1 sachet fast-action dried yeast
1 teaspoon salt
2 tablespoons olive oil
1 egg, beaten

FOR THE TOPPING
150 ml (¼ pint) double cream
150 ml (¼ pint) fromage blanc
2 tablespoons olive oil
salt and black pepper
2 onions, finely chopped
225 g (8 oz) smoked streaky bacon, de-rinded and cut into tiny strips

Mix the flour, yeast and salt in a bowl, then mix in the oil and egg, gradually adding enough water to make a pliable dough. Knead the dough, then cover with a clean, damp cloth and leave in a warm place to rise for about 45 minutes or until doubled in size.

Knock the dough back and divide it into one or two pieces. Roll or spread each piece into a thin round and place on oiled baking sheets.

Mix together the cream, fromage blanc, oil and seasonings and spread the mixture over the bases. Sprinkle the onions and bacon on top and bake in the oven at 230°C (450°F, gas mark 8) for about 15 minutes or until golden.

Green Beans Szechuan-style

Szechuan food is famously 'hot', spiced with chillies and Szechuan peppercorns, a reddish-brown aromatic with a distinctive flavour obtainable in Chinese stores. This simple treatment of green beans brings out their own flavour, through the pungent accompaniments. It would make a good follow-up to Peking Dumplings (see page 226) served with a little plain rice. I have adapted the recipe from one given by Ken Hom in *The Taste of China*.

6 SERVINGS

450 g (1 lb) fresh green beans
2 mild green chillies
1½ tablespoons peanut (groundnut) oil
3 garlic cloves, crushed
1 teaspoon salt
1 dried red chilli (optional)
1 tablespoon white wine vinegar or rice vinegar
2 tablespoons dry sherry (optional)
2 teaspoons sugar
2 tablespoons water
1 teaspoon Szechuan peppercorns

String the beans, if necessary, and snap in two. Cut the green chillies in half, de-seed and slice thinly. Heat the oil in a wok or large frying pan, add the garlic and salt and turn over a high heat for a few seconds. Add the green chillies and stir-fry for about another 10 seconds or until the chilli is softening. If you are using a dried red chilli, de-seed it and crush it finely. Add it to the pan with the beans and all the other ingredients, except the peppercorns. Stir-fry for about 5 minutes or until the beans are just tender. Add a little more water if they look like drying out and catching. Heat the peppercorns in a small saucepan until they release their aroma and are roasted. Crush the peppercorns and sprinkle over the dish before serving.

Baked Brie in pastry

A whole Brie or Camembert cheese baked till molten in a pastry case is spectacular, and so easy it deserves a place in pauper party food. It might be acceptable to vegetarians too, if they can overlook the use of rennet. Admittedly, a whole cheese is not cheap, but so rich cooked like this it could feed 8–10 people as a main course accompanied by a large bowl of crisp salad – lettuce hearts, rocket, corn salad, raddichio, strips of spring onion, whatever.

Most recipes call for home-made shortcrust (see page 107), but I first ate it encased in puff pastry (buy this frozen), which looked even more billowing and impressive. For a lighter result you could wrap your cheese – ripe but not runny – in many sheets of filo (also obtainable frozen) overlapped and lightly oiled. In the case of short or puff pastry, you need to cut two discs large enough to enclose the cheese when wetted round the rim and pinched together to seal. Cut a few slashes in the top layer so steam can escape. Bake in the middle of a hot, preheated oven for 20 minutes, or till the pastry case is crisp and golden brown. Filo cooks so rapidly that you may need to lower the heat after ten minutes or so to prevent it burning. Use a sharp knife to cut slices, with a spoon to collect up hot melted cheese.

Spicy Chickpeas

This is a delicious 'munchy' with drinks.

450 g (1 lb) chickpeas
salt and black pepper
3 onions, chopped
3 tablespoons vegetable oil
3 garlic cloves, chopped
1 tablespoon cumin seeds
1 tablespoon coriander seeds
½ teaspoon chilli powder or dried chilli, de-seeded and chopped
1 tablespoon tomato purée
a bunch of fresh coriander or parsley, chopped

Soak the chickpeas for at least 4 hours or overnight. Drain them and put them in a saucepan. Cover with water, bring to the boil and boil hard for 20 minutes, then turn the heat down and simmer for about 2 hours. (The cooking time will vary according to the chickpeas, but chickpeas never seem to overcook however long you boil them.) When they are nearly ready, salt the water. If you do this when the chickpeas are raw it will toughen them.

In a heavy-based frying pan large enough to take the chickpeas, fry the onions in the oil for a few minutes, then add the garlic. After a minute or two, add the spices and fry for 1 minute, then stir in the tomato purée and cook for 1 minute. Put in the chickpeas, stir round and heat through. Sprinkle with chopped coriander and black pepper before serving.

Ginger-Stuffed Chicken Legs

Transforms sinewy drumsticks into exciting spicy parcels.

6 SERVINGS

2 small onions, finely chopped
5 cm (2 inch) piece of fresh root ginger, peeled and finely chopped
1 fresh or dried chilli, de-seeded and finely chopped
grated rind of 1 lemon
a generous bunch of fresh parsley or coriander, finely chopped
225 g (8 oz) minced pork
soy sauce
black peppercorns, ground
6 chicken legs
2–3 tablespoons vegetable oil

Mix the onions, ginger, chilli, lemon rind and parsley or coriander with the pork, a generous splash of soy sauce and ground peppercorns.

Remove the bones from the drumsticks by turning them inside out and cutting the bones free with a small sharp knife – tear the skin as little as you can but don't worry too much about what happens inside the drumstick. Turn them the right way out again and stuff with the pork mixture. Pull the skin around the re-formed legs and sew up with a large needle and thick thread.

Heat the oil in a flameproof casserole and fry the chicken parcels gently for 5 minutes or until they begin to brown, then transfer to the oven at 180°C (350°F, gas mark 4) and cook for 25 minutes or until they are well browned and the juices run clear.

Serve with rice.

Grilled Aubergines and Sesame Chicken Breasts with Garlic Rice

6 SERVINGS

6 chicken breasts, boned
2 tablespoons sesame oil
2 tablespoons sunflower oil
4 garlic cloves, chopped
salt and black pepper
3 large aubergines
125 g (4 oz) sesame seeds
1 teaspoon finely ground sea salt
700 g (1½ lb) long-grain rice

Cut the chicken breasts down the middle into two thin fillets. Mix together the sesame oil, sunflower oil and garlic in a bowl. Add the chicken, stir to coat, then leave to marinate for 30 minutes.

Remove the chicken pieces from the marinade, reserving the marinade. Sprinkle the chicken pieces with salt and grill them quickly.

Cut the aubergines into slices about 2.5 cm (1 inch) thick. Brush with some of the reserved chicken marinade, sprinkle with salt and grill until soft and golden.

Toast the sesame seeds in a dry pan, then stir the sea salt in with them while they are very hot. Arrange the aubergine and chicken fillets overlapping alternately on a serving dish and sprinkle with the toasted sesame seeds and black pepper.

Meanwhile, cook the rice in boiling salted water for about 12 minutes or according to the manufacturer's instructions. Put the remaining chicken marinade in a heavy-based saucepan large enough to hold the rice. Add a little extra oil if necessary and cook until the garlic is just golden. Drain the cooked rice and stir it into the garlic oil. Serve immediately with the chicken and aubergines.

Chicken Liver Pilaff

Most supermarkets stock plastic tubs of frozen chicken livers, which are relatively cheap and multi-purpose – thread on to kebabs, mash into a pâté, spread on to crostini, or use to add flavour and protein to a simple rice dish like this pilaff, zapped up with currants, pine nuts, herbs and enriched – if possible – with a little chicken stock; easier than a risotto but tasty and quick. After thawing out, frozen chicken livers need to be picked over to cut off any greenish, discoloured bits, which taste bitter. Keep a tub of livers in your freezer, they are endlessly useful.

4–6 SERVINGS

600 g (1¼ lb) frozen chicken livers, thawed and trimmed
400 g (14 oz) patna or basmati rice
½ litre (18 fl oz) chicken stock
200 g (7 oz) dried Italian porcini, soaked
200 g (7 oz) streaky bacon, or pancetta, cut into small strips
1 large onion, peeled and chopped
1 clove garlic
a handful of fresh herbs in season, chopped
1 tablespoon currants
2 tablespoons pine nuts or almonds, toasted

Pick over the chicken livers, trimming off greeny bits, and slice in half. Set the rice to boil in salted water for 8 minutes, drain well, then turn into an earthenware casserole and keep warm. Heat the chicken stock and porcini soaking water, season with salt and pepper, and stir into the rice. Set the dish, loosely covered with foil, in a low to moderate oven so the part-cooked rice can absorb the stock.

In a heavy pan fry the streaky bacon, till the fat runs, then add the chopped onion and garlic. When these are softening (not burnt) add the chicken livers and cook gently, stirring, for 2 minutes or till the livers are just pink in the middle. Stir these ingredients into the rice, which by now should be al dente, adding the chopped herbs, soaked currants and toasted nuts. Fork to mix well. Heat through for another 5–10 minutes, with some shavings of butter on top.

Serve with green beans, hot or as a salad.

Jiaozi (Peking Dumplings)

As a child reared on northern Chinese cooking, jiaozi were food to dream about, a birthday treat. I used to watch Lim, our cook, and the amah gossiping with much cackling laughter as they filled tray after tray with these savoury dumplings, plump as little goldfish in their pleated cases of white dough. Fillings vary in detail, but a mixture of finely chopped pork, prawns and Chinese cabbage, spiked with soy sauce and aromatic sesame oil, is a constant. Sealed throughout cooking, the concentrated flavour as you munch is mind-blowing.

Reading Ken Hom's book, *The Taste of China*, reminded me that steam-frying jiaozi saves much last-minute flap. This is a treat for a celebration with close friends – crude food, but incomparable. Quantities here yield about six jiaozi each. Serve them piping hot, in bowls, with dipping sauces, and eat with chopsticks. Finish, perhaps, with a thin, clear, palate-cleansing Egg Drop Soup (see page 125).

6–8 SERVINGS

FOR THE JIAOZI DOUGH
350 g (12 oz) strong white flour
about 350 ml (12 fl oz) very hot water

FOR THE FILLING
275 g (10 oz) Chinese cabbage, finely chopped
175 g (6 oz) minced pork
175 g (6 oz) prawns, preferably uncooked, peeled and chopped
6 spring onions, finely chopped
2 garlic cloves, finely chopped
1 tablespoon light soy sauce
1 tablespoon dark soy sauce
1 tablespoon dry sherry (optional)
25 g (1 oz) dried Chinese black mushrooms, soaked in warm water for
30–60 minutes, then drained and chopped
1 tablespoon sesame oil
1 teaspoon salt
a generous grinding of black pepper

4 tablespoons peanut or safflower oil, for frying
300 ml (½ pint) hot water

Make the dough first. Sift the flour into a large bowl and pour in the hot water, whisking steadily until the ingredients come together in a ball. The dough should not be sticky, but moist enough to gather up tidily. Transfer to a floured board and knead until smooth and elastic. Return to the bowl and cover with a clean, damp cloth. Set aside.

Combine the filling ingredients in another bowl, mixing thoroughly with your hands, and set aside.

Knead the dough again on a floured board, then shape it into a long sausage about 2.5–4 cm (1–1½ inches) in diameter. Cut off a slice about 2 cm (¾ inch) wide, flatten it with the palm of your hand, then roll it out thinly with a floured rolling pin to make a circle about 9 cm (3½ inches) across. Continue rolling slices until you have used up all the dough, covering the rounds with a clean, damp cloth meanwhile.

To shape and fill the jiaozi, pinch three or four pleats in one side of each dough circle to create a concave shape. Pop 2 teaspoons of the filling into each hollow, fold the two sides together and pinch to close (a trace of water along the join can help), making a plump little crescent shape. Lay these on a lightly floured tray, cover with a clean, damp cloth and set aside until you have filled all the jiaozi.

To steam-fry the jiaozi, heat the oil in a wok or large frying pan, then pack the jiaozi in closely in a single layer. Cook over a moderate heat until the bases of the jiaozi are browned. Pour over the hot water, cover and cook over a high heat for 2 minutes. Lower the heat to a simmer and continue to cook, still covered, for another 8–10 minutes or until most of the cooking water has been absorbed. Uncover and continue cooking until the pan is dry and sizzling and the dumplings are crisp and golden brown on the bottom.

Serve at once with the following dipping sauces, either in larger communal bowls or little individual bowls: dark soy sauce; light soy sauce with a dash of white wine vinegar; chilli bean sauce.

NOTE: *Unless you have two pans on the go, the jiaozi will need preparing in relays, but compared with the boiling procedure, the involvement at this stage is minimal.*

Choucroute à l'Alsacienne

This recipe is indebted to Sue Style's *A Taste of Alsace*, though I have pruned it a little to bring it within pauper budgets. This is a fine dish for a winter party, a peasant feast of pungent flavours, particularly easy to prepare and the kind of big hotpot that can be left to cook longer without spoiling if you turn the oven down a notch.

6–8 SERVINGS

1.5 kg (3 lb) sauerkraut, canned, bottled or sold in plastic packs
15 g (½ oz) butter, lard or bacon fat
2 onions, chopped
2 garlic cloves, crushed
450 g (1 lb) belly of pork in one piece, rubbed with salt
and left overnight
100 g (3½ oz) smoked bacon in one piece
1 smoked sausage ring
1 bay leaf
1 teaspoon juniper berries
1 teaspoon coriander seeds
2 cloves
6 peppercorns
600 ml (1 pint) dry white wine
600 ml (1 pint) stock or water
1.5 kg (3 lb) large potatoes
6–8 canned frankfurters

Tip the sauerkraut (choucroute) into cold water and wash well, changing the water once or twice. Drain, then squeeze out the moisture. Melt the fat in a large flameproof casserole and soften the onions and garlic over a low heat. Wipe the belly of pork free of salt. Lay half the choucroute on the bottom of the pan, add the bacon, pork belly and smoked sausage ring on top, scatter the herbs and spices over, cover with the remaining choucroute, pour over the wine and stock or water, and bring to a gentle simmer. Cover, transfer to the oven and cook at 180°C (350°F, gas mark 4) for 2 hours. Check that the liquid level is okay, topping up with water if necessary.

Meanwhile, steam the potatoes briefly in their skins, then peel and cut into chunks. Prick the frankfurters, and gently heat through, but do not boil or they will burst.

Dish up on your biggest platter thus: a mound of choucroute in the centre, potatoes at each end, and sliced meats, sausage and frankfurters spread appetizingly on top. Serve with mustard.

Pigeon Casserole

Unless you know an obliging farmer, pigeons are not all that much cheaper than cheap chickens. On the other hand, their firm, dark meat has infinitely more flavour and interest than factory-farmed chickens. Young birds are good plainly roasted, wrapped in bacon, but if there is any doubt about their age this casserole method is a safe bet.

4 rashers streaky bacon
4 plump pigeons
250 g (½ lb) small or pickling onions
butter
flour
300–600 ml (½–1) pint cider, stock, or water plus bouillon cube
125 g (¼ lb) mushrooms
handful of raisins or sultanas
thyme
bay leaf
salt and pepper

Chop up the bacon, rinds removed, into small squares. Bacon, pigeons and onions should be lightly browned, separately, in that order, in a little butter. Use the same fat for all three frying operations, unless it blackens too much, in which case, wipe out the pan and add fresh butter. Put each lot aside as it is done. Stir the flour into the remaining fat in the pan, pour in 300 ml (½ pint) cider, stock or bouillon and bring to the boil. Simmer for a few minutes, until the sauce has thickened.

If you are doing this preliminary cooking in a frying pan, you will now have to transfer everything to a casserole large enough to take the pigeons and other ingredients. Put the bacon and onion in the bottom of the casserole, then add the pigeons, sliced mushrooms, raisins or sultanas, and herbs. Pour over the stock, which should come about three-quarters of the way up the sides of the birds, and bring to the boil again. (If there is not enough stock, add a little more – hot water will do.) Add a pinch of salt and some black pepper.

Cover with greaseproof paper (or foil) and the lid, and cook in a hottish oven (200°C, 400°F, gas mark 6) for 1 hour. Now remove the lid, turn the birds over and cook for a further 45 minutes, uncovered. If the sauce seems very thin you can strain it off into a saucepan (leaving the pigeons and other ingredients in the casserole in the oven) and boil it fiercely for a few minutes to reduce it, before returning it to the casserole dish for serving. But this should not be necessary.

Serve with baked potatoes, or boiled rice, and peas.

Home-made Venison Sausages

A home-made sausage, let's face it, has real style. Made with venison, this is dinner party food, a bother to make but on the other hand brilliantly easy to cook. Venison is too lean to make a juicy sausage, so the fatty pork makes up for this deficiency as well as reducing the cost. Serve with one of the mixed vegetable purées, or lentils, braised red cabbage, and Onion Compote (see opposite), or Cumberland sauce.

4–5 SERVINGS

1 kg (2 lb) belly of pork
1 kg (2 lb) venison off the bone
225 g (8 oz) hard back pork fat
1 tablespoon coriander seeds
6 allspice berries
6 cloves
1 tablespoon black peppercorns
3 garlic cloves, crushed
2 tablespoons salt
1 glass of red wine or port
pig casings (see Note)

Cut the rind and rib bones from the belly of pork and put it through the mincer with the venison. Cut the pork back fat into tiny cubes and mix these with the meat. Pound the spices to a coarse powder in a mortar, and mix into the minced meat with your hands, together with the garlic and salt. Pour over the wine or port. Mix again, then leave to stand for about 2 hours. Stuff the sausage casings to make short, fat links. Leave in a cool place for 24 hours to develop the flavours before cooking.

NOTE: *Some family butchers stock animal casings, or you can order them by post. (One good supplier is Smithfield Casings & Sundries, West Burrowfield, Welwyn Garden City, Herts AL7 4TW. Tel: 01707 328557.) Packed in salt in a jar, they will keep for ages in the fridge. Soak in water before use.*

Onion Compote

This is a delectable way to make use of little pickling onions or shallots, and is no trouble once you have peeled the onions. Serve with cold meat, or sausages, or alone with dark rye bread as an original starter.

4 SERVINGS

450–700 g (1–1½ lb) pickling onions or shallots
200 ml (7 fl oz) water
1 tablespoon wine vinegar
3 tablespoons olive oil
1 tablespoon brown sugar or honey
2 tablespoons tomato purée
3 tablespoons raisins, sultanas or currants
a sprig of fresh thyme, a bay leaf and a sprig of fresh
rosemary, tied together
salt and pepper

To peel the onions or shallots, blanch them in a large saucepan of boiling water for about 10 seconds, then drain them and rinse under cold running water. Trim off both ends and slip off the skins.

Put the onions or shallots in a large heavy-based saucepan with the remaining ingredients. Bring to the boil, then turn the heat right down and simmer gently, half-covered, for 30–45 minutes or until the onions or shallots are tender and most of the liquid has evaporated. Check from time to time that the liquid is not catching and burning – always a danger with a mixture that includes sugar or honey. Add a splash more water if this looks likely. Remove the herbs and season with salt and pepper. Serve warm or cold.

Boiled Salt Silverside

I am indebted to Arabella Boxer's *English Food* for this traditional British dish. It costs less per pound than a roasting cut and I find it makes an impressive dinner party dish, its fine red colour set off by boiled potatoes and carrots.

6–8 SERVINGS

a rolled cut of salt silverside, weighing 1.4–1.6 kg (3–3½ lb)
3 carrots
2 onions, each studded with two cloves
1 celery stick
1 tablespoon black peppercorns
1 bay leaf

Wash the rolled beef, then put it in a heavy-based saucepan large enough to take the beef and vegetables. Cover with cold water to about 2.5 cm (1 inch) above the beef. Bring very slowly to the boil, skimming off any froth. When boiling, add the carrots, onions, celery, peppercorns and bay leaf. Turn the heat down and cook, partly covered, for 2 hours, topping up with hot water if the liquid drops below the beef.

If eating hot, remove to a warmed serving dish, cutting off any string. Serve surrounded by separately cooked carrots, and boiled potatoes. If the broth is not too salty, stir a little mild mustard into a gravyboatful and pass this round, to moisten the beef.

For eating cold, let the beef cool in its liquid. This keeps it juicy. Don't be put off by the greyish exterior of the silverside; once cut, the inside is an almost garnet red.

Bollito Misto

8–10 SERVINGS

2 celery sticks, cut into short lengths
2 carrots, roughly chopped
1 onion, roughly chopped
1 kg (2 lb) piece of beef brisket
salt
1 chicken

FOR THE SAUCE
a large bunch of fresh parsley
1 garlic clove
1 tablespoon capers, drained
6 anchovy fillets, drained
½ teaspoon mustard
½ teaspoon wine vinegar
175 ml (6 fl oz) olive oil
a pinch of salt (if needed)

Put the celery, carrots and onion in a very large saucepan or flameproof casserole with enough water to cover the meat and chicken when they are put in. Bring to the boil, then put in the piece of brisket. Return the water to the boil and skim off any scum that comes to the top. Add a little salt, put the lid on so that it almost covers the pan, and turn the heat down so that the water just simmers. Let the beef simmer for 2 hours on its own, then put in the whole chicken and continue simmering for a further 1 hour.

To make the sauce, chop the parsley, garlic and capers together finely. Mash the anchovy fillets and mix all the ingredients together, seasoning with more vinegar or a pinch of salt, if necessary.

When the meat and chicken are cooked, remove them from the hot stock and cut slices off them to serve. Return the leftover meat and chicken to the hot stock. Serve the slices of meat with just a very little of the stock, some plain boiled potatoes and a generous tablespoon of the green sauce. The stock and whatever meat is left will provide an excellent soup for the next day.

Chinese Spiced Beef

For this dish, you must have star anise, a pretty star-shaped spice, which can be bought cheaply at Chinese food stores and some supermarkets. It gives the meat an absolutely unique and delicious taste and aroma. For the rest, it is a gratifyingly easy recipe to prepare, the kind you can leave quietly cooking while you talk to your guests.

8 SERVINGS

1 kg (2 lb) shin of beef in one piece
2 tablespoons oil
1 tablespoon soy sauce
2 teaspoons wine or wine vinegar
pepper
2 garlic cloves
1 star anise
1 tablespoon sugar
buttered noodles, to serve

If the meat is ragged-looking, tie it up neatly with string. Heat the oil in a frying pan, add the meat and cook until browned all over. Add the soy sauce, wine or vinegar, pepper, garlic cloves (whole), and 4 tablespoons water, and simmer slowly, covered, for 10 minutes. Add the star anise. Turn the heat right down, cover, and cook very slowly for 1 hour. Add the sugar, turn the meat over, re-cover and simmer for another hour.

To serve, boil up a lot of egg noodles in salted water. Stir a little butter and soy sauce into them, and pile up in one large dish. Take the meat out of the pan, cut the string and slice on to a warmed plate. Pour over the juices from the pan. Serve the meat and juice with the buttered noodles.

If you must serve a vegetable, it should be a Chinese-style vegetable dish – stir-fried cabbage or bean sprouts would be excellent.

Guinea Fowl and Lentils

The guinea fowl is a terrific bird, far more festive and deliciously gamey than chicken. It feeds more people than any game bird and usually costs less. Serve it with a dish of lentils and some salad and it will be a feast.

8 SERVINGS

2 guinea fowl
10–12 garlic cloves
175g (6 oz) butter
12 shallots, skinned (optional)
2 sprigs of fresh rosemary
olive oil
salt and (preferably coarse) black pepper
800 g (1¾ lb) green (Puy) or brown lentils
250 ml (8 fl oz) hot water
grated rind of 1 lemon (optional)

Finish plucking the guinea fowl – butchers and supermarkets often leave a few feathers in so you can be sure what you're getting. Crush four or five garlic cloves and put them with a generous knob of butter into each bird. Oil a casserole or earthenware baking dish and put the shallots on the bottom, then the rosemary sprigs on top of the shallots. Rub the guinea fowl with oil and salt and lay them on their sides on the shallots and rosemary. Cook them in the oven at 220°C (425°F, gas mark 7) for 20 minutes, then turn them on to their other side for a further 20 minutes, basting every so often with the butter that runs from them. Finish them breast-up so that this browns.

Meanwhile, heat the remaining butter and 4 tablespoons oil in a large sauté pan and put in the remaining whole garlic cloves. Stir for a minute, then put in the lentils. Turn the lentils about in the oil for 1–2 minutes, then pour over the hot water. Let it sizzle, then cover the lentils with hot water and keep them over a fairly robust heat, topping up with water if you need to, until they are ready. Don't stir them too much or they will get knocked about and become a bit mushy. When they are ready, but still firmish, season with salt to taste and plenty of black pepper and just before you bring them to the table, a splash of good olive oil and lemon rind if you are using it.

Dorset Rabbit Pie

Rabbit can sometimes be dry – this is an old-fashioned way of sealing in their moisture and flavour. Eat it on its own (perhaps after a first course of salad) or with some simply cooked broad beans.

6 SERVINGS

2 rabbits
seasoned flour
450 g (1 lb) fresh breadcrumbs
8 large onions, very finely chopped
grated rind of 1 lemon
salt and pepper
a small bunch of fresh sage, finely cut
2 eggs
2 tablespoons milk
5 rashers of unsmoked streaky bacon, de-rinded

Joint the rabbits, dust them with seasoned flour, and put them in a straight-sided casserole. Mix the breadcrumbs, onion, lemon rind, salt and pepper and the sage leaves together and bind with the eggs and milk. Cover the rabbit with the rashers of bacon and lay the 'stuffing' over the top. Cook in the oven at 200°C (400°F, gas mark 6) for 2 hours, covering it with greaseproof paper if it seems to be browning too soon.

Tuscan Rabbit with Prunes

Serve with plenty of pappardelle or wide noodles and a green salad.

8 SERVINGS

2 rabbits
boiling tea
about 12 prunes
olive oil
1 glass of red wine
1 glass of Marsala
6 garlic cloves, chopped
1 sprig of fresh thyme or marjoram
salt and pepper

Joint the rabbits, cutting the saddles into two pieces so that more people can get the best bits. Pour boiling tea on to the prunes and leave for 15 minutes. Drain the prunes and put them with the rabbit in a marinade of a glass each of olive oil, wine and Marsala. Cover and leave for at least 1 hour or the whole day (if it's for supper) in the fridge.

In a heavy flameproof casserole, heat 2 tablespoons olive oil and brown the rabbit pieces. Add the garlic with the herbs to the rabbit, cook for a scant minute, then pour over the reserved marinade and the prunes. Season with a little salt and plenty of black pepper, put the lid on tightly and cook in the oven at 180°C (350°F, gas mark 4) for at least 2 hours. You may cook it harder for a shorter time but the gentle simmering makes for the richest flavour.

'Peking' Breast of Lamb with Pancakes and Slivered Spring Onions

This is the pauper's version of a famous Chinese feast dish. Breast of lamb is a very cheap cut which, like duck, is fatty and flavoursome, and during long slow cooking in a honey glaze will become crispy on the outside with rich shreds of meat on the inside. You can make the pancakes yourself, following the recipe below or, if you can get to a Chinese supermarket, buy them ready-made. There's no pretending it isn't time-consuming making the pancakes, but it should make you pretty proud of yourself!

1 breast of lamb
salt
4 tablespoons honey
2 bunches of spring onions, cut into 5–7.5 cm (2–3 inch) slivers
Hoisin sauce (see Note), to serve

FOR THE PANCAKES
175 g (6 oz) plain flour
a pinch of salt
100 ml (4 fl oz) boiling water
sesame oil

Immerse the lamb in boiling water for 3 minutes, then drain it, pat it dry with absorbent kitchen paper and place it on a rack to dry. Rub it with salt. Dilute the honey with enough boiling water to make it liquid and brush it on to the lamb until it is completely saturated. Leave it on the rack to dry out again overnight or for as long as possible.

Place the breast of lamb on a rack over a roasting tin and cook in the oven at 170–180°C (325–350°F, gas mark 3–4) for 1 hour or until it is brown and crisp. With a sharp knife and fork, cut the lamb off the bone and serve with a heap of steamed pancakes, a plate of slivered spring onions and a bowl of Hoisin sauce. Each diner should spread his pancake with some of the sauce, a piece or two of the spring onion and some of the sweet crispy meat.

To make the pancakes, sift together the flour and salt in a deep bowl, pour on the boiling water and mix. The mixture will seem rather dry to begin with, but should end up as a dryish dough. Since flours vary in absorbency, you may need more boiling water, but use it sparingly.

Knead the dough until it stretches fairly elastically, then put it on a floured board and pat with a rolling pin or milk bottle, until it is a long oblong roll about 2 cm (¾ inch) thick. Cut this across into chunks 4 cm (1½ inches) wide, and divide these into 4 cm (1½ inch) squares. Take two squares, flatten each slightly with the rolling pin, dip a finger into a saucer of oil and smear it over one side of one square. Then clap the other square on top, like a little sandwich, and roll them both out together until very thin and roughly circular.

Put a few drops of oil in a frying pan and spread it over the base of the pan with greaseproof paper – it must be greaseproof or it will absorb the oil. When the oil is moderately hot, put in the pancake and leave for a minute until it is light brown or a deep cream colour underneath. (If black spots appear your pan may be too hot, or the heat may be uneven.) Turn the pancake over and cook the other side the same way. The pan may need re-oiling before starting the next pancake.

As the pancakes are cooked, keep them warm by standing them on a saucer in a colander which is resting on the bottom of a large pan with a little water simmering in the bottom. This keeps them warm without drying them out.

Repeat the process, oiling the pan as needed, until all the pancakes are cooked. Serve with the lamb, Hoisin sauce and spring onions.

NOTE: *If you cannot get Hoisin sauce, use soy sauce with a little sugar added.*

Chicken Maryland

What sets Chicken Maryland apart, I think, is the trimmings – corn fritters and fried bananas. Sweet potatoes, or yams, which can be bought in some large markets, particularly in London, would be an authentic accompaniment.

4 SERVINGS

1 young chicken, cut into 4 joints, or 4 chicken portions
1 tablespoon plain flour, seasoned with salt, pepper and paprika
1 egg, beaten
dry breadcrumbs
15 g (½ oz) butter
2 tablespoons vegetable oil
a little soured cream
watercress, to garnish

FOR THE TRIMMINGS
about 225 g (8 oz) canned corn kernels, or 2 fresh or frozen corn cobs
2 eggs, separated
salt and pepper
1 teaspoon baking powder
125–150 g (4–5 oz) soft white breadcrumbs
butter, for frying
4–5 bananas

To prepare the chicken, put the seasoned flour in a polythene bag with the chicken pieces, and shake until well coated. Dip the chicken pieces in beaten egg and roll in breadcrumbs until covered. Heat the butter and oil in a pan large enough to take all the chicken, and fry the pieces gently, over a moderate heat for 30–45 minutes or until well done all over, turning occasionally. Add a little soured cream to the juices in the pan a few minutes before serving, scraping up the debris with a wooden spoon, and leave to bubble gently.

Meanwhile, in a second frying pan, make the corn fritters. For these, you must drain the corn, if canned, or boil it for about 10 minutes and scrape it off the cobs, if fresh or frozen. Beat the egg yolks and add to the corn. Season with salt and pepper. Beat the egg whites until stiff and fold in. Add the baking powder, and enough breadcrumbs to make the mixture thick and dry enough to handle. Shape into little cakes. Melt some butter in a large frying pan and fry the corn fritters until brown on both sides. Put them in a dish and keep them warm in the oven at 130°C (250°F, gas mark ½).

Peel the bananas, slice them lengthways and fry them gently in butter until soft.

If the corn fritters seem like too much of a performance, you could serve the kernels just as they are, with a little butter or soured cream stirred in. But don't skip the fried bananas.

Serve the chicken on a long plate, garnished with watercress and the fried bananas. Serve the corn separately. Baked sweet potatoes, with butter, or plain baked potatoes, would be a nice easy accompaniment.

Steak and Kidney Pudding

This is an excellent dish with which to impress. It is actually rather easy to make, but doesn't look it. The quantities given make a large pudding – it might be better to try a half-size pudding first.

6–8 SERVINGS

**3–4 sheep's kidneys or 450 g (1 lb) ox kidney
1 kg (2 lb) stewing steak or shin of beef
seasoned flour
225 g (8 oz) plain flour
salt and pepper
125 g (4 oz) shredded beef suet**

Clean the kidneys well, removing all gristle and the cores. Skin them and chop them into small pieces. Cut the beef into 2.5 cm (1 inch) cubes and roll them in seasoned flour.

To make the suetcrust pastry, sift together the flour and a pinch of salt. Add the suet and stir in 6–8 tablespoons water, enough to make a stiff dough. Roll this out and use to line a pudding basin, keeping about a third of the pastry to cover the top with. Put in the beef pieces and kidney, and add enough water to come within 2.5 cm (1 inch) of the top. Season with salt and pepper, then put on the pastry lid. Crimp the edges together and press them down over the rim of the bowl. Place a piece of foil over the top, tied with string round the ridge at the top of the basin.

Put 5 cm (2 inches) of water in the bottom of a large saucepan with a tight-fitting lid. If possible, stand something on the bottom to rest the bowl on – an inverted saucer would do. Put the pudding in when the water boils. Cover the pan tightly and simmer steadily for 3–4 hours. About 30 minutes before the meal, take the pudding out, remove the foil cap, and put the pudding in the oven at 190°C (375°F, gas mark 5) to brown the top. (This part is not essential, but it does improve the appearance.)

If the pan lid is not tight fitting you will have to check from time to time to see if the water has boiled away. It will almost certainly need replenishing with more *boiling* water.

With a classic dish like this, serve Brussels sprouts or cabbage, boiled for 5 minutes or so, well drained and braised in a little butter.

Brawn (Fromage de Tête)

A dish that could make your reputation in foodie circles, because it is so rarely offered. A good brawn, pale nuggets of meat in a clear jelly, is a fine thing. Not for the fainthearted cook perhaps, but can Hugh Fearnley-Whittingstall be the only man around who can deal with pig parts without fuss and panic? You need a friendly butcher. A classic brawn is made from a half pig's head, lightly cured, and lengthily simmered with tongue and ear (this supplies gelatine) till tender. The butcher should separate tongue and ear, and remove any bristles. Traditionally, saltpetre was included in the cure, to give it a rosy tint. If you can source it, use it, but it will taste fine without.

SERVES 10–16

half a young pig's head, brains removed, tongue and ear separated
100 g (3½ oz) brown sugar
225 g (8 oz) salt
250 ml (½ pint) red wine vinegar

Wash the head, tongue and ear in cold water. Pat dry. Mix the salt and sugar and rub this very thoroughly into the pig pieces. Cover and leave for 24–48 hours in the fridge or a cool place. Now add vinegar to the brine and turn the pieces over in it. After another 24 hours (longer will not hurt) wash the pieces, then soak in cold water for an hour or two to remove as much salt as possible.

Put the pieces in a large pan, cover with cold water, bring slowly to simmering point, skimming frequently, and continue simmering for 2–3 hours, or until the meat is tender and the tongue skin can be removed easily. You could add a couple of cloves and a bay leaf to the cooking liquid, but dishes like this were rarely cooked with vegetables for fear the keeping properties would be interfered with – a plain meat stock/jelly keeps longer.

Transfer the head, tongue and ear to a chopping board, and remove meat (mostly cheek) from the head, cutting it into neat pieces. Skin the tongue, removing the gristly root, and slice or cube. Discard the ear. Pack the meats into a good sized pudding bowl or pâté dish.

Reduce the cooking liquid by fast boiling if there seems too much to just cover the contents of the bowl. Pour the stock over the meats through a fine strainer. The brawn needs to be cooled, and set, under pressure. For this stand the bowl in a dish on a draining board, stand a smallish plate on top (one that fits inside the bowl) and weight this with kitchen weights, tins or whatever is available, keeping any stock overflowing the bowl for other purposes. Let the brawn cool, and solidify overnight, or longer, in a cool place or in the fridge.

Turn out on to your best serving platter, garnish with parsley and cress, and serve sliced on its own, as a starter, or with Dijon mustard, baked potatoes and green salad for a substantial main dish.

Chilli con Carne

This fiery, spicy stew of meat and frijoles (cooked black or borlotti beans) is hugely popular with men, washed down with cold beer or lager. It belongs to the Tex Mex tradition, with the emphasis on Tex – Mexicans look down on it as touristy, but it would be an excellent choice to feed a mob of partying teenagers or 20-somethings, served up with lots of plain rice, bowls of salsa, guacamole, and stacks of hot tortillas.

My recipe is adapted from one in Lourdes Nichols' *Mexican Cookery*. I have substituted mince – beef, pork – for stewing meat (easier to serve and eat), suppressed some seasonings and used real chillies instead of chilli powder. Frijoles can be bought canned, but I suggest you cook your own, remembering to put them into soak the night before. My version, I realize, much resembles South African bobotie, if a mite hotter, which is indisputably great party food.

500 g (1 lb) black pinto or borlotti beans
1 kg (2 lb) pork mince
1 kg (2 lb) beef or lamb mince
4 tablespoons wine vinegar
4 fresh or dried red chillies, de-seeded and chopped finely
1 tablespoon mixed herbs – thyme, oregano, marjoram
salt, pepper and a pinch of sugar
4 tablespoons oil
4-6 cloves of garlic, minced
2 medium cans peeled tomatoes
3 large onions, peeled and chopped
1 onion stuck with half a dozen cloves
1 teaspoon cumin seeds
1 teaspoon aniseed
1 teaspoon sesame seeds

Put the beans to soak in cold water. Using your hands, mix the two kinds of mince together with the vinegar, chillies and herbs and season with salt, pepper and sugar. Leave overnight in the fridge.

Next day, put the beans to cook (see Frijoles, below). Heat the oil in a wide, heavy pan and fry the mince mixture, half at a time, till browned, breaking up lumps with a fork. Turn the mince into a large oven dish, adding the garlic, tomatoes and onions. Add water to barely cover and cook in a low oven, 160°C (325°F, gas mark 3), for an hour or so, till the mince is tender and the liquid rich and reduced.

Put the spices into a blender, or crush with pestle and mortar. Add to the cooked mince, stir, add the cooked beans and let cook for about 20 minutes longer for the flavours to blend. Taste and adjust the seasoning. Add more chopped chilli if the mix is not fiery enough, tomato purée if it needs more roundness, more salt and pepper almost certainly, maybe a squeeze of lemon or lime to sharpen the flavour, a spoonful of soy sauce or Worcestershire sauce for punch. If the chilli seems a touch dry, add hot water, a little at a time. Stir in a generous handful of chopped coriander just before serving.

Serve spooned over a mound of plain rice, boiled for 12 minutes, drained and dried out in a shallow dish in the oven, at lowest setting.

Frijoles

Cover the soaked beans with fresh cold water, bring to the boil and cook, part covered, for 2–3 hours, or until they can be squashed between your fingers. Always add boiling – not cold water – to cooking beans if the water is boiling away. Refried beans would now be cooked up with garlic and other seasonings to be truly Mexican, but the Chilli con Carne is already so spicy they can be added just as they are, drained. Cooked beans soak up liquid, so you may need to extend the chilli stock after including them.

Baked Gammon

Gammon, baked with a glistening brown crust of molasses, mustard and vinegar, studded with cloves and surrounded by spicy fruit, is one meat I could happily eat for weeks on end.

Cuts of cheaper boiling bacon, sold in plastic packs, can be cooked in the same way. These can be extra salty. To deal with this, place the meat in a large saucepan, cover with water and bring slowly to the boil. Throw away the water and repeat with fresh water.

4–6 SERVINGS

1 small corner of gammon, weighing about 1–1.5 kg (2½–3 lb)
a few dried apricots
1 onion, studded with 2 cloves
1 carrot
1 bay leaf
vinegar
cloves
molasses or brown sugar
mustard

Soak the gammon and dried apricots separately overnight in cold water. Drain the meat and put it in a pan of fresh cold water with the onion, carrot and bay leaf. Bring very slowly to the boil over a low heat. Keep the water only faintly simmering, and cook for roughly 20 minutes per 450 g (1 lb), stopping a little short of the full time allowance, as the joint will be finished off in the oven. If you don't want to bake it straight away, leave the meat to cool in the cooking water – this keeps it moist and tender.

While the gammon is cooking, drain the apricots and cook in a little water with 1 tablespoon vinegar and a clove or two. Drain when soft and reserve the water.

To bake the gammon, first remove it from the water and strip off the rind with a sharp knife, leaving most of the fat. (This part does not apply to boiling bacon cuts.) Score a lattice pattern on the fat with the point of a knife and stick a clove into the middle of each little pane of fat. Mix some molasses or brown sugar, vinegar and mustard together – the amount varies with the size of your joint, but the proportions are roughly 1 tablespoon molasses to 2 teaspoons vinegar and 1 teaspoon mustard.

Put the gammon in a roasting tin and spoon the mixture over it, scooping it out of the tin and repeating the process until the fat is brown and sticky. Surround the meat with apricots and bake in the oven at 180°C (350°F, gas mark 4) for about 30 minutes, basting once or twice with the juices in the pan, supplemented with a little apricot water if necessary.

To serve, transfer the joint to a large plate, with the apricots all around. Dilute the juice left in the roasting tin with a little more apricot water, heat and serve as gravy.

I think ham and gammon need only the plainest accompaniments – baked jacket potatoes, a dish of buttered peas, or a faintly bitter salad with curly endive, and lots of freshly made mustard.

Tagine of Lamb and Dried Fruit

A tagine is a Middle Eastern/North African meat or chicken stew, slowly cooked till meltingly tender, often coloured with saffron, buzzed up with various spices and characteristically given a haunting sweetness by adding various dried fruits. I use halal lamb (closer to mutton, hence stronger tasting) from Asian shops, where it is sold for curries. I prefer prunes or dried figs for the fruit element; dried apricots are oversweet. If your budget won't run to saffron, substitute turmeric; the taste will be different, but good, and the golden colour is appetizing. Tagine is one of those good-tempered dishes which can sit in a low oven without spoiling. Serve with couscous, and harissa (a fiery condiment sold in small tins) so fire-eaters can step up the heat at the table.

SERVES 6–8

1 kg (2 lb) lamb, cut into chunks
2 tablespoons cooking oil
3 large onions, peeled and roughly chopped
4 cloves garlic
a pinch of saffron filaments or 1 heaped teaspoon powdered turmeric
1 tablespoon coriander seed
250 g (9 oz) dried fruit (prunes, figs, apricots, apples)
salt and pepper
a handful of fresh coriander or parsley, chopped

Trim excess fat from the meat, and fry in hot oil till lightly browned all over. Transfer to a casserole dish. Fry the chopped onion and garlic briefly in the same pan till just coloured. Add to the casserole. Soak the saffron in a little hot water for 30 minutes, then add the saffron and soaking liquid to the cooking pot. If using turmeric heat with coriander seeds in a dry pan till you can smell the aroma – about 3 minutes. Crush together roughly in a mortar. Add to tagine. Add the dried (unsoaked) fruit, whole or chopped. Stir all together, then add cold water to cover ingredients.

Cover the pot with foil, then the lid and cook in a low oven for 2 hours at 150°C (300°F, gas mark 2). After 1 hour check the contents – the dried fruit will have absorbed much of the water, so you may need to add a little more before replacing the lid. If the tagine is swimming in liquid cook on without the lid to reduce it. Add salt and pepper to taste.

A few minutes before serving stir in chopped coriander or parsley, and if you fancy the extra kick, a heaped teaspoon of harissa.

New, Improved Hand of Pork

This is a recipe from the original *Pauper's Cookbook* that has not only been reinstated, but made hugely more exciting by a) salting overnight, b) rubbing in a paste of garlic/chillies/aniseeds, and c) cooking for eight to ten hours in a very slow oven. It fed ten people hot, four more cold, and was unanimously voted top recipe for cooking pork. And the beauty of it is that a hand of pork is much cheaper than a leg or shoulder, a bit untidy looking in its raw state, but turns out to be ideally suited to this cooking method, gaining flavour from being on the bone and succulence from the fat which melts slowly and prevents the meat drying out. A good family butcher should provide you with a hand, weighing 4–5 kg (9–11 lb). Get him to score the skin.

SERVES 10–12

1 hand of pork
125 g (4 oz) pouring salt
8–10 cloves garlic, peeled
5 dried red chillies, seeds removed
3 tablespoons aniseed
2 lemons
olive oil

The day before, stand the hand in a roasting pan and rub salt into it all over. Leave in a cool place; in the fridge if there are flies about. By next day the salt rub will have leached out some liquid. Pour this away. Rinse the joint in cold water to remove as much salt as possible. Pat dry with kitchen paper. Stand the meat on a rack in the roasting pan. Crush garlic, chillies and aniseed in a mortar to a thick paste; rub this into the joint generously. Put the meat in its pan into a hot oven – 200°C (400°F, gas mark 6) – for approximately 30–40 minutes, or till the skin begins to brown and crisp, then turn the heat right down to 100°C (200°F, gas mark ¼), brush olive oil over, followed by a squeeze of lemon juice, then leave to cook for 8–10 hours, turning it over two or three times and basting with more lemon juice and a little oil.

Towards the end of cooking, you might add some water, cider or wine to the pan to make the basis of a gravy with the fat and juices which have dripped off the meat, more juice than fat. Turn the joint crackling side up too. Take it out and let it rest while you make the gravy. If it is too salty dilute with water/wine/cider. The meat will be so soft carving is simple – slice towards the bone with a sharp knife.

I served it hot with a potato and swede mash and Hot Greens (see page 186), and cold with baked potatoes, braised endives and salad. Brilliant.

Hand of Pork Candied Chinese-Style

At the time of going to press, the butcher was selling hands of pork for £4 each, one of the cheapest things in his window. In this recipe, the highly flavoured pork can be served as part of a Chinese meal with other vegetable and rice dishes – a way of making this small joint satisfy a party.

6–10 SERVINGS

1 hand of pork
10 cm (4 inch) piece of fresh root ginger, peeled and thickly sliced
3 spring onions, halved lengthways
6 tablespoons thick soy sauce
3 tablespoons dry sherry
25 g (1 oz) brown sugar

Put the pork in a heavy-based saucepan and cover with cold water. Bring to the boil and boil, uncovered, for 5 minutes. Pour off the water and scum, then return the pork to the pan, skin side down (Yan Kit recommends resting it on a bamboo mat if possible, to prevent the pork sticking to the bottom). Add the ginger, spring onions, soy sauce, sherry, sugar and about 1 litre (2 pints) water. Bring to the boil, then put on the lid and reduce the heat. Leave to simmer for 1 hour, occasionally loosing the joint from the bottom of the pan.

After the first hour, turn the joint over and put more water in, if necessary, to make sure it comes one third of the way up the pork. Replace the lid and continue to simmer gently for a further hour, again moving the joint about occasionally to prevent it sticking.

Remove the lid and turn the heat up a little so the liquid boils and reduces. Baste the joint with the sauce as it thickens. When you are satisfied with the texture of the sauce, discard the ginger and spring onions and pour the sauce over the steaming pork.

Pot-roasted Venison

In 1970 I wrote, innocently, that the 'best cuts of venison cost the same as the cheapest cuts of beef', giving a convincing recipe for loin marinated in port, and slowly roasted. But venison is now something of a luxury meat, and loin one of its prized – hence expensive – cuts. Instead I suggest haunch of venison, which is both cheaper and a generous and handsome joint for a dinner party. It should be marinated, being a lean meat, and slowly pot-roasted, or braised, to make it tender, with the traditional pot vegetables. Use red wine if you are out of port, coriander berries if you have no juniper berries, but don't skimp on the streaky bacon which gives extra flavour and helpful lubrication to the meat. Any of the following would be good accompaniments: crisply sautéed potatoes, potato and celeriac mash, purée of lentils or chestnuts, braised celery, 'Hot' Greens (see page 186). The Scots serve venison with rowan jelly but any sharp fruit jelly is a good counterpoint to this dark, rich meat.

SERVES 6–8

round of venison haunch, weighing approx 1.5–2 kg (3–5 lb)

MARINADE
½ litre (18 fl oz) port or red wine
4 tablespoons olive oil
1 sliced onion
1 clove garlic
1 tablespoon crushed juniper or coriander berries
2 sprigs rosemary or thyme
1 teaspoon black peppercorns

POT ROAST INGREDIENTS
1 onion
1 carrot
1 stick celery, chopped
300 g (11 oz) streaky bacon
1 teaspoon dried orange peel or 1 tablespoon Seville orange marmalade

SAUCE
2 tablespoons orange or lemon juice or red wine vinegar
salt to taste

For speed the marinade ingredients can be simply combined and poured over the venison, in a deep bowl. For greater pungency they can be briefly cooked together, cooled and poured over the meat. Leave the meat, covered, in a cool place or the fridge for 1–2 days, turning now and then.

About 4 hours before dinner, take out the venison, wipe dry with kitchen paper, and brown all over in oil or goose fat. Place the chopped vegetables in the bottom of a heavy casserole, sit the joint on top, cover with bacon rashers, pour over the strained marinade, add the dried orange peel or marmalade, cover the casserole with a sheet of foil, then the lid. Cook in a low oven (150°C, 300°F, gas mark 2) for 4 hours.

Transfer meat and bacon to a hot serving dish, cover with foil and leave in the oven (turned off) while you make the sauce. Strain and rapidly sieve the cooking liquid and reduce by boiling fast in a wide pan till it thickens. Add juice or vinegar, adjust seasoning and serve in a hot jug or sauceboat at table, along with carved meat and vegetables of your choice.

Venison cools exceptionally quickly, according to Elizabeth David, so everything – plates, serving dish, sauce boat, needs to be presented really hot, and served up fast.

Steamed Lemon Mousse

This is a lovely pudding, fragrant and delicate – English cooking at its most harmonious. It has a summery feel about it, but as lemons are available all year round you could equally well serve it as a refreshing sequel to a heavy winter meal.

4 SERVINGS

6 eggs, separated
150 g (5 oz) butter
150 g (5 oz) granulated sugar
grated rind and juice of 1 lemon

Put the egg yolks, butter, sugar, lemon juice and grated lemon rind in the top of a double saucepan or in a heatproof bowl over barely simmering water. Stir with a wooden spoon until the custard thickens.

It must not boil, or the eggs will scramble. The secret is to keep the water underneath only just simmering, and to stir until the mixture reaches custard thickness, and no longer. Remove from the heat and continue to stir until cold (this takes less time than you would expect – a few minutes).

Stiffly whisk the egg whites and fold them into the mixture. Turn into a buttered or oiled (vegetable oil, not olive oil, which has too pronounced a taste) pudding basin, then cover the basin with a plate or a cap of foil. Stand the basin in a saucepan with about 2.5 cm (1 inch) of gently boiling water in the bottom. Cover the pan itself and steam for about 1 hour or until the mousse is firm.

Leave to cool, then turn out on to a dish.

Orange Jelly

This makes the most delicious jelly – soft and wobbly, with an incomparably fresh flavour. Blood oranges are especially good in this recipe, when available.

4 SERVINGS

9 large oranges
1 lemon
125 g (4 oz) caster sugar
15 g (½ oz) powdered gelatine
2 tablespoons water

Thinly peel the rind from one orange and half the lemon. Put the sugar in a small saucepan with 4 tablespoons water and heat gently, stirring occasionally, until the sugar dissolves. Bring to the boil and boil for 5–10 minutes to form a syrup. Pour on to the orange and lemon rind while still boiling.

Squeeze the juice from all the oranges, and the lemon, and strain through a nylon sieve. Put 2 tablespoons water in a cup and sprinkle the gelatine on top. Leave to soften for 5 minutes, then stand the cup in a saucepan of gently simmering water and heat until the gelatine has dissolved. Strain the syrup and add to the fruit juices with the dissolved gelatine. Pour into a bowl or separate glasses and leave until set.

Chocolate Mousse

Many cookbooks seem to feel the need to apologize for including a recipe for chocolate mousse. I don't see why, myself. It is true that it is not exactly an original offering, but it is one everyone should know – not only good to eat, but ideally simple to make.

4 SERVINGS

175 g (6 oz) plain chocolate
a small lump of butter
3 eggs
a drop of vanilla essence or rum if you have any

Melt the chocolate till soft, with a spoonful of water, in a bowl in a warm oven. Stir it, add the butter and, when amalgamated, the egg yolks and vanilla or rum. Beat the egg whites stiff, but not too dry, and fold into the chocolate mixture. Mix lightly till the mousse is uniformly brown. Pour into a shallow bowl or – if possible – into separate cups. Leave to stand overnight.

Dur Mou

This old French family recipe starts with a basic chocolate mousse mixture made with lots of eggs, and ends up with something between a soufflé and a squidgy cake. You then sandwich a layer of the chocolate mousse between two layers of the *dur mou* for an unbelievable, wickedly rich result.

6 SERVINGS

300 g (11 oz) plain chocolate
225 g (8 oz) unsalted butter
225 g (8 oz) sugar
9 egg yolks
a pinch of salt
5 egg whites

Preheat the oven to 150°C (300°F, gas mark 2). In a bowl placed over a pan of simmering water, melt the chocolate with the butter. Beat the sugar with the egg yolks until smooth. Mix this with the chocolate away from the heat, adding it gradually.

Beat the egg whites in a clean bowl with a tiny pinch of salt until stiff. Fold into the chocolate mixture gently but thoroughly. Have ready two greased 18 cm (7 inch) cake tins. Divide about two-thirds of the cake mixture between the pans and bake in the oven for 1 hour. Meanwhile, keep the remaining chocolate cake mixture/mousse in the fridge.

Let the cakes cool. Spoon the mousse over the cake base and sandwich the two halves together. Eat warm or cold.

Meringues and Cream

Home-made meringues have nothing in common with the commercial variety, which explode into brittle shards when you take an incautious bite. The home-made meringue is faintly crisp outside, tacky within and the palest honey colour. Two meringues per person, sandwiched with whipped cream and topped with a trickle of melted chocolate, are a delectable dessert, which is simple to make.

One egg white gives you four smallish meringues. But this is such a popular pudding it is best to make a few over.

4 SERVINGS

4 egg whites
8 heaped tablespoons caster sugar
a few drops of vanilla flavouring
300 ml (½ pint) whipping cream
225 g (8 oz) plain chocolate

To make the meringues, whisk the egg whites until they stand in peaks. Add the caster sugar a little at a time whisking constantly until the mixture is smooth and thick. Add a few drops of vanilla flavouring and whisk briefly. Drop the mixture in spoonfuls on to a greased baking sheet, and cook in the oven at 110°C (225°F, gas mark ¼) until faintly tinged with colour. If you are not in a hurry, it is a good idea to stand the meringues in a draught for a while to dry off before putting them in the oven.

To make the filling, whip the cream until it is fluffy. You can sweeten it, but I find the plain cream contrasts well with the sweet meringue. Sandwich the meringues together with the cream. Melt the chocolate in a little water in a low oven, just before serving. Stir it until smooth, and make a little doodle over each meringue sandwich.

NOTE: *Meringues are the ideal way to use up leftover egg whites.*

Lemon Meringue Pie

This is a particularly foolproof version of an American classic. It makes a large pie – you will need a pre-baked 23 cm (9 inch) shortcrust shell. If this seems too much use half the quantities in an 18 cm (7 inch) shell, but as the pie tastes equally good hot or cold there is usually no trouble with leftovers.

1 pre-baked 23 cm (9 inch) shortcrust shell (see page 108)
4 egg yolks
175 g (6 oz) sugar
rind and juice of 2 lemons

MERINGUE
125 g (4 oz) sugar
4 egg whites

To make the pie filling, beet egg yolks vigorously with sugar, adding the strained juice and grated rind of the lemons. Cook in the top of a double boiler over barely simmering water till thick. Beat the egg whites till stiff and dry with the remaining sugar. Take about half the egg whites and fold into the lemon custard mixture. Pour into the pie shell. Cover with the rest of the egg white, spooning it on lightly so that it looks peaked on top. Brown in moderate oven at 180°C (350°F, gas mark 4) for 15–20 minutes.

Mont Blanc

A sumptuous pudding, this, and like so many of the best inventions, simplicity itself – a mound of sieved, sweetened chestnut with a cap of whipped cream. The only problem is peeling your chestnuts. Easier to do while they are piping hot and you are wearing rubber gloves.

4 SERVINGS

450 g (1 lb) fresh chestnuts
a little milk
vanilla sugar or sugar and vanilla flavouring
whipping cream
grated chocolate, to decorate (optional)

Score the chestnuts crosswise across the top and drop them into boiling water. Boil for about 8 minutes, then take out a few chestnuts at a time and remove the outer shell and inner brown skin.

When you have peeled the chestnuts, put them in a saucepan with a little milk sweetened with vanilla sugar (or sugar and vanilla flavouring), and stew for 20–30 minutes or until they are soft. Drain the chestnuts and press them through a sieve, or small colander, so that the chestnut drops like short lengths of vermicelli on to a serving dish.

Don't press this into shape, but hollow out the top. Whip the cream until stiff with a little caster sugar and a drop of vanilla flavouring. Spoon it into the hollow on top of the chestnut and sprinkle with grated chocolate, if using.

Sussex Puddle

For this pudding you will need a large (about 1.4 litre/2½ pint) pudding basin and a saucepan big enough to hold it – worthwhile investments if you want steamed puddings in your life (see the other recipes on pages 111, 112 and 240).

6–8 SERVINGS

1 large lemon
225 g (8 oz) self-raising flour
125 g (4 oz) shredded suet
about 150 ml (¼ pint) milk and water mixed
125 g (4 oz) slightly salted butter, cut into pieces
125 g (4 oz) soft brown sugar

Scrub the lemon to remove any sprays or waxes and prick it all over with a fork. Mix the flour and suet together and gradually add the milk and water until you have a firm dough.

Put the dough on a lightly floured surface and roll it out to a large circle. Cut out a quarter of the circle for the lid of the pudding, and use the remainder to line a buttered 1.4 litre (2½ pint) pudding basin. Put in half the butter, half the sugar, and the lemon. Put the rest of the butter and sugar on top. Roll out the last quarter of the suet to make a lid, wet the edges and press it on, with a large piece of foil, pleating it to allow for swelling. Tie it round the rim with string.

Lower the basin into a large pan of boiling water so that the water comes at least halfway up the basin. Cover and leave to simmer for 3–4 hours, replenishing with boiling water as necessary.

After steaming, remove the pudding from the saucepan and take off the foil. Bake in the oven at 180°C (350°F, gas mark 4) for about 20 minutes or until the suet is browned. To serve, loosen the pudding from the basin with a palette knife and turn it out on to a plate.

Ginger Ice Cream

This is by no means a thrifty recipe except that nobody ought to eat very much of it. Make Almond Biscuits (see opposite) to go with it.

8 SERVINGS

250 ml (8 fl oz) full cream milk
1 whole egg plus 2 egg yolks
3 tablespoons syrup from the bottle of preserved stem ginger
250 ml (8 fl oz) whipping cream
5–6 nuggets of preserved stem ginger, finely chopped
2 tablespoons soft brown sugar

Bring the milk to the boil and pour it very slowly on to the egg and egg yolks, beating hard all the time. Return to the pan and stir over a very low heat until the custard thickens. The moment it is thick enough to coat the back of a wooden spoon, put the base of the pan in a bowl of iced water and stir the ginger syrup into the custard. Pour the custard into a freezerproof container and freeze for 30–40 minutes or until the custard has set solid round the edges.

Whip the cream until it is stiff. Turn the frozen custard into a bowl, stir it up well and quickly stir in the ginger pieces and whipped cream. Taste and add sugar cautiously. Return to the freezer and freeze for 1 hour, then give it another gentle stir, so that the ginger pieces do not sink to the bottom. Freeze until hard.

NOTE: *It is not vital to use the exact quantities of preserved ginger and syrup; the contents of a small jar will do.*

Almond Biscuits

Another good recipe for using up egg whites.

MAKES 6

2 egg whites
a pinch of salt
50 g (2 oz) caster sugar
2 teaspoons flour, sifted
grated rind of ½ lemon
a pinch of ground cinnamon
50 g (2 oz) ground almonds

Whisk the egg whites, adding the salt halfway, until it forms soft peaks. Gradually add the sugar and continue to whisk until stiff. Gently fold in the flour, lemon rind, cinnamon and almonds. Line a baking sheet with greaseproof or rice paper. Drop tablespoons of the mixture on to it and bake in the oven at 150°C (300°F, gas mark 2) for about 20 minutes or until the little biscuits are golden brown.

Private
Enterprise

Most of the recipes in this chapter are for what might be called extras, things which are not essential, but nice to have. Jams, marmalade, sauces and relishes, breads, cakes and biscuits. This type of cooking is fun to do when you are in the right mood. You save some money too, but the real point of home-made items like these is that they taste so much nicer than anything you could buy at a comparable price. They are a luxury paupers can afford.

Many of these recipes can be made equally well by people living in the town or country. But I have included some recipes especially for country-dwellers, because this is where private enterprise really does pay off. Without going to the lengths of buying a gun or fishing tackle, you can still supplement your eating, free, if you know where to look (ask a sympathetic local), and what to look for – a little research in the public library may help here. Quite a few good things grow wild: blackberries, of course, sloes and elderberries. Dandelion leaves for salads (the French actually grow them for the purpose), wild sorrel, highly pungent wild garlic, young nettle shoots for soup. Mushrooms take some tracking down, but they can still be found in suitable spots (hayfields where horses have been pastured are supposed to be ideal) if you get there before other people. This is one subject you must learn up, though. Death caps, which look deceptively like edible mushrooms, are deadly. The safest thing is to get some knowledgeable countryman to show you the difference between the two.

Living by the sea opens up a whole new range of delicacies. Shellfish, straight from the beach and still tasting of the sea. Mussels are a lucky find, but remember that only mussels off the rocks are safe for eating. Those attached to wooden groins or metal are risky, and you should check that there are no sewage outlets nearby. Other shellfish to hunt for are cockles, whelks, winkles, but again check that they are safe for eating. Standing one of the local fishermen a pint will probably supply all the information you need, and a lot more besides. A large shrimping net might be a good investment. A friend who lives on the Kent coast trails one of these along the beach, and boils up the catch – small fish, shrimps, baby crabs – into a good fish soup, bouillabaisse style, with lots of garlic and herbs, and a little cream.

Chatting up local farmers can also be helpful, and might produce an occasional hare, rabbit or pigeon, as well as odd things like buttermilk. Not for free, of course, but cheaper than shop prices.

French Dressing (Vinaigrette)

The most commonly used dressing for both cooked and raw salads, this is composed, in its classic state, of nothing but oil, vinegar, salt and pepper. Three parts oil, to one part vinegar, a good pinch of salt and pepper to taste.

Unless you are using the best quality ingredients, however – French wine vinegar, fine olive oil – the dressing will almost certainly be improved by adding various other flavourings. The choice is huge and there is nothing to stop you working out your own formula. But the usual garlic and mustard one, with or without chopped fresh herbs, is hard to beat. In this case you can use 1 crushed garlic clove and 1 teaspoon French mustard (or a pinch of mustard powder) with the basic oil/vinegar mixture, and as many chopped herbs – chives, tarragon, parsley, thyme, chervil, basil are a few often used – as you like. About 1 teaspoon sugar is an improvement if you are using malt vinegar and powder mustard. If you like a suggestion of garlic more than the actual bulb, rub a cut clove round the salad bowl, or on a crust of stale bread, sprinkled with a few drops of oil, which you bury at the bottom of the salad, to exhale, as the French writers lyrically put it, its incomparable fragrance.

You can mix up the ingredients in the salad bowl itself, as the French do, mixing the various extras into the vinegar before adding the oil (the French say this helps blend the flavours better) or, as most of us do, shake the mixture up in a screw-topped jar or bottle. Whichever way, make sure the ingredients are well mixed before dressing the salad, and toss the salad with a couple of spoons (less fastidious people can use their fingers) until it is all well coated. Once dressed, try not to leave the salad standing too long – this applies to lettuce, cress, chicory and curly endive in particular – or it will begin to go flabby and the oil and vinegar will separate.

Other ingredients which turn up in salad dressings include grated orange rind, crumbled blue cheese (an American fad this), a whole range of fancy vinegars – cider, tarragon, garlic – honey, nuts, sultanas, white wine, Tabasco, Worcestershire sauce, lemon juice, sieved hard-boiled egg yolk, pounded anchovies. A soft-boiled egg yolk scooped out and mixed with your vinaigrette helps the dressing cling nicely to a cooked vegetable salad; the white, chopped, can be sprinkled on top. Also more exotic herbs, like fennel and dill. There is no harm in experimenting a little, though I would not advise trying them all out at once.

Mayonnaise

Mayonnaise seems to share with soufflés an undeserved reputation for being as unpredictable as an operatic diva. I can't really see it myself. It can, and occasionally does, curdle, for no very clear reason, but it can almost always be rescued by starting again with a fresh egg yolk and beating in the curdled substance little by little. Make sure all the ingredients are at room temperature. Remove eggs from the fridge or cool larder in advance. It is also a good idea to preheat the jug for the oil by rinsing with boiling water, then drying, before filling with oil.

For a smallish quantity of mayonnaise, allow one egg yolk to approximately 300 ml (½ pint) olive oil. *Do* use real olive oil. The flavour of the oil is the whole point of the sauce.

To make it, you need a bowl, a wooden spoon, a small jug for the oil, a little mustard powder, salt and pepper to mix into the egg yolk, and a little vinegar or a squeeze of lemon juice to finish off with.

Break the yolk into the bowl. Stir well with your spoon, blending in the dry ingredients until smooth. Now start adding the oil, a drop or two at a time, stirring between each addition. After a minute or so the mixture in the bowl should be getting the smooth, shiny look and firm consistency of a successful oil-and-egg-yolk emulsion, which is what a mayonnaise is. When it gets to this stage you can step up the oil doses a little – a drip instead of a drop, but make sure you stir it in thoroughly before adding more. By the time you have used up more than half the oil, you can increase this to a small splash.

When your oil allowance is gone, you should have a firm, pale yellow substance, rather similar to a packet custard in consistency. A squeeze of lemon juice or a dash of vinegar stirred in rapidly will thin it down. If it still seems too firm you can add more oil, or a little boiling water (about 1 tablespoon) to lighten it, though personally I think a rather solid mayonnaise has more pungency. The sauce is now ready to be mixed into salads, or used to coat hard-boiled eggs, cold fish, chicken, and so forth.

When your mayonnaise curdles, you will be confronted by a queasy mixture with a runny texture which refuses to jell as a mayonnaise should. If you are in any doubt, leave the mixture to stand for a few minutes – if it *has* curdled, or separated, one look will confirm the fact. What you do now is break another egg yolk into a fresh bowl, add the usual ingredients, stir in the oil, drop by drop, until firm and only then add your curdled mixture, little by little, alternating with oil. The only snag to this is that you will need to use more oil to get the consistency right, so you will have more mayonnaise at the end. The surplus can be stored in the fridge for a few days in a glass jar with a screw top.

Basic mayonnaise can be converted into various other classic sauces by adding certain ingredients. Sauce Rémoulade, for instance, a sharp sauce which is delicious with grilled meat, is plain mayonnaise (300 ml/½ pint) with rather more mustard added (2 teaspoons) plus some chopped gherkins and capers, a dash of anchovy essence and a spoonful of chopped herbs, in this case parsley, tarragon and chervil. (If you can't get them all never mind.)

The celebrated Sauce Tartare, which is excellent with rather fattier, fried food (fish, chops, etc.), has 1 hard-boiled egg yolk worked into the raw egg yolk before proceeding as for mayonnaise. At the end, add rather more vinegar and chopped gherkins, capers and herbs as for Rémoulade, plus the chopped white of the hard-boiled egg.

Lemon juice, freshly squeezed, and a few shreds of lemon rind, give zing to a fluid mayonnaise, excellent with summer salads. Adding crème fraîche or yoghurt gives a milder flavour. Curry powder or paste (see page 212) makes it exotic.

Aïoli

Aïoli is a mayonnaise powerfully flavoured with garlic. In Provence, where it comes from, they eat it with plainly boiled fish or beef and an assortment of vegetables – carrots, beans, potatoes – hard-boiled eggs, and boiled chicken. If you like garlic, you will probably find yourself thinking up excuses for eating aïoli.

Start by pounding two or three cloves of garlic (3 garlic cloves, 1 egg yolk and 500 ml/18 fl oz oil is about right for four people) to a pulp, then stir in the egg yolk and add the oil drop by drop to start with, beating all the time with a wooden spoon. When it starts to thicken, you can add the oil in slightly larger quantities. The procedure, in other words, is exactly as for mayonnaise. (See above for what to do if it should curdle.) When you have made as much as you need, add a squeeze of lemon juice and a little salt, and stir again. This yields a stiff, almost solid yellow emulsion, which can be extended with tepid water to soften the taste and make a more fluid sauce. Up to a third of the mayonnaise volume is fine. Add a little at a time, beating until smooth.

Try this with boiled cod steaks, and an assortment of vegetables.

Skordalia

Garlic lovers should try this Greek relish/sauce because it delivers the adorable pungency of the bulb, like aïoli, but without the same degree of oiliness – olive oil is used, but a base of breadcrumbs or mashed potato give it a pasty rather than oily consistency. Excellent with fried or grilled fish or meat, or roasted vegetables. Or serve up in a little dish with a Mediterranean meze, or hors d'oeuvre. The proportions given here are elastic – four garlic cloves may be enough for you where some use as much as a whole head. Lemon juice can replace vinegar.

1 thick slice stale bread, crusts removed
4 large cloves garlic, peeled
2 tablespoons white wine vinegar or lemon juice
110 ml (4 fl oz) olive oil
salt

Soak bread in water for 5 minutes, then squeeze out most of the water. Put the bread in a liquidizer with the garlic and the vinegar, and process briefly. Add the olive oil bit by bit, processing till blended. Add salt to taste, more water and oil if the sauce is too thick.

For skordalia with a mashed potato base, liquidize the garlic, vinegar and oil, then add this to one large boiled potato mashed separately, and adjust seasoning.

Bread Sauce

Bread sauce and Cumberland sauce are Britain's most distinguished creations in the sauce line. Even the French, who like to damn our cooking with the faintest of praise, are impressed by these two. Bread sauce, as you doubtless know, is eaten with roast chicken. Even if you don't have roast chicken very often, the sauce is worth knowing about because it is easily made and always popular.

2 cloves
1 medium onion
1 bay leaf
300 ml (½ pint) milk
3–4 tablespoons fresh white breadcrumbs
a little butter or cream
salt and pepper

Stick the cloves into the onion and put this and the bay leaf with the milk in a saucepan. Cover and set on a very low heat for 10–20 minutes or until the milk is well flavoured. Take out the onion and bay leaf, stir in the crumbs and simmer for a few minutes or until the sauce is thick but not stodgy. Season with salt and pepper and add a little butter (or cream if you have any to spare). Heat through and serve.

Basic White Sauce

Basic white sauce, like basic stock, is a neutral-tasting compound which absorbs the flavours you add to it. I don't think there is much to be said for the practice of pouring it over boiled vegetables to make them look more genteel, but as a binding for certain casserole dishes – fish pie, onion, bacon and potato hotpot – and as a base for cheese and onion sauces, it is extremely useful. A thick white sauce is also the foundation for most soufflés.

For some reason, the making of this sauce is surrounded with complications in most cookbooks. The milk, they tell you, should be heated separately, added little by little to the flour-and-butter mixture, and the whole preparation needs constant stirring to prevent lumps or burning. The method suggested here, which was given to me by a wise and experienced cook, is beautifully simple, uses only one pan, and you don't even need to stir – though I must admit I usually do once or twice to be on the safe side. The whole operation only takes three or four minutes.

MAKES 600 ML/1 PINT

15 g (½ oz) butter
1 heaped tablespoon plain flour
600 ml (1 pint) milk

Melt the butter in a saucepan over a moderate heat, stir in the flour thoroughly, pour in the milk (cold), increase the heat and bring fairly rapidly to the boil. I usually give it a stir at this point to make sure it is not sticking to the bottom of the pan, though if you don't cook it over fierce heat it shouldn't do so. In a few minutes it will have thickened to the right consistency. If there are any lumps you can disperse them with a few turns of the rotary whisk.

If you are using the white sauce as a base for cheese or onion sauce, you should simmer it gently for a while to get rid of the taste of the flour. Twenty minutes, on a very low heat, would be ideal, but 10 minutes is adequate. If it is to be used in a dish which requires further cooking anyway, like fish pie, you can dispense with the extra simmering and it will be ready as soon as it has thickened.

Green Sauce

A pungent sauce to serve with fish, and fatty meats like pork chops.

1 slice of white bread, crusts removed
1 tablespoon wine vinegar
1 garlic clove, roughly chopped
2 teaspoons capers, drained
2 anchovies
a bunch of parsley, chopped
olive oil
black pepper

Soak the bread in the vinegar. Pound the garlic with the capers and anchovies in a mortar or in a strong bowl with the end of a rolling pin. Squeeze the vinegar out of the bread and add it to the mortar or bowl with the parsley. Pound again, then stir in enough olive oil to make a thick sauce. Add pepper to taste.

Agresto

This Italian pasta sauce can be made with any nuts you have, including those cocktail packets of 'mixed nuts'. The only nuts I think are really unsuitable are peanuts, which would give the sauce too oriental a flavour. It's a reliable store cupboard standby.

1 lemon
50 g (2 oz) walnuts or hazelnuts
50 g (2 oz) almonds
2 garlic cloves
1 thick slice of white bread
a sprig of parsley, finely chopped
a pinch of sugar
black pepper

Wash the lemon vigorously to rid it of sprays and wax, then grate the rind from the skin, being careful not to include any pith, and squeeze out the juice. Remove the skin from the nuts by covering them in boiling water for a couple of minutes, then rubbing the skins off in a tea towel.

In a mortar, blender or food processor, blend the nuts together with the garlic, lemon juice and rind, and when it's a paste add the bread, parsley and sugar. Continue to blend until it's smooth. Heat the mixture gently in a small heavy-based saucepan, adding enough water to give it a more sauce-like consistency, but do not let it boil. Season generously with black pepper.

Serve it more or less diluted depending on the shape of your pasta and quite thick if it is to be a sauce to go with poultry, game or beef.

Garlic Purée

a whole string of garlic bulbs
salt
olive oil

Wrap the unpeeled heads of garlic together in kitchen foil and cook in the oven at 190°C (375°F, gas mark 5) for 1 hour. Leave them to cool, then unwrap them and skin them. Press the cloves through a sieve, cover with olive oil and keep in a jar in the fridge. Add to sauces, pasta or stuffings, or use to rub on meat or fish for grilling or roasting.

Aubergine Purée

3 aubergines
1–2 garlic cloves, crushed
3 tablespoons olive oil
juice of 1 lemon
2–3 tablespoons chopped fresh parsley or coriander
salt and black pepper
1 teaspoon paprika

Char the aubergines under the grill or over a gas ring, or place them in the oven at 230°C (450°F, gas mark 8) until they soften. Peel the aubergines, squeeze out the excess juice and pound them with the garlic in a mortar or blender. Mix in the oil gradually, then the lemon juice, herbs and salt, pepper and paprika.

Serve as a dip for pitta bread.

Pauper's Pesto

4 SERVINGS

50 g (2 oz) almonds
3 garlic cloves
a large bunch of fresh parsley and/or other herbs
50 g (2 oz) Pecorino cheese (or Parmesan, but Pecorino is cheaper)
5 tablespoons olive oil
salt and black pepper

In a pestle and mortar, crush the nuts with the garlic cloves. Tear up the herbs and crush these along with the nuts and garlic. Grate the cheese into the mix, pour over the oil, season with black pepper and a little salt and pour over freshly cooked pasta.

Mint and Yoghurt Dip

Local Bangladeshi restaurants serve this to dip onion bhajis in, but lately I have noticed it migrating to city wine bars, as one of various dips for crudités. It is an absolute cheat but simple and refreshing.

150 g (5 oz) carton of natural yoghurt
a little fresh coriander, finely chopped
2–3 tablespoons bottled mint sauce or jelly

Mix all the ingredients together well in a bowl. You may like to add a little salt or lemon juice.

Guacamole

The main ingredient is mashed avocado, making guacamole a smoothie compared with salsa, though the additions are much the same. Guacamole can be made in a blender, or processor, more speedily, but aficionados prefer the rougher texture of a hand mixed, hand chopped version. Your choice. The proportions given make about 600 ml (1 pint); double up for a party.

2 large ripe tomatoes, peeled and chopped
a small bunch of coriander, chopped
1 small onion, peeled and finely chopped
2 fresh green chillies, de-seeded and chopped
juice of 1 lemon or lime
salt and pepper
2 ripe avocados

Combine all ingredients except the avocados ahead of time, and chill under clingfilm. Close to eating time, cut the avocados in half, removing the stones, scooping out and mashing the flesh with a fork. Stir into the chilled ingredients. Putting the stone in the mix is said to prevent the avocado discolouring. A squeeze of lime or lemon can also be helpful. Prepare close to eating time. Guacamole can be used as a dip, a relish or a salad; both delicious and good for you.

Salsa Tipico

Freshly made, this is not dissimilar to an Indian raita – chopped tomato and onion, made searing with fresh chilli. Breakfasting in L.A. I discovered what a spoonful can do to spark up hotel buffet scrambled eggs.

SERVES 8 UPWARDS

8 ripe tomatoes
1 onion, finely chopped
1 small bunch coriander, finely chopped
4 fresh green chillies, de-seeded and chopped
1 lemon, squeezed
salt and pepper

Combine all the ingredients, mix thoroughly, and let stand for at least 10 minutes before serving.

Onion Relish

Some startlingly simple ideas can make good eating. This primitive but tasty relish was dished up at a café in Lincoln with ham and eggs.

3 large onions, sliced quite thinly
1 tablespoon salt
wine or cider vinegar and chopped parsley, to serve

Salting the onions and leaving them overnight, or for a few hours, sweats the 'fire' out of them and makes them limp but juicy. Shake the onions with the salt. Rinse quickly in cold water to remove excess salt, and dry on absorbent paper.

Serve with a sprinkling of vinegar and very finely chopped parsley.

Home-made Spiced Olives

This is a simple way to buzz up the flavour of those Greek olives preserved in brine and sold in plastic packs. Covering them with oil preserves them, herbs and spices improve their flavour, and as a bonus, the oil itself – a mixture of olive and sunflower or safflower – takes on an intensity of flavour which adds life to salad dressings, pasta, etc.

575 g (19 oz) pack of black olives in brine
2 teaspoons coriander seeds
1 teaspoon black peppercorns
2 large garlic cloves, unpeeled but crushed slightly
several dried red chillies
1 teaspoon salt
2–3 sprigs of fresh rosemary and thyme
olive and sunflower or safflower oil, to cover

Drain the olives in a colander or sieve. Heat the coriander seeds and peppercorns for a minute in a small frying pan to make them more aromatic, then bruise them in a pestle and mortar or in a strong bowl with the end of a rolling pin. Layer the olives, garlic and whole chillies, with a sprinkling of salt and the crushed spices, in a glass jar with a lid. Push the herb sprigs down the sides. Pour in enough of the mixed oils to cover the ingredients, seal the jar and store for a few days before eating. Rather than using the oil for cooking, you could simply replenish the jar with more olives.

Potted Cheese

Cheese should really be kept in a cold larder, rather than the fridge, but mostly it gets bunged into the latter and all of a sudden one is feeling guilty about waste, contemplating a rubble of dry hunks and heels of assorted cheese. Potting it, which means breaking it down in the processor to mix with soft butter and other seasonings, recycles the cheese scraps very satisfactorily, to eat with biscuits or on toast. Many people like potted cheese better than ordinary.

odds and ends of cheeses, hard or semi-hard
about half the weight of cheese in softened butter
enough dry or made mustard to taste
salt and pepper
a splash of any spirits available – port, whisky, sherry, etc.
a splash of Worcestershire sauce
½ teaspoon cayenne pepper

Cut the rinds off all the cheeses and process with all the other ingredients until smooth. Taste. You may need to add more of something; it rather depends on what cheeses you used. If you are eating it immediately, you can slurp ends of cream cartons in too, to give a 'spreading consistency'. Keep in the fridge.

Dandelion Salad

Young tender dandelion leaves make a tasty salad, either mixed up with the usual green stuff, or on their own. If the dandelions are growing in your garden, you can make them more tender by laying a tile over the plant. With wild ones just take the youngest leaves, but pick them from a clean spot – not a roadside verge.

Dress either with French Dressing (see page 259) or this hot bacon dressing. De-rind a few rashers of bacon and cut them into cubes. Put them in a frying pan and cook over a moderate heat until the fat has melted a bit and the bacon pieces are crisp. Quickly stir 1 tablespoon vinegar into the pan and pour the whole lot over your salad.

NOTE: *This dressing also goes well with curly endive (frisée) and the coarser varieties of lettuce.*

Rillettes

A nice starter to eat with fresh bread, gherkins and a bowl of radishes.

6–8 SERVINGS

1 kg (2 lb) belly or shoulder of pork, cut into narrow strips
250 ml (8 fl oz) water
2 cloves
2 bay leaves
chopped fresh thyme
2 garlic cloves, crushed
salt and pepper
quatre-épices

Put the pork in a heavy-based saucepan with the water, cloves, bay leaves and some thyme. Cover and cook over a very low heat for 4 hours. Alternatively, put the ingredients in a casserole, cover and cook in the oven at 140°C (275°F, gas mark 1) for 4 hours.

Drain the meat and fat through a sieve over a bowl and press the meat to extract as much fat as possible. Reserve the fat. Pound the meat in a pestle and mortar or in a strong bowl with the end of a rolling pin. Transfer the meat to a large bowl. Using two forks, pull the meat fibres apart, separating it into strands. Season with a little garlic, ground black pepper, quatre-épices and more thyme, then return the meat to the pan and cook for a further 30 minutes without the fat.

Pack the meat tightly into several small sterilized pots. Spoon some of the fat from the first cooking from the top of the bowl, leaving any juices or jelly behind, and melt it once more. Pour it over the rillettes to a depth of 1 cm (½ inch). Cover the fat closely with a piece of foil or greaseproof paper, and tie a large piece over the top of each pot. The rillettes will keep in a cool place for 6 months.

Argentine Chorizo

My mother's family come from the Argentine, and this is the sort of sausage they made on the *estancia*, for drying out slowly in a warm kitchen. Beef is naturally included, and helps the drying process as it dries quicker than pork. Paprika provides the characteristic bright orange-red colour.

12–14 SERVINGS

2 kg (4 lb) belly of pork
½ nutmeg, grated
1 teaspoon ground cloves
½ bottle red wine (a Rioja or Portuguese Douro)
6 garlic cloves, crushed
3 tablespoons dried thyme, rosemary and oregano mixed
2–3 tablespoons paprika or pimenton (see Note)
3 tablespoons salt
½ tablespoon black peppercorns, crushed
1 kg (2 lb) shin of beef
pig casings (see page 231)

Strip the rind from the pork, cut out any bones, and cut off the thick outer layer of fat. Dice this and set aside. Grind the spices together in a mortar. Put the wine, garlic, ground spices and herbs in a saucepan and boil for 1–2 minutes. Add the paprika or pimenton, salt and crushed black peppercorns, then remove from the heat and leave to cool. Cut off as much gristle as possible from the beef, dice roughly with the leaner pork and then put through a coarse mincer. Pick out any stringy bits which eluded the mincer. Strain the marinade, and pour over the meats. Add the diced pork fat. Mix well with your hands and leave to stand overnight.

Next day, stuff the casings, making 15 cm (6 inch) links. Hang in a warm, dry place for 1–2 weeks, or until hard and knobbly, then transfer to a cool, dry place. As they dry out, the sausages will get smaller and harder, and need longer cooking. The flavour is magnificently concentrated; this is a sausage to add sparingly to stews and casseroles and bean dishes, or dice into piperade or a cabbage stuffing.

NOTE: *Pimenton, if you can get it, is a sweeter version of paprika and what chorizo would be made with. My mother used to get her ingredients in bulk and have them minced and stuffed into casings by her obliging butcher, a possibility worth exploring.*

Chicken Liver Pâté

6 SERVINGS

450 g (1 lb) chicken or turkey livers
125 g (4 oz) butter
2 garlic cloves (or more if you like), chopped
1 sprig of thyme, basil or marjoram
salt and pepper
100 ml (4 fl oz) sherry
100 ml (4 fl oz) brandy
30 g (1 oz) butter (optional)

Chop the livers, removing any greenish or discoloured bits carefully as these will give a bitter taste. Melt the butter in a heavy sauté or frying pan and put in the garlic. Let it soften just a little – don't allow it to brown. Put in the chicken livers and turn them about until they are firm and brown all over. Leaving them pink inside used to be recommended but with the risk of salmonella it's as well to cook them through.

Sprinkle over the finely chopped herbs. Spoon the chicken livers into a sieve over the serving dish (reserving the pan juices) and press through with a wooden spoon – you could use a food processor for this job if you have one, or if you like a coarser pâté, simply chop the livers up on a board (a large knife or mezzaluna is helpful for this). Season with a pinch of salt and plenty of black pepper. Pour the sherry and brandy into the hot pan, let it sizzle for a few moments, then stir the juices in with the livers. Let the mixture cool.

If you want it to keep for a few days, pour some melted butter over to seal it and keep it in the fridge. Eat with hot toast for a starter or with toast and salad as a supper or light lunch dish.

Mutton Ham

16–20 SERVINGS

**a leg of lamb
a bunch of fresh herbs
a few peppercorns
a blade of mace
honey, to glaze**

FOR THE MARINADE
**125 g (4 oz) brown sugar
2 teaspoons ground cloves
1 teaspoon pepper
1 teaspoon ground mace
½ teaspoon ground ginger
125 g (4 oz) salt**

Mix together all the marinade ingredients, except the salt, and rub well into the lamb and down by the bone. Let it stand for a few hours and then rub in the salt. Place in a large dish and leave to stand for 6 days, turning the joint twice a day and spooning the juices over it assiduously.

To cook the lamb, soak the joint in water for a few hours, then place in lukewarm water in a large saucepan to which you have added the herbs, peppercorns and mace.

Bring to the boil, then reduce the heat and cook slowly until tender, allowing 25 minutes per 450 g (1 lb), plus 25 minutes. Just before serving, glaze the joint by brushing it with honey (dissolved in a little boiling water if it's very thick). Serve hot.

Fleur Kelly's Roman Loaf

The bread that fresco artist Fleur Kelly bakes regularly for her family looks just like the loaf you might spot in a Pompeian dining room fresco – an irregularly rounded golden pillow patched with brown. I first ate a big slice of it with baby beets in mayonnaise, a green salad and glasses of rosé, basking in the sun, and it was just how I like bread – crusty, dense of crumb and alive with the flavour of organic flour. An honest bread, good to the last crust and crumb. The charm of her recipe, which she freely passed on, was its insouciance – no lengthy kneading, one long raising, a sojourn in her Aga oven and *mirabile dictu*, the Roman loaf. My first attempt was pitiful, soggy in the middle and heavy as stone. But I have begun baking it regularly now that my supermarket stocks all the correct ingredients and each loaf is an improvement on the one before. The *sine qua non*, I have decided is the 'very large – 9 L, 2 gallon – bowl' Fleur stipulated; in too small or shallow a container the dough expands so fast it outgrows its strength. I have taken to using an old and battered 'panshon', like a very large glazed flowerpot (which might well substitute), a traditional bread-making utensil whose thick baked clay and generous depth seem to give yeasted dough an ideal environment. Unlike Fleur, I knead the first 'sticky' mass for a few minutes, I leave it to rise no more than eight hours, and I move the loaf down from the middle of my oven to the bottom after about forty minutes so the crust doesn't burn. My loaf needs to be cut with a serrated-edge knife too – a new experience for soft supermarket bread fanciers. It is not *quite* there, but it is the real thing and half the price of a 'peasant loaf' at the Borough Market. If you don't have an Aga (and it must be admitted that few urban paupers do), you will need to experiment a bit with temperatures, but pretty satisfying results have been obtained by putting the loaf in at 220°C (425°F, gas mark 7), reducing the heat to 180°C (350°F, gas mark 4) after 20 minutes and baking for a further 30–40 minutes, till done. *Per ardua ad astra* seems a fitting Roman comment.

Here is Fleur's recipe:

MAKES 1 LARGE LOAF

1.4–1.8 kg (3–4 lb) unbleached strong white flour
1 sachet fast-action dried yeast
1 tablespoon salt
1 tablespoon sugar

Mix together all the ingredients in a very large (9 litre/2 gallon) bowl. Add enough warm water to make a loose, sticky mixture. Stir the mixture rapidly with your hand, just enough to combine the ingredients. Cover the bowl with a clean, damp cloth and leave to rise overnight, or even until the following lunchtime, in the warm near the Aga. The next morning, give the mixture a quick scoop round with your hand, then turn it on to a baking sheet sprinkled with flour. Put it in the bottom of the Aga's top oven for 45–60 minutes, or until the crust is firm and the loaf feels springy. Stand the loaf up sideways after taking it from the oven, or the base is liable to become soggy.

VARIATION: *Sprinkle a handful of sesame or poppy seeds over the loaf after the first thirty minutes of cooking.*

Soda Bread

This traditional Irish bread, made without yeast, is a useful standby for holidays, and other times when bread supplies might run out. A handful of currants or sultanas added to the dough makes a nice teabread, eaten with butter, hot from the oven. Ideally the bread should be made with buttermilk, which can now be bought from good grocers and delicatessen shops and costs a little more than the same quantity of milk. You can substitute sour milk (thickened but not separated).

MAKES 1 LOAF

**450 g (1 lb) plain flour
1 teaspoon salt
1 teaspoon bicarbonate of soda
1 teaspoon sugar (optional)
buttermilk**

Sift the dry ingredients together into a bowl. Make a well in the centre and gradually add the buttermilk, stirring in the flour until you have a soft dough and the bowl is fairly clean. Turn the ough on to a floured surface and knead lightly. Pat into a round about 3 cm (1¼ inches) thick. Lay it on a lightly greased baking sheet and, using a sharp knife, make a cross-shaped cut in the centre. Bake on the middle shelf of the oven at 220°C (425°F, gas mark 7) for about

35 minutes. Remove the bread from the baking sheet and tap the bottom to make sure it is cooked thoroughly – it should sound hollow. Leave to cool or eat warm.

Buttermilk Scones

These scones are quick and easy to make and should preferably be eaten warm from the oven.

MAKES ABOUT 12 SCONES

225 g (8 oz) plain flour
1 level teaspoon baking powder
a pinch of salt
25 g (1 oz) butter or margarine
¼ teaspoon bicarbonate of soda
150 ml (¼ pint) buttermilk

Sift together flour, baking powder and salt. Rub in the butter or margarine as for shortcrust pastry till the mixture forms fine crumbs. Dissolve the bicarbonate of soda in the buttermilk and stir into the dry ingredients, till you have a soft, elastic white dough. Knead lightly till the dough is smooth and the sides of the bowl clean. Roll the dough out on a floured board, about 2 cm (¾ in) thick. Stamp out into rounds about the diameter of a coffee cup. Lay these on a greased baking sheet or baking tin.

Bake in a hot oven (220°C, 425°F, gas mark 7) for 10 minutes, then reduce the heat to 200°C (400°F, gas mark 6), and cook for another 5–10 minutes, or until the scones are lightly browned.

Caraway Tea Bread

A traditional feature of nursery teas, this is far too good to disappear along with nannies and starched tablecloths. Tea bread in this case means a plain cake which should be baked in a loaf tin, to be sliced and eaten with lots of butter. The caraway seeds – beloved of Victorian cookery – give it a unique flavour.

350 g (12 oz) strong white flour
2 teaspoons baking powder
175 g (6 oz) caster sugar
75 g (3 oz) butter
150 ml (¼ pint) milk, boiled
1 egg, beaten
3 teaspoons ground caraway seeds

Sift the flour and baking powder twice, add the sugar and lightly rub in the butter. Mix the scalded milk, which has been left to cool a little, with well-beaten egg and ground caraway seeds. (To achieve the best flavour, lightly heat the seeds in a frying pan for a minute, then pound in a mortar or whizz in an electric coffee grinder.) Stir the milk and egg mixture into the dry ingredients, beat until well mixed, turn on to a floured board and knead quickly into a loaf tin measuring about 20 x 10 cm (8 x 4 inches). Bake on the middle shelf of the oven at 190°C (375°F, gas mark 5) for 1 hour or until it feels firm on top. Cover the top with buttered paper to prevent scorching, if necessary.

Cinnamon Biscuits

The cinnamon gives these biscuits a pleasant, not-too-sweet flavour, more popular with adults than children.

MAKES 24

75 g (3 oz) butter, softened
75 g (3 oz) caster sugar
1 teaspoon ground cinnamon
175 g (6 oz) plain flour
1 egg, beaten

Cream the butter and sugar together. Sift together the cinnamon and flour and gradually beat it into the creamed butter and sugar. Finally, add the beaten egg and mix it all together to a stiff paste. Roll out on a floured surface and cut into rounds with a cutter or glass. Lay these on a lightly oiled baking sheet and bake in the oven at 180°C (350°F, gas mark 4) for about 30 minutes or until crisp.

Oatcakes

Useful when you run out of bread as they are quick to make. Oatcakes freeze well.

MAKES 30

175 g (6 oz) fine or medium oatmeal (not porridge oats)
50 g (2 oz) plain flour
½ teaspoon salt
¼ teaspoon bicarbonate of soda
40 g (1½ oz) butter, margarine or lard
2 tablespoons boiling water

Mix the dry ingredients (oatmeal, flour, salt and soda) together in a bowl. Melt the fat in boiling water, add it to the dry mixture and knead lightly (adding a drop more water if needed to give a firm dough). Roll out thinly on a surface floured with a handful of oatmeal and cut into triangles with a knife. Place on a greased baking sheet and bake in the oven at 200°C (400°F, gas mark 6) for 15 minutes or until crisp. Leave on a rack in a warm place to dry out.

Jam-making

The essential article for jam-making is a very large saucepan. Traditionally, these were made of copper, but an aluminium pan is just as satisfactory. It must be perfectly clean to prevent the sugar catching and burning. Where the recipe calls for warmed sugar, this means sugar which has been poured out into a large shallow baking tin and warmed in the oven for ten minutes or so. The oven must be set at a low temperature (about 150°C, 300°F, gas mark 2) so that the sugar does not actually melt. You can test when it is warmed by sticking your finger in. The idea of this is to ensure that the sugar melts almost instantly on contact with the hot fruit mixture.

Testing for setting is not, I must admit, a magically simple process. The usual advice is to pour a little of the jam on to a saucer, and put it in the fridge or outside the window to cool off for a few minutes. If the jam is going to set, the stuff in the saucer will have formed a slight skin which wrinkles when you blow on it. Unless the recipe specifically instructs you to stop cooking after a certain time, you may need to go on testing and boiling for rather longer than indicated. It all depends on the amount of pectin (natural setting agent) in the fruit, and this can vary with the age and quality of the fruit. When in doubt, though, it is often better to chance the jam being a little runny than to boil on grimly, as the sugar does tend to burn or thicken drastically after a certain point, and jam which has to be hacked out of its container with a stout blade is a mixed blessing. Boil, in the case of jams, means boil *hard*, unless otherwise indicated. The stuff is liable to spit and splutter, so approach it cautiously, and use a long-handled wooden spoon for stirring or testing.

Having delivered all these warnings, I would just like to add that making jam satisfies some streak of the alchemist in one, in a way most cookery does not. Filling up your row of little jars (they should all be thoroughly washed, dried and warmed in the oven) is a triumphant experience. If you are planning to keep any jams for a longish time, seal them carefully with the wax discs and cellophane tops sold for the purpose. Otherwise, I find screw-on lids are adequate.

Gooseberry Jam

Gooseberry jam is one of the easiest to make, as the fruit has a high pectin content and sets readily. If you like a slightly tart jam, it is also one of the nicest. Unripe gooseberries are best for jam as their skins are less tough.

MAKES 3.5–4.5 KG (7–9 LB)

2 kg (4 lb) under-ripe green gooseberries, topped and tailed
3 kg (6 lb) sugar, warmed
1 litre (2 pints) water

Put the gooseberries in a large saucepan with the water and bring slowly to the boil. Mash the berries with a spoon and cook for 20 minutes. Add the sugar and allow it to dissolve, then bring the jam to the boil and boil for 10 minutes. Test for setting by dropping a little jam on a cold saucer and putting it in a cool place for a minute or two. If setting point has been reached, the jam on the saucer will form a slight skin which will wrinkle when you blow on it or push your finger through it. You may need to go on boiling the jam for 15–20 minutes to reach setting point.

NOTE: *If you can cook the gooseberries in a copper preserving pan they will keep their green colour. Otherwise they will turn a pinkish-amber shade.*

Bramble Cheese

This has more texture than bramble jelly, but without the seed you find in bramble jams.

equal quantities of blackberries and cooking apples
granulated sugar

Wash the berries. Peel but do not core the apples and cut them up roughly. Put the fruit in a saucepan with water almost to cover and cook slowly, covered, until reduced to a pulp. Rub through a coarse sieve, adding a little more boiling water. Weigh the strained pulp and to each 450 g (1 lb), add 450 g (1 lb) sugar.

Warm gently, stirring, until the sugar has dissolved, then bring to the boil and boil until setting point is reached. Test (see above) after only a few minutes as this preserve reaches setting point very quickly.

Pot and seal in the usual way.

Seville Orange Marmalade

This is a coarse-cut, bitter marmalade.

MAKES ABOUT 1.5 KG (3 LB)

450 g (1 lb) Seville oranges
1 litre (2 pints) water
1 kg (2 lb) sugar, warmed

Wash the oranges and put them in a saucepan with the water. Cover and simmer slowly for about 1½ hours, or until a blunt wooden skewer pierces the orange skin easily. Take the oranges out of the liquid, let them cool and then cut them up into small thick strips, keeping all the pulp and juice which oozes out of them. Extract the pips, put them in the liquid in the pan and boil steadily for 10 minutes to extract the pectin. Remove the pips and put in the cut orange pulp. Bring to the boil, and stir in the sugar. Remove the pan from the heat and go on stirring until all the sugar is dissolved. Return to the heat and boil rapidly until the marmalade reaches setting point. This may not take very long, so, to be on the safe side, start testing (see above) after 15 minutes. Pot and seal in the usual way.

Orange Marmalade

A medium-sweet marmalade.

MAKES ABOUT 2.3 KG (5 LB)

450 g (1 lb) Seville or bitter oranges
1.5 litres (3 pints) water
1.5 kg (3 lb) sugar, warmed
juice of 1 lemon

Cut or mince the oranges finely, removing the pips. Tie the pips in a small piece of muslin. Soak the peel and pulp overnight in the water, together with the pips.

The next day, put the fruit, water and pips in a saucepan, cover and simmer slowly for about 1½ hours or until the peel is quite soft. Remove the bag of pips and stir in the sugar and lemon juice. Bring to the boil and boil rapidly for about 20 minutes or until setting point is reached (see page 280).

Dumpsideary Jam

A traditional English country jam, made with mixed orchard fruit – apples, plums, pears – which are ripe at the same time. The Irish version, 'Mixty Maxty', is much the same except that it omits the spices.

MAKES ABOUT 2.5–3.2 KG (5½–7 LB)

1 kg (2 lb) green cooking apples
1 kg (2 lb) pears
1 kg (2 lb) plums
600 ml (1 pint) water
grated rind and juice of 2 lemons
6 cloves
1 small cinnamon stick
4.5 kg (9 lb) sugar

Quarter the apples, slicing off the core and any brown parts. Do not peel. Chop the pears somewhat smaller, also removing soft or brown parts. Put them all, with the whole plums, into a large pan, with the water and cook gently and slowly until the flesh is all soft. Turn into a large nylon sieve, and rub through into a preserving pan. Keep some of the plum stones, cracking them with a hammer to extract the kernels. Weigh the pulp and warm the sugar. Add the grated lemon rind and lemon juice to the fruit. Tie bruised spices in a muslin bag and add. Stir in the warmed sugar, set over a moderate heat, stirring until the sugar melts, then boil rapidly, stirring often, until it reaches setting point (see page 280). Stir in the plum kernels, pot and cover.

INDEX